THE
STRANGLEHOLD
OF THE I.Q.

Benjamin Fine, Ph.D.

THE STRANGLEHOLD OF THE I.Q.

Doubleday & Company, Inc.

GARDEN CITY, NEW YORK

1975

Portion of "Under Which Lyre," copyright 1946 by W. H. Auden from the book *Collected Shorter Poems 1927–1957*. Reprinted by permission of Random House, Inc.

Library of Congress Cataloging in Publication Data

Fine, Benjamin, 1905–
    The stranglehold of the I.Q.

    Bibliography: p. 252
    Includes index.
    1. Mental tests.   2. Educational tests and measurements.   I. Title.
BF431.F436   153.9′3
ISBN 0-385-01576-3
Library of Congress Catalog Card Number 75–5260

Contents

DEDICATION

To my beloved and affectionate wife . . .
LILLIAN ROSE FINE
who, for four decades, has been my stimulating companion,
happy helpmate, and inspiring life partner . . . coauthor of
our four delightful daughters
ELLEN SYDNEY
JILL BARBARA
CARLA COLEMAN
JANET EVA
this book is joyfully dedicated with growing understanding and
never-ending love.

REDEDICATION

This book, published posthumously, embodies the philosophy of Benjamin Fine, a pioneer in educational journalism, winner of the Pulitzer Prize for the New York *Times* in 1944, the only Pulitzer Prize it ever received for writing on education.

He was a creator of educational history and a visionary who foresaw and crusaded for higher teacher salaries, school integration, wider academic freedom, and revolutionary and creative educational procedures long before they became today's realities.

In this book, he writes: "Not every child can define a sonata. Music is not part of every house. But every child has the right to be happy, to be treated with humanity, with compassion, and with respect and honesty." His definition of education was not so much the accumulation of factual knowledge as much as the warm meaningful relationship between the understanding teacher and the student whose imagination and intellect might reach unknown lands under his or her tutelage. The school experience of every child, he felt, should be one of lasting beauty and significance to both teacher and pupil.

He will be remembered as an innovative educator and journalist who truly believed that education was the enduring basis for the perpetuation of our democratic way of life. We know him, especially, as a great humanitarian, tolerant and forgiving of human error, who saw in the flowering of young minds under sympathetic and intelligent guidance the true purpose of education.

This book is thus rededicated to you, Ben, with our love and the unforgettable remembrances of your joy and excitement in the process of your living.

Lillian, Ellen, Jill, Carla, and Janet

June 16, 1975

1

The I.Q. re-examined

The current controversy over the I.Q. (Intelligence Quotient) among eminent psychologists, geneticists, educators, and even a Nobel Prize physicist has focused attention on a sore but vulnerable aspect of education. As never before, the very essence of the I.Q. tests is being challenged.

In a real sense, the I.Q. battle has become a fight for survival for many youngsters who are damaged for life as they are pigeonholed by I.Q. testing into academic and rigid lifetime molds. While the caste system is still accepted as a way of life in various countries, it may become so in our nation through the insidious I.Q. tests.

Of course, the principle of testing children, or adults for that matter, is not new. It has been with us for nearly a century. But the unhealthy emphasis that is now placed on I.Q. scores, and the grip that they hold in the academic world, is new.

Where did it begin?

Is it reliable or, as critics claim, is it a devious plot, designed to keep certain minority groups with nonwhite pigmentation, or those economically and socially deprived, in an inferior status?

Let us examine, or rather re-examine, the entire issue of the I.Q. Where does it fit into American education? How has it been used and abused in our schools, colleges, graduate institutions, business firms, and corporations? Then let us see what can be done to counteract this growing menace that is poisoning our intellectual well-being.

This is not intended to be a discussion for clinical psychologists, geneticists, psychometricians, test makers, or guidance counselors. Rather, it is designed for parents and other lay people who have more at stake than the purveyors of the hundreds of I.Q. tests that have sprouted as thickly and as indiscriminately as toadstools following a summer rain.

I am concerned with the fathers and mothers of schoolchildren who say to me, worried, concerned, and overwrought:

"Does my child have a high enough I.Q. to go to college?"

"How can I raise my child's I.Q.?"

"Why is my child placed in a retarded class? He is so bright around the house."

"Shall I believe Billie's teacher, who says he has a low I.Q. of 95 and should go to a vocational school rather than academic high school?"

Parents are unhappy! Perhaps that is why growing numbers have concluded: Away with the I.Q. tests! Though parents are not versed in psychological jargon, they know that schools place too much stress on achievement scores, math scores, reading scores, raw scores, percentiles, stanines, standard deviation errors, and the other I.Q. verbiage, entirely meaningless to them and to many of us, too.

They are distressed, as I am, at the I.Q. numbers game. A battle is raging in the educational fraternity. Sides have been drawn. Issues delineated. Positions taken. Passions run riot, replacing reason.

On the one hand, we find proponents of the infallible I.Q. and its ironbound hold on children championed by such eminent authorities as Arthur R. Jensen of the University of California, William Shockley of Stanford, Richard J. Herrnstein of Harvard, Hans J. Eysenck of the University of London, and the late Sir Cyril Burt of Great Britain. To them, and the group they represent, the I.Q. is to a large degree static. They believe it is largely determined by heredity and race.

According to their reckoning, 80 per cent of the intelligence that an individual has is inherited. They hold further that blacks are inferior, on the average, by 15 I.Q. points to whites. They maintain that a child is born with a good mind, which shows in a high I.Q. score, or he is born with a slightly deficient brain, shown in a low I.Q. score. It is as basic an inheritance as the color of his eyes or the shape of his nose and does not change to any extent during his lifetime.

However, no one has yet been able to prove that the I.Q. score and intelligence have any correlation whatsoever. Actually, the I.Q. measures what the child has already learned, not his capacity to learn as Professor Jensen and his colleagues would have us to believe.

To be fair to those who uphold the sanctity of the I.Q. and its rigidity, they maintain that there is room for improvement—at a ratio of 80 to 20. Since, they are convinced, 80 per cent of one's intelligence, as measured by the I.Q. tests, is inherited, some leeway exists to raise the score. The 20 per cent that is not inherited but which lowers the child's I.Q. may be due to environment, poor schooling, misguided teachers, inability to function properly in a ghetto city, or just plain laziness. This is, in my opinion, a reckless and unwarranted assumption.

But these eminent scholars have not been left unchallenged. Many believe that the I.Q. test does not measure intelligence. It does not separate blacks from whites, Indians from Chicanos, Jews from Orientals, or race from race. Among those who take issue with the sanctity of the I.Q. are professors Jane R. Mercer of the University of California, Carl Senna of the University of Massachusetts, J. McVicker Hunt of the University of Illinois, Ray C. Rist of Portland State University, Leona E. Tyler of the University of Oregon, and Martin Deutsch of New York University. These educators, and many more throughout the land, discount the rigidity of the I.Q. test, doubt the 80–20 formula established rather arbitrarily by Jensen, and disagree that an I.Q. score and general intelligence can be equated.

Among the serious questions raised by knowledgeable men and women, in and out of the education profession, who disagree over the I.Q. controversy are issues that may affect hundreds of thousands, if not millions, of children, adolescents, and parents.

How valid are I.Q. scores?

Do they prove anything about the intelligence of the child?

Shall we continue to base our educational system on the I.Q. as we now do to such a large extent?

Are I.Q. scores and intelligence synonymous?

Which I.Q. test shall be used?

How can a parent tell whether the examiner is biased or adequately trained to conduct an accurate test?

What do the final scores mean in relation to a child's future school or college program?

Shall the I.Q. scores follow the child from grade to grade, school to school, into adult life, as if they were branded into his skin?

After working with gifted children for many years, I have reached the conclusion that the I.Q. tests should not be used as the main device to separate superior from average or below-average children. When I first started to work with gifted children, I believed strongly that the I.Q. was sacrosanct. When the tests showed a child with an I.Q. score of 126, and my cut-off point for the "gifted" category was 130, I would say: "Sorry, Tommie won't keep up with the high academic standards our private school demands. We can't accept him into a gifted program."

Gradually my viewpoint changed. I came up against hard reality. I found that a student may have an I.Q. of 175, but if he is not motivated, if he does not want to work or study, if he has emotional problems, he is likely to fail. On the other hand, I discovered that a youngster with an I.Q. of 110—about the average range—might zoom to the top of his class and manage nicely if he is encouraged, stimulated, and motivated to succeed. On retreats, I sometimes found that the 175 I.Q. had dropped to 115, and the 110 I.Q. had reached 145.

It is more important to watch children at work and at play, to check their actual performance in the classroom, to find out whether they have emotional problems at home or with their friends, rather than place full faith in an ephemeral I.Q. score that can bounce around like a ball at the end of an elastic string.

I had fallen into the same I.Q. trap that has enmeshed countless other educators, teachers, psychologists, parents, and gullible laymen. Everything was either black or white—there was no gray. If a child had a superior I.Q., he was intellectually bright. If not, he was doomed to fail.

By now I am thoroughly convinced that the I.Q. tests have outgrown their original purpose, which was to predict academic success. American educators, led by the famous Professor Lewis M. Terman of Stanford University and followed by the equally renowned professors Edward L. Thorndike, L. L. Thurstone, S. L. Pressey, Charles Spearman, Irving Lorge, Rudolf Pintner, and David Wechsler, magnified the validity and significance of the I.Q. tests and equated them with intelligence. As a result, many young boys and girls have been cast into categories that they do not deserve and from which they often find escape impossible.

I am also opposed to the various group standardized, aptitude, vocational, and achievement tests now in use both in schools and the business world, to the extent of $300 million annually. While I would not designate this as a multimillion-dollar racket, I can safely refer to it as an unhappy $300-million-dollar misunderstanding. That is what the schools of our nation now pay the publishing firms that provide them with assorted tests, charts, manuals, score sheets, questionnaires, and other endless, often dubious, testing paraphernalia. On July 1, 1973, at its fifty-second representative assembly, the influential National Education Association, with more than one million members, adopted this resolution on standardized tests:

"The National Education Association strongly encourages the elimination of group standardized intelligence, aptitude, and achievement tests to assess student potential or achievement until completion of a critical appraisal, review, and revision of current testing programs."

Thereupon the educators called for an immediate national moratorium on standardized testing, plus the establishment of a Task Force to continue its research in this controversial area. As of now, the Task Force believes that certain measurement and evaluation tests are either invalid and unreliable, out of date, or unfair, and should be withdrawn from use. To quote the NEA report:

"The unfairness of some tests to some students was brought to the attention of the Task Force from a variety of sources. A group of minority students told of being placed in special education classes on the basis of being below grade level on standardized achievement tests, placements that could be adjusted only after three years."

Instances were related of black students being denied participation in extracurricular activities on the basis of tests. Teachers reported that group tests applied to very small children are unreliable because of their varying attention spans and maturity levels.

In its monumental study, the National Education Association found that teachers were frequently unfamiliar with the tests they were required to administer, the purposes of the over-all evaluation programs they used, and the objectives of the testing programs. The teachers complained that neither preservice in college nor inservice programs in their schools provided them with adequate preparation for administration and interpretation of tests to prescribe learning activities based on the findings.

Only thirteen states have instruction in tests and measurements as a prerequisite for teacher licensure. Some of these apply only to specific groups of teacher trainees, such as special education and guidance counseling.

Also, considerable research over the years has led to the conclusion that the most commonly used group intelligence tests measure only two aspects of intelligence—verbal capacity and mathematical reasoning. Even if it were agreed that these functions are important predicators of capacity to be successful in our society, conventional intelligence tests still are grossly flawed and can be considered biased.

We have ample evidence to suggest that the scores on tests of mental ability are so influenced by past experiences and cultural backgrounds that they are highly biased in favor of those groups whose experience and culture the items reflect: white, middle-class values. Tests are often characterized by an ambiguity that confuses those who think critically and in depth. Intelligence tests reflect mainly the ability of children to converge on single, predetermined answers. Divergent thinking, an important prerequisite to creativity, is not measured in the typical intelligence test.

Nor can we condone the harm done to children when the test results are misused by educators or parents. False and capricious labeling can damage the confidence and self-concept of many students, sometimes fatally and irreversibly. It is a statistical fact, the way tests are constructed, that 50 per cent of any population tested will always end up below the average mathematical "norm" that has been arbitrarily established and 50 per cent, above. This leads many teachers, and particularly parents, to believe that being below "average" means poor-quality performance. But no matter how brilliant the student body tested may be, half will always fall below the average base.

I want to reassure parents and students: The mathematical average may, or may not, be related to competent performance. Most parents do not realize that the "norming" process automatically places half the students below average, no matter how well they perform. A student who places below average when tested in a select private school may well place near the top percentile if tested in a run-down, neglected, understaffed ghetto school.

To examine another facet of the I.Q. controversy, often overlooked, we must consider the stake that the testing industry has in the entire I.Q. and standardized testing program in the United States. That an overkill exists in the use of the multitude of tests is apparent. At least 200 million achievement tests are used each year in our nation's schools. To this must be added the numerous I.Q. tests, the aptitude and vocational inventory tests, the criterion-reference tests, as well as the millions of teacher-constructed, or regional and state, tests.

In his current *Mental Measurement Yearbook* (1972), Dr. Oscar Buros, world-famous authority on testing, renowned author, psychologist, and educator, lists more than two thousand tests now in use. Each of these claims virtue and value for its own product. Do you know that there is as much competition in selling a specialized test as there is in peddling different brands of tooth paste?

Some tests remain on the market for many years beyond a time when much of their content and objectives has become irrelevant. They are not withdrawn simply because there continues to be a market for them. Just as the automobile manufacturers, thanks in large part to the efforts of Ralph Nader, frequently recall their cars to make major or minor adjustments, so should the testing industry overhaul and withdraw tests found to lack validity, reliability, or proper standardization. The I.Q. field needs a Ralph Nader of its own. Its closest counterpart is Dr. Buros, who has continued doggedly, year after year, to point to the need of better supervision in the testing field.

Is there a place for any kind of testing program in our schools? Yes. But the use to which the I.Q. or achievement tests are put should be to improve instruction, diagnose learning difficulties, and prescribe activities in response to these needs. As the National Education Association suggests in discussing the place for I.Q. and other tests in our schools:

"They must not be used in any way that will lead to labeling and classifying of students, for tracking into homogeneous groups as the major determinants to educational programs, to perpetuate an elitism, or to maintain some groups and individuals 'in their place' near the bottom of the socioeconomic ladder. In short, tests must not be used in ways that will deny any student full access to equal educational opportunity."

In his *Tests in Print,* Dr. Buros notes that at present, no matter how poor a test may be, if it is nicely packaged, and if it promises to do all sorts of things which no other can do, it will find many gullible buyers. Evidently counselors, personnel directors, psychologists, and school administrators are ready to believe the exaggerated claims of tests authors and publishers.

Distressed at this gullibility, Dr. Buros laments: "Bad usage of tests is probably more common today than good usage. Must it always be this way? We are afraid so."

What, then, is the answer?

Dr. Wilson Riles, California Superintendent of Public Instruction, insists that we must develop more effective assessment techniques—instruments and methods which are more useful to the teacher in diagnosing the strengths and weaknesses of youngsters than are most I.Q. or standardized tests. He is opposed to the injustice of putting students into pigeonholes and then believing that such placement is either infallibly correct or that children are static, not complex, dynamic, and constantly changing.

What do the I.Q. tests actually reveal? I'd sum it up this way: The amount of verbal aptitude the child possesses. His mathematical abilities. What he has retained from the books he has read. The fluency of the language used at home. His ability to memorize names and places. The attention paid to him by his parents. In essence, the accumulated knowledge of his young life span.

What do the I.Q. tests conceal? Traits such as imagination, curiosity, creativity, the thinking process, motivation, ingenuity, kindness, tolerance, honesty, integrity, nonconformity, and a hundred or more everyday living characteristics. None of these can be labeled with an I.Q. score.

Listen to Dr. Margaret Mead, the noted anthropologist, as she speaks from her vast lifetime experience:

"The idea that we can test to measure children's imagination, sensitivity, or sense of understanding of the world is incredibly stupid. There are no tests which will measure appreciation of literature or the ideas children have in their heads when writing. You cannot measure anything that really matters."

What a pity that we have become brainwashed and grovel at the feet of an I.Q. idol that has no substance or bearing in the areas of life that really matter! But the tyranny of the I.Q. dies hard. As a friend of mine said to me recently:

"Of course, I don't actually believe in the I.Q. tests. Just the same, I'm taking my two young sons to a psychologist next week to find out their scores. I want to know how bright they are."

Contradictory? Of course. But he wanted, as so many parents also want, self-gratification, satisfaction, or a sense of security, although it is false and meaningless. Why do so many parents agree that the I.Q. tests are invalid or unfair, yet feel flattered if, when their children score high, they are patted on the back by the psychologist and told that they have budding young geniuses on their hands?

To determine the growth of the I.Q. fetish, we should explore the reasons behind this irrational phenomenon. The American public swings from one fad to another. But the devotion to the I.Q. goes beyond mere superficial attitudes or attractions. We have made the mistake, in embracing the I.Q. syndrome, of confusing the psychological scores with innate intelligence.

No general agreement exists as to the meaning of intelligence and its relation to the measured I.Q. When asked to define intelligence, the nation's leading psychologists differed vastly in their views. The pioneer of them all, Dr. Edward L. Thorndike, defined intelligence as the power of good response from the point of view of truth or fact. Even among our brightest children, a correlation does not exist between verbal and mathematical concepts. A child with the highest I.Q. score in a group of one thousand children of his age will not be, necessarily, among the top when it comes to moral issues, accuracy in perception, or accuracy in memory. Life and the training he receives can determine a child's approach to different forms of intellectual operation.

Another giant in his field, Dr. Terman, whose longitudinal study on the gifted is still making history after half a century (it began in 1922), suggests that an individual is intelligent in proportion as he is able to carry on abstract thinking. In the long run, he observes, it is the races which excel in abstract thinking that eat while others starve, that survive epidemics, master new continents, conquer time and space, and substitute religion for magic, science for taboos, and justice for revenge.

What are the two levels of intelligence? A person who flounders in abstraction, but is able to handle tools skillfully, play baseball for the All-Stars, become a Joe Namath, a Willie Mays, or a Hank Aaron, is not less intelligent than the person who can solve mathematical equations, acquire a huge vocabulary, write a novel, or become President of the United States. The man, or boy, who works with his hands may have a different kind of intelligence than the person who works with his mind, but, nonetheless, he does have a specific ability.

Here is the way the intelligence syllogism goes: the pick-and-shovel man does his thinking on the sensor-motor and perceptual levels. Mere ability to think can repair your automobile while greater ability to associate in abstract ideas can draft plans for a skyscraper, discover a curative serum, or send a man to the moon.

Accordingly, educators who are involved in I.Q. testing maintain that these tests should correlate highly with school educability. Therefore, we find the I.Q. tests studded with items that involve arithmetical reasoning, language completion, naming opposites, matching proverbs, completing analogies, or understanding difficult or obscure passages from literature.

Are these inherited functions? Hardly. Much depends on where you were born, where you went to school, what kind of education you received, and how fortunate you were in the acquisition of well-to-do parents who could provide you with a good environment and a finely developed sense of child rearing.

An inspection of virtually all the I.Q. tests now in use shows that the items on them are not confined to the use of the intellect. Rather, scores are determined largely in terms of what the child has learned in school, at home, on the street, or in his clubhouse. If the child has the requisite skills and knowledge, he can usually get a high I.Q. score. As we examine the I.Q. tests, we find that they measure information that has already been learned if the environment so permitted. Tests that demand verbal or mechanical ingenuity favor those children who have had the opportunity to master these traits prior to taking the I.Q. test.

As Professor Pintner points out, intelligence is shown in dealing with things as well as words, with living men and women as well as with symbols, with the chisel, paintbrush, or the laying of bricks as well as with verbal responses. This means, therefore, that we need various types of I.Q. tests, to measure general ability and to do many things, as opposed to educational tests specifically designed to measure knowledge which an individual has been directly taught or has acquired through life experiences.

For example, the untutored savage may have high intellectual capacity, but without knowledge we would not call him an intelligent man. We could say that he had a fine mind, high intellectual powers, or splendid native intelligence. No existing I.Q. test would bring out these qualities. A test must be developed, if we are to use the I.Q. measurement at all, to ascertain the capacity to learn in more ways than the use of words, signs, or symbols.

No single test can measure pure intelligence. Yet many psychologists have equated intellect with mental ability. They have thereby overlooked the vast number of special abilities that help make up the mind. A person's mind never stops growing, regardless of age. Special abilities continue to accumulate throughout a lifetime. One's intelligence continues to grow, change, develop, and redevelop as long as he lives. However, the mind can expand its powers or it can deteriorate, depending on whether it is used or permitted to vegetate.

The I.Q. test is used not only to determine comparative mental endowment, capacity to learn, presence of special abilities, degree of mental deficiency, but also as the basis for school placement, vocational guidance, psychiatric diagnosis, prediction of adjustment potentials from infancy to old age, and a host of other related, or unrelated, items. These might include child adoption, juvenile delinquency, fitness for military service, college success, old-age counseling, or placement in mental institutions.

Is it any wonder, then, that the I.Q. controversy has not abated but grown steadily more virulent? If we accept the I.Q. scores as sacrosanct, as being the last word in a child's, or adult's intellectual process, we must assume that they are meaningful. They are, admittedly, to a very limited degree. They can often predict success in school or college—assuming the presence of motivation, accurately evaluated tests, an above-average community environment, and an economically stable home. But then, that was the original purpose of the I.Q. tests.

Let us always remember, though, that changes in the I.Q. can be produced by a variety of social and environmental factors. And we must likewise bear in mind that we possess many types of intelligence, from abstract to social, to practical and emotional.

Our knowledge of components of human intelligence has come mostly within the last twenty-five years. At the University of Southern California, a project, founded in 1949, has been studying cognitive and thinking abilities. Five basic groups of intelligence factors have been isolated: cognition, memory, divergent thinking, convergent thinking, and evaluation.

What determines human intelligence? This question must be answered if we are to understand more fully the controversial aspects of the pro- and anti-I.Q. psychologists. In *Human Intelligence,* Professor Hunt attempts an answer. He expresses surprise that educators still conceive of intelligence tests as indicators of fixed capacity or innate potential. It is wrong, he stresses, to predict an adult's intellectual competence from his score on a test taken at an early age, without specifying the circumstances he would encounter in the interim.

We know that children with lower socioeconomic backgrounds, once widely considered to be born stupid or lazy, may instead be viewed as having been cheated of an equal opportunity to gain an education. Although genetic limits do exist, they can be altered through environmental changes.

Enough evidence has accumulated to discard the time-worn notion of a fixed, static I.Q. Schooling makes a difference. If you tested a farm boy, who never left his home and dropped out when he completed the third grade in elementary school, and compared him with an affluent suburbanite attending a first-rate private school with all its advantages, the differences in I.Q., measured, say, at age twelve, would indeed show the city child "brighter," if brightness and a higher I.Q. score are equated. Why shouldn't he have a higher score, with his many educational, economic, social, and physical advantages?

Let us look deeper into the comparison. Would the city child have greater curiosity, more imagination, more tender regard of wild life, a deeper love of nature, or the ability to name the wild flowers in the cow pasture than the farm boy?

The child from the city may have an I.Q. score 30 points higher than his country cousin. And why not? The untutored boy had not learned about analogies, proverbs, mathematical formulae, similarities, poetry, nor even the meaning of the everyday simple words used in the I.Q. tests, let alone the difficult abstract ones.

All that the test would show is that one child had the advantages of a good schooling; the other had the natural training that comes with living close to nature on a farm.

If the farm lad were to receive an education equivalent to that of his city counterpart, undoubtedly the I.Q. difference would shrink substantially, or even go above that of the city boy. It is not unusual to find changes of 40 to 50 points in individual cases over a period of years, or even months.

A tragic result of theory that the I.Q. remains relatively constant and unchanged throughout life, despite growing evidence to the contrary, is that schools still use scores based on the performance of children made in earlier years. Unfortunately, we find that the I.Q. score made by a child in the first grade may follow him doggedly throughout his academic life, and beyond. Many educators and guidance counselors still accept the fallacious belief that tests administered at one age can reliably predict what the child will do at a later stage of his life.

I do not believe that long-range prediction is possible from test scores alone. We would have to know the circumstances of the child's development, his environment, family status, emotional or financial outlook. Many events can take place in the interim—a change in Father's job, a move to another state, improved or reduced socioeconomic status.

As Dr. Hunt so aptly puts it, trying to predict what a person's

I.Q. will be at at age twenty, on the basis of his I.Q. at age four or five, is like trying to predict how heavy a two-week-old calf will be when he is two years old, without knowing whether he will be reared in a dry pasture, in an irrigated one, or on a feed lot.

Teachers and others who deal with children in the classroom are hypnotized by the I.Q. scores. If a child does poorly in class, and the teacher notes that somewhere along the line the youngster had a group Otis Lennon Mental Ability Test and scored 101 points, the teacher is often likely to say:

"Oh well, Bill is doing about what can be expected. After all, what can you ask of a child with average intelligence? No use pushing him any further. He won't make it."

Or, if the child is moving along rapidly, and the I.Q. score on the accumulative record sheet is high, the teacher may say smugly:

"Mary is working to her capacity. She is a bright child. With an I.Q. of 138, she certainly deserves to get all A's in school. I'm glad I have at least one bright kid in my class."

We must re-examine the whole question of the I.Q. and determine how the tests are to be used, if at all. Better still, a moratorium on all I.Q. and achievement tests should be declared until we know more about their value, their place in our schools, and the role they should play in the lives of millions of young boys and girls in school systems throughout the United States.

It is for these reasons that I would like to eliminate the term I.Q., or Intelligence Quotient, from our lexicon. Since we really do not know what the term means—even our foremost scientists, school psychologists, eminent scholars, and child experts argue loudly over an acceptable definition—why continue its use?

Unfortunately, for the children, at any rate, the commonly accepted meaning of an I.Q. score is "innate intelligence." To put it simply, if your child has an I.Q. of 150, he is "gifted" or a potential genius; at 120 he is "superior" but not in the gifted category; a score of 100 places him in the "average" range; 85 puts him the slow class, while anything below 75, or in some states 80, relegates him to a class for mentally retarded.

This is unfair! Our children are cheated!

2

What is the I.Q. test?

Many types of I.Q. tests exist. Some are designed to measure the verbal intelligence of children. Others stress spatial or mathematical information; still others measure creativity. Tests also are designed to discover musical ability, social poise, emotional stability, vocational skills, or future high school or college success.

Strictly speaking, though, the I.Q. has a niche of its own. Proponents hold that it measures pure intelligence, whatever that may mean. It would take volumes to list and delineate the numerous I.Q., aptitude, achievement, and intelligence tests now in use in schools, colleges, business, or governmental agencies.

These tests fall into various major classifications: tests of character and personality, vocational tests, I.Q. tests, math tests, English and reading tests, social studies and history tests, science tests, as well as fine arts, foreign language, music, and inventory tests. The bulk of them is used in the United States. A much smaller number is found in Great Britain, Canada, Australia, the Union of South Africa, Switzerland, Holland, New Zealand, and Sweden. The United States outpaces all the other nations combined by a long stretch.

The I.Q. testing began, for all practical purposes, with the development of the Binet test in 1905. About the year 1900, the French Government commissioned Alfred Binet and Theodore Simon to prepare a method that could predict which French children would be likely to benefit from regular school education, and which should be placed in special schools for slower learners. Thus, the original purpose of these tests—and it should be noted that the word I.Q. was not used at that time—*was to predict which child could succeed academically.* No other purpose was intended, nor were the tests constructed in any way that might possibly lead to any other conclusion. Thus, the I.Q. tests, stripped of all the verbiage that now surrounds them, are measures of academic readiness rather than measures of intelligence. This point must always be remembered.

One of Binet's basic assumptions in preparing his test was that a child, regardless of age, could be considered "normal" if he were able to do things and answer test questions comparable to other children of his own age. On the other hand, he was slow or even retarded if his test performance showed that he could not function academically at the level of children in his age bracket. The further below his level he performed, the lower would his intelligence be considered.

On the other hand, if he went above his age group and was consistently more advanced, he was listed as a superior or bright child. An eight-year-old who could answer the questions designed for the ten-year-olds was called bright. If he could only go to the six-year-old level, he was termed slow-witted or retarded.

Here we hit a basic fallacy that the I.Q. testers have promulgated: by no stretch of the imagination can we say that a score on an I.Q. test can serve as an indication of hereditary capacity or scholastic potential. All we know from the I.Q. test is that Billy, age nine, is doing as well as Mary, age nine. But Billy is doing better than Nellie, age eight, and poorer than Harry, who is age twelve. The age of the child is the all-important determinant in calculating the I.Q. score.

Yes, but what about late bloomers? Since age and mental progress are assumed to be correlated, do we likewise assume that each child develops along a similar mental or intellectual pattern? By the same token, would we say that Billy at four feet tall is physically inferior to Johnny, who is four feet, five inches tall, even if both are exactly seven years old? Perhaps Billy may spurt and overtake Johnny before the year ends or by the time they both achieve their maximum growth. Isn't it just as likely that the intellectual growth of these two seven-year-olds will also change, develop, and grow along different patterns, just as their physical growth will?

Alfred Binet, whose test methods are probably among the most widely used today, recognized the limitations of his selection program when he challenged and criticized psychologists who even as far back as the year 1909 began to misuse the results of the Binet tests. He knew that the I.Q. is merely a score that is offered as an index of a child's rate of learning, compared with the learning rate of others with whom he can be reasonably compared.

A child's mind, said Binet, is like a field for which an expert farmer has devised a change in the methods of cultivation, with the result that in place of a desert land, we now have a forest. Binet explained his theory of testing further, in these words:

"It is in this particular sense, the one which is significant, that we say that the intelligence of children may be increased. One increases that which constitutes the intelligence of a school child, namely the capacity to learn, to improve with instruction."

The Binet test was revised in 1916, for use in this country, by the late Dr. Terman of Stanford University—hence the name, Stanford-Binet. It could just as readily have been called the Terman-Binet test. Somewhere along the line, Theodore Simon dropped out of the testing domain.

But Terman went further than Binet had intended. The revision of the Binet scale incorporated the features that characterize scales of the Binet type: the use of age standards, the kind of mental functions brought into play, and the concept of the measurement of general intelligence. The 1916 Terman scale provided standards of intellectual performance for average American children from the age of three to sixteen.

From Binet's original fifty-four questions, the number was increased to ninety. Items involving the more complex mental processes were retained. The 1916 Stanford scale was standardized on a sample of 1,000 children and 400 adults.

In 1937, the Stanford-Binet test was again revised. As the Manual for the Third Revision Form L-M explains, during the years intervening between the publication of the 1916 scale and the beginning of work on the second revision, much information had accumulated on the behavior of various types of mental tests and the relative merits of specific tests as measures of intelligence. Certain types of tests had generally proven to have higher correlations with the various independent estimates of the trait than others.

As revised in 1937, the test retained the characteristics of Binet-type questions. It utilized the same assumptions, methods, and principles. Moreover, it made use of age standards of performance and the assumption that general intelligence is a trait which develops with age. It remained a measure of general ability rather than of specific or related groups of abilities.

Prominent among the subtests used (and this is true of virtually all other I.Q. tests later devised) are analogies, opposites, comprehension, vocabulary, similarities and differences, verbal and pictorial completions, absurdities, drawing designs, and memory for meaningful material and digits. And analysis of the revised test shows that it is still weighted with situations in which verbal ability is an essential element.

The standardization group for the 1937 Stanford-Binet revision consisted of 3,184 native-born white children. Approximately 100 children were tested at each half-year interval from one and half to five and a half years; 200 at each level from ages six to fourteen, and 100 each from ages fifteen to eighteen. Each group was equally divided between the sexes. The final sample was slightly higher on the socioeconomic level than the census population. Disproportionately more urban than rural children were used.

Finally, the third revision took place in 1960. Now the test included in a single form the best subtest questions from the L and M scales. These were two different tests, made comparable, so that either could be given to the children tested, without fear that they had already seen the "answers."

Those revising the test held that there was less need for alternative forms of equivalent difficulty than in 1937 because other well-constructed individual tests were available to the clinicians who worked in the field of child testing. The selection of subtests included in the 1960 scale was based on the records of tests administered during the five-year period from 1950 to 1954. Children from various types of communities in different parts of the country were included in the new assessment groups.

A total of 4,498 children between the ages of two and one-half and eighteen are represented in the 1960 test. The choice of samples was determined by the occupational grouping of fathers and, in the case of the fifteen-year-olds, by grade placement also. Six occupational groups of fathers were selected as the basis, for standardization: professional and technical workers; managers, officials, proprietors, farm managers, and farm owners; clerical and sales workers; craftsmen, foremen, and operatives; private household and service workers; and laborers, farm and nonfarm. The percentage of each was based upon 1950 census figures.

Changes in the test have been of two significant types: content and structure. In content, items were eliminated that duplicated questions. As far as structure is concerned, changes were made where the items appeared to be too difficult. However, the 1960 revision was based on the validation made in the 1937 scale. Less than 4,000 children were used as the basis for validation, with approximately 100 each from kindergarten through twelfth grades. No nonwhites were included.

Whether the revised Stanford-Binet is any better than the previous ones in measuring intelligence is still a highly debatable question. Since it is based on items used on children some forty years ago, might there not be substantial differences in the reaction that could be expected from children today? Moreover, this revised test, as is true with virtually all current I.Q. tests now in use, selected only white, native-born American children as subjects. Blacks, Orientals, Chicanos, Spanish-speaking persons, or other minority groups were eliminated.

It is important to note that the 1960 revision—the one currently in use—did not update the older 1937 standardized test on the validation process. This was not done, despite the fact that it may affect the academic or professional lives of millions of children for years to come.

Probably next in importance, if not equally so (some psychologists say more so), is the Wechsler series of I.Q. tests. The best known of the series, which range from preschoolers to adulthood, is the Wechsler Intelligence Scale for Children—the WISC—standardized in 1949 on a sample of 2,200 English-speaking white children. This brief sample attempted to cover all geographic areas of the United States and nine occupational categories held by the fathers of the children tested. What about mothers? Aren't they important in the life of a child? I certainly believe so.

The occupation of the mother was not considered of any importance, even though large numbers of mothers are today the "head" of the household, especially where the family is broken through divorce, or the mother is the breadwinner. As was the case in the Stanford-Binet, no blacks, Chicanos, or Orientals were included in the standardization sample.

Unlike the Stanford-Binet, the WISC divides the child's knowledge or intelligence into various categories, each measured separately, and then averaged into the total I.Q. score. These subtests are included: verbal, comprehension, arithmetic, similarities, picture arrangement, block design, picture completion, object assembly, mazes, coding, and total performance. The raw scores on the subtotals are added to arrive at a final I.Q. score, based on a specific formula built into the test.

It matters little, in this test, whether one child gets a score of 100 on his vocabulary and 150 on block design, while another child gets 150 on vocabulary and 100 on the design section. Both would have a total performance score of 125. Yet the first child would be mechanically oriented, while the second, with the high verbal score, would definitely veer toward the verbal and language arts.

The total I.Q. score on the WISC has little relationship to the specific knowledge that the child possesses, assuming that you believe the scores are in any way significant.

That may be why critics have taken issue with the claims made by those who sponsor the WISC tests. Typical is this comment by Professor David Freides, Emory University psychologist:

"This twenty-one-year-old test is probably more directly instrumental in influencing life decisions on school-age children than any other. Yet the greatest part of its content was borrowed from a test for adults, Form 2, of the Wechsler Belleview Intelligence Scale. Many of the questions in the WISC are clearly inappropriate for children and should be replaced."

For example, such items on the WISC as "Why is it generally better to give money to an organized charity than a street beggar?" or "Why is it better to pay bills by check rather than by cash?" are unsuitable for many children and far beyond their comprehension as to the social implications. Indeed, many adults would find the proper answers difficult.

Yet, they are part of the testing procedure, not only in the WISC but in other highly respected and universally adopted I.Q. tests. The WISC norms are based on tests given to children prior to 1955. The test originally was issued in 1949. Are the norms of a generation ago an honest reflection of 1975 or the years beyond? Does the Stanford-Binet, with its norm based on standardizations made in the 1930s, cope with the changes that have taken place in the last twenty to forty years?

Examples can be cited of how far off the "norms" are in these outdated tests, still found in every guidance counselor's office in the nation's schools. The WISC Manual, which gives the directions for those administering the test to follow, lists the scoring limits for a correct answer to the question, "What is the population of the United States?", as between 130 and 190 million.

That is definitely unrealistic. Our population has already passed the 220-million mark! Yet, if the examiner followed his Manual implicitly, as he has been admonished to do, he would have to mark the answer wrong. This, in turn, would lower the I.Q. score of the child who answered the question correctly, and give credit to the one who may have answered it incorrectly.

Some of the items on the various I.Q. tests are unfair to foreign students, recently arrived in this country from Cuba, Puerto Rico, or elsewhere, or children from disadvantaged slums, from the Appalachian Mountains regions, or poorly supported rural schools. Could you reasonably expect these children to identify the poems of Longfellow, distinguish between two abstract concepts, or recall the names of the early Presidents of the United States?

All of the WISC subtests use words, pictures, and materials that are more familiar to middle-class white Americans than to any other social or ethnic group. Three of the eleven subtests require knowledge of factual information—definition of a word, an author, or a socially acceptable rule of behavior.

Other questions ask children to remember a series of numbers, detect the similarity between varying concepts, discover a missing element in a line drawing, arrange blocks in a design, arrange pictures into a coherent story, solve a puzzle, or decode and copy a series of simple designs that grow progressively more complicated.

Children who are well read, it is obvious, are most likely to secure higher I.Q. scores on the vocabulary and information sections of the test. Professor Jerome Kagan of Harvard University lists five questions taken from the vocabulary or information subtests found in the WISC and five designed by a psychologist, Adrian Dove. The latter items were chosen as being familar to urban poor blacks, while the Wechsler questions presumably favored middle-class white Americans.

Wechsler Test

1. Who wrote *Hamlet?*
2. Who wrote the *Iliad?*
3. What is the Koran?
4. What does audacious mean?
5. What does plagiarize mean?

Dove's Test

1. In C. C. Ryder, what does C. C. stand for?
2. What is a gashead?
3. What is Willie Mays' last name?
4. What does "handkerchief head" mean?
5. Whom did "Stagger Lee" kill in the famous blues legend?

Observes Dr. Kagan: "Is it unreasonable to ask whether high scores on either test measure anything to do with basic mental capacity? A person's score reflects the probability that he has been exposed to the information requested."

If the Wechsler tests were translated into Spanish, Swahili, or Chinese, and given to every ten-year-old child in Latin America, East Africa, or China, would many get above the retarded mentality score? Would we then say that almost all children in these lands were full-witted or mentally deficient? Not at all. We would recognize immediately that the tests were not valid. They were not standardized on the populations that were being tested. A similar situation exists in this country. Invalid tests will give invalid results.

The Child Growth and Development Center at The Johns Hopkins University, under the direction of Dr. Janet Hardy, examined some Wechsler subtests that were given to poor, disadvantaged minority children. The outcome threw much further light on the stranglehold of the I.Q. Many children failed, or received much lower scores than they should have, because they did not understand the question, and often not even the speech pattern of the examiners.

Although their answers seemed reasonable enough to the children, they did not receive any credit for them. Thus their I.Q. scores were substantially lowered. When the Center staff adjusted its approach to meet the needs of the different cultures with which they were dealing, the scores were raised significantly.

Numerous examples of cultural bias are cited by the Johns Hopkins team of examiners. Take this question: "What is the thing to do if a child much smaller than yourself starts to fight with you?"

The white, or perhaps the black, middle-class child usually indicates that he would try to avoid a fight. He receives a maximum credit for this answer, raising his I.Q. score. Many of the disadvantaged children said they would fight back. They received a minus credit, thus lowering their score.

When asked why they would fight back, a typical reply was:

"My mother says if someone mess with you, you mess 'em back."

Each child is giving what he believes to be the correct answer, which it is to him and to the standards of the group to which he belongs. But now we find that mental capacity has been equated with ethnic mores or a different cultural attitude from that held by mainstream children.

Take the question of pronunciation. When the middle-class examiner in the Johns Hopkins study asked the children to define "fur" some said:

"That's what happens when you light a match."

Evidently, the words "fur" and "fire" sounded alike to them, as did the words "sword" and "saw." Answered incorrectly, not because of an intelligence lag but because of a pronunciation misunderstanding, these wrong answers might cause a drop of five, ten, or twenty I.Q. points. These examples cover only a small proportion of the questions that lend themselves to serious bias in the tests as presently constructed.

There are many other intelligence tests, in addition to the Stanford-Binet and Wechsler, designed ostensibly to measure I.Q., aptitude, achievement, or vocational potential. Many of them, even when viewed through a nonpsychological, layman's eyes, are inept, inadequate, fallacious, and even dangerously open to misuse. Imagine finding a child's I.Q. at the age of two months and then projecting his future intellectual growth, as the Bayley Scale of Infant Development presumes to do!

Standards have been established by the Mental Measurement Yearbooks. They are sound, solid, worthwhile criteria, whose adoption is long overdue. When will the I.Q. multimillion-dollar industry adhere to them? Dr. Buros comments pessimistically:

"Many of the tests on the market today would cease to exist if these standards should become the accepted criterion for evaluating test manuals."

A number of experienced psychologists point out that the I.Q. scores change, that the tests reflect only one or two out of a huge range of possible mental abilities. The tests are not a fair indicator of the potential performance of such groups in the United States as ghetto blacks, reservation Indians, economically deprived poor whites, or those attending fund-starved rural schools.

We know that the early preschool years give the child from a disadvantaged home too few experiences that produce proper learning attitudes or environment. Since the child cannot, or does not, find success in school, he seeks it in the streets or through his own peer group. Because they must concentrate on bare economic survival, parents in the lowest economic brackets have little time to devote to their children's intellectual growth, nor are they motivated to do so.

It is obvious that children will do poorly on the I.Q. test when they are apathetic, withdrawn, unmotivated, hostile, and in constant conflict with their teachers or supervisors.

As Dr. Martin Deutsch, Director of the New York University Institute for Development Studies, points out, not only do the culturally deprived youngsters fall behind in basic skills, such as reading and arithmetic, they also do not respond to any other aspect of the learning process. Education simply passes them by, and going to school becomes an ever-growing chore to which they respond only in negative terms.

The effect of the I.Q. score can be devastating to the child and to his parents. If a child scores low on an intelligence test because he cannot read, notes Dr. Kenneth B. Clark, nationally known psychologist, and then is not taught to read because he has a low score, the child is imprisoned in an iron circle from which he cannot escape. He becomes the victim of an educational self-fulfilling prophecy. The I.Q. score showed he could not read. Since he is then not taught, the prophecy of the I.Q. is fulfilled—he never learns to read properly.

The I.Q. does not determine how much a child will learn, or the ceiling of what he can learn, if permitted to grow to his full potential. Rather, it suggests the rate of the child's learning ability and the amount of time and effort that will be required to teach the child. We have enough evidence to show that all children are able to learn. But we must recognize that it may take some longer than others, that they will need more encouragement, more stimulation, a greater challenge.

Let us recall that the original purpose of the Binet test was to predict which children would succeed academically and which would fail. But psychologists have gone far beyond that point today. They have broadened its base and insist that the I.Q. score is a measure of intelligence, which of course it is not.

We would not have fallen into the current bitter and acrimonious controversy over racial and ethnic intellectual differences, as well as the gross misunderstanding of the purposes of the I.Q. scores, if Binet had labeled his original test, back in 1905, as a general measure of academic readiness rather than a measure of intelligence. The I.Q. label should be changed to A.Q.—from Intelligence Quotient to Academic Quotient. Isn't that what the I.Q. controversy is all about?

The early psychologists who promoted "intelligence" testing in the United States interpreted the I.Q. score as a measure of academic and biological potential. Such interpretations have continued to muddy the testing movement for three quarters of a century. As a consequence, too often the I.Q. test score is correlated with the child's mental ability, not his scholastic attainment.

Although many psychologists do not accept a unitary and constant conception of intelligence, the term, through usage, does have just that connotation. The Binet test, as we have seen, was developed for a highly specific and prescribed purpose, not as a measurement of intelligence. It was only later, in 1912, that Dr. Wilhelm Stern of Germany devised the I.Q. score, calling the test a measurement of intelligence and the score an indicator of mental capacity. From that step it was a short hop, to 1916, when the I.Q. became popularly known as a test to measure intelligence, even though that term was still undefined.

With the increasing potency of the Binet score to predict scholastic success, the unitary concept of intelligence evolved. The protests of psychometricians, critical psychologists, and concerned educators went unheeded.

Even if the I.Q. scores are accepted as a reflection of intelligence, the data are hardly consistent with this concept. Researchists have found that the failure to predict childhood I.Q. from infancy plus the data on the extent of I.Q. change during childhood argue against constancy. As early as the turn of the century, educators found that performance on some mental tests was independent of performance on other tests of equal difficulty.

Even if we separate the I.Q. tests from the issue of intelligence, this will not condone the application of the scores as a basis to predict what the individual will be able to do, or to select him for special consideration. Psychologists have found that performance varies within an individual. Since in many instances changes can be substantial, testing, if done at all, should take place at frequent intervals, particularly if any change takes place in the living conditions of the student involved.

Shall we continue to give I.Q. tests? Not if we value the emotional, social, intellectual, academic, and physical health of our millions of schoolchildren.

Commercially, the I.Q. has sometimes deteriorated into cheap, parlor-game gimmicks. I have seen, at some newsstands or corner drugstores, gadgets that resemble the pinball or soft drink machines. "Get your I.Q. tested for 25¢!" proclaims a bold sign above the gadget. Put in a quarter and answer the questions that flash into view. If you get fifteen out of the twenty right, your I.Q. is slated as 150. If you get ten right, it is 100. And, under five correct answers, you are a mental retardate. The other day I tried it and answered six of the twenty questions. What does that make me? Who knows; maybe the machine knows something that I don't about my intellect!

Not long ago the newspapers carried a story about a Canadian psychologist, John Ertl, who has developed a new method of testing brain power. While the old test measures what you have already learned, his test, says Ertl, will measure your potential to learn. The idea for his new measuring device occurred in 1959, after he scored 77 on a traditional I.Q. test. This put him among the mentally retarded group. No wonder he decided to build his own I.Q. testing machine, to prove that he was just as bright as the next person.

Ertl's test uses a "neural efficiency analyzer" which has five basic parts: a device to amplify the waves, a helmet sporting a pair of electrodes to pick up brain waves, an oscilloscope on which the waves can be viewed, a flashing light to stimulate the brain, and a computer to analyze the efficiency with which the brain produces the flashes.

The test is painless, takes three minutes, and works equally well for an illiterate, a newborn infant, or an established genius. The score is computed to be the average time the brain takes to respond to some 200 flashes. The lower the number, the better the performance. A normal score ranges between 120 and 140. Ertl claims that he has found that the 15 I.Q. points that Dr. Jensen says blacks average below whites are wholly the product of cultural bias in the conventional tests. In his astoundingly different I.Q. test, all those tested, black or white, rich or poor, urban or suburban, showed an equal response.

A gimmick? Some might say so. But Ertl's findings are under study by two independent research authorities. And his technique is undergoing extensive examination at ten different research institutions. If it is found to be legitimate, and if its validity can be proven, the analyzer will be mass produced. Another I.Q. test will be on the overcrowded but ever-receptive market.

One thing appears self-evident: there should be less emphasis on I.Q. testing and more stress on learning. The I.Q. testing apparatus is a blot on American education. No other country in the world places as much emphasis on the I.Q. as we do. Among other nations, China has outlawed it completely.

It is time that we dropped out of the race to see who has the highest I.Q. Our emphasis should be placed on methods of creative teaching in the schools. The long overdue moratorium on I.Q. testing should take top priority on the nation's educational agenda.

3

How is your child's I.Q. determined?

Francis Galton, cousin of the noted Charles Darwin, evolved the idea of measuring mental ability on an objective basis. Just about the time that Darwin began his *Origin of Species,* Galton published, in 1869, *Hereditary Genius,* which dealt with the question of intellect. Galton noted that excellence ran in families. He had evidence, he said, that statesmen, judges, prime ministers, scientists, poets, or even outstanding athletes frequently tended to be related by blood. And therefore, he concluded, inheritance played a major role in the inheritance of intellect.

Motivated by this conclusion, Galton tried to test mental ability. He was unable, however, to develop a workable formula. That was to come at a later date in another country. But Galton did, in 1881, establish a laboratory where people, for a fee, could have their vision, hearing, and other senses tested.

Nothing came of this ambitious but unsound project. Nonetheless, he continued to search for a practical intelligence test, which he could not find.

But in 1890, Professor James McKenn Cattell coined the phrase "mental test." This was based on the work he was doing, as a psychologist, with children at the University of Pennsylvania. Cattell expanded on Galton's experiments and attempted to measure the mental, as well as the physical, aspects of an individual. The Cattell inroads in the testing field, while substantial, were only a pioneering venture.

Still later, Dr. Franz Boas explored various traits of 1,500 children in Worcester, Massachusetts. Clark University, in Worcester, had attracted many notable psychologists, and it was here that Dr. Boas conducted his experiments in testing. He included the usual physical measures such as hearing and vision but added a new, more all-embracing, area—that of memory. In his memory test, children were asked to repeat a list of digits that they had just heard and to record the longest list of numbers that they could accurately remember.

This "immediate memory span" is found in many I.Q. tests today. The work of Cattell and Boas attracted attention outside their own laboratories. By the mid-1890s, testing became more than a theoretical topic of discussion among psychologists, but earned the support of various professional organizations.

However, the vital spark flickered and almost became extinguished, until it blazed forth in its full light overseas, through the efforts of Binet. He made testing practical and showed that it could become a useful, if limited, tool in the schooling of children. As far back as 1895, ten years before he developed a workable test that he felt would be valid, Binet suggested that mental testing should be based on the psychological processes of thought involving intelligence, rather than on sensory and motor functions.

Binet had no idea what type of test might evolve, but he suggested a variety that could be considered: tests of memory, mental imagery, imagination, attentiveness, mechanical and verbal comprehension, aesthetic appreciation, moral sensibility, or even the child's capacity to sustain muscular and visual judgment of distance.

Incidentally, most of these traits are now included in the standard I.Q. tests, still in use eighty years after the original suggestion. Binet began to test his theories on children. For the first time, he correlated intelligence with age. In one experiment, Binet tested 500 children by reading them a sentence and then asking them to write down as much as they could remember. He found that as children grew older, they performed more skillfully on the tests.

However, Binet wanted to find a test that could measure the difference between bright and dull children. With the help of teachers, he placed children in two categories—the brightest and the dullest in their grades. Then he gave each group a series of tests, ranging from simple sensory discrimination to perceptual speed tests.

As Binet continued with his work, he attracted the attention of the French Minister of Public Instruction who wanted a better method to determine which were the subnormal children in the Paris schools.

Working with another psychologist, Dr. Theodore Simon, Binet developed a series of tests graded as to difficulty, and standardized for normal children of various ages. The innovation made by these two psychologists rested on what is now the commonly accepted premise: chronological age must be taken into consideration when determining mental ability. The correlation between age and intellect is vital in this testing procedure.

Here is the crux of the entire I.Q. evaluation, as envisioned by the French psychologists and continued until the present day wherever I.Q. tests are given: if a child outperforms other children of his own age, he is automatically and arbitrarily assumed to be bright. If he does as well as his age group—and the majority do—he is called an average child. But, for whatever reason, if he does not do as well, he is listed as being dull, of below-average intelligence.

As their first experiment in putting their theories into actual practice, Binet and Simon drew up a list of thirty test items covering what they felt to be the range of a child's mental capacity. The list included such items as the imitating of gestures, following instructions, naming familiar objects, repeating sentences, and distinguishing between abstract words. This test was given to fifty normal children between the ages of three and eleven, and to fifty children diagnosed as retarded. To their delight, Binet and Simon found that their test could pick out the retarded children more quickly, cheaply, and accurately than had been done previously through hit-and-miss methods of evaluation.

The Binet-Simon test, as it was then known, caught the imagination of the educational and psychological world. It swept across borders to America, primarily, but to other nations as well. In 1908, the authors published a revised series of tests, to be used to rate all children, not just a device to separate the normal from the abnormal.

In his final version, published in 1911, a year before he died, Binet listed five problems which the average child of various age levels could reasonably be expected to solve.

Six-year-olds, for example, were expected to distinguish between morning and afternoon; define familiar objects in terms of use; copy a diamond shape; count thirteen pennies, and distinguish between an ugly and a pretty face.

An average ten-year-old was considered to be acting mentally within his age group if he could arrange five blocks in order of weight; draw two designs from memory; criticize absurd statements; answer comprehension questions, and use three words in not more than two sentences.

At this point it is essential to stress that Binet did not use the term Intelligence Quotient, or I.Q., when developing and later conducting his tests. His primary objective was to find, if possible, ways to distinguish between an average child and one who might need special help as a mentally retarded youngster and be placed in a school where such help might be more readily available.

But the German psychologist, Dr. Stern, took Binet's findings one step further, and what a lasting, controversial step it has been! He proclaimed that a child who was a year behind his peer group at age six was more retarded than a child who was a year behind his peer group at age twelve, and that there was a distinct relationship between mental and chronological age.

What does this mean? To get the child's I.Q., according to the Stern formula, and the one now universally accepted, divide one's mental age by chronological age; then multiply by 100 to get rid of decimals. Hence a child who is five years old and has a mental age of eight years and two months, as measured by an I.Q. test, is as bright, under this formula, as a child who is eight years old and has a mental age of thirteen years. Both will be found, upon careful computation, to have identical I.Q. scores of 160.

Contrary-wise, a child of ten who has a mental age, as measured by the Binet scale, of seven years will be considered dull with a mental I.Q. of 70. If the child has a mental age of fifteen, he will be considered superior or gifted, with a computed I.Q. of 150. Despite various revisions of the Binet and the host of other I.Q. tests that came in its wake, the basic concept remains unchanged—the I.Q. is considered to be the mental age divided by the chronological age.

Although most I.Q. tests have been standardized for use with children, a number of tests now in general use, such as the Wechsler Adult Intelligence Scale, attempt to go into the adult area. I.Q. tests have even been designed for use in the employment of men and women in business concerns or industrial corporations.

Can intelligence be designated in terms of a number, or a symbol? Is Robert brighter than Mary because his I.Q. score is 133 and hers is 121? Is there any way to correlate comprehension, inventiveness, or critical judgment with an arbitrary figure, whether it be 133, 117, or 97? Existing evidence does not uphold these contentions.

Stressing this point, the Harvard psychologist, Dr. Herrnstein, whose *Atlantic Monthly* article on the I.Q. followed by his book *I.Q. in the Meritocracy* catapulted him into the ongoing controversy, observes that common sense insists on a multiple concept of intelligence. He comments further:

"Some people are adept at words, some at numbers, some at spatial imagination, some at visual or auditory remembering, some at deductive reasoning, some at inductive inference, and so on. We expect some people to be broadly talented, others to be narrowly so, and still others not to be talented at all."

Quite true. But here we come to another significant aspect of the I.Q. issue: Who does the testing? The *Stanford-Binet Intelligence Scale—1972 Norms Edition* gives specific instruction. The most essential requirement to determine a valid score, it points out, is an examiner who knows how to use the test and is sensitive to the needs of the child being tested. Moreover, examiners are warned, unless the tests are given in strict accordance with the procedures by which they were standardized, the results will be invalid.

Unfortunately for the child who is being tested, an examiner may be letter perfect in following directions and still get inaccurate results. If the psychologist or teacher who does the testing is unable to motivate the child to do his best, it is certain that the I.Q. score will be lower than it otherwise might be. The examiner may fail to follow up ambiguous responses, or be unable to gain a good rapport with the child. In either case, the I.Q. score will not be an accurate indication of the child's ability as measured through these tests.

Moreover, the Manual cautions the examiner against being influenced by any general impression he may have formed of the child's ability before the testing even begins. There is a natural tendency to overestimate the ability of a sprightly, self-confident, talkative child, and to underestimate the thoughtful, timid, or insecure youngster.

Since the scoring is done entirely by the examiner, in the case of individual tests, or by teachers in the group I.Q. tests, the margin for errors is enormous. Not only can there be, and often are, wrong mathematical computations, but the personal judgment of the examiner can sway the results by a substantial margin. Although referred to as an "objective" I.Q. test, it is far from that. Human mistakes, errors, and personal biases are not only possible but have been found to occur far more frequently than the testing profession is willing to admit.

The Manual on the Stanford-Binet concedes that the margin for error exists and is difficult to overcome. It says frankly:

"While one could wish that the Binet scales were entirely free from subjectivity of scoring, this limitation is the price that is paid for the great flexibility and richness as compared with tests which are stencil-scored. The price is not excessive in view of the greater psychological insight that the Binet type of test affords."

The examination of a young child can usually be completed in thirty to forty minutes. An older child may require as much as ninety minutes. The experienced examiner requires considerably less time than the novice.

Let us look at that terrifying statement again.

A test that takes from half an hour to an hour and a half may determine a child's academic life, his profession, the courses he will take, the classmates with whom he will associate for many years, the attitude of the teacher toward him or the school or college he may enter.

Incredible!

Yet this is not unusual. And at the same time, the psychologist who administers the I.Q. test has the problem of deciding whether the child should get full, partial, or no credit on the I.Q. scale. The ability of anyone to make this judgment accurately is dubious. For example, a child of six will find, on one of the I.Q. tests, the question:

"What is the difference between a bird and a dog?"

The correct answer is, "A bird flies and a dog runs." But a minus answer would be: "A bird can go faster than a dog," or perhaps, "A dog chases a bird."

As a farm lad from Briggs Corner I know that a dog will chase a bird in the meadow or across the corn patch, and I also am certain that a bird can go faster than a dog. This is logical to a rural farm child who probably takes for granted that a bird flies and a dog runs and goes deeper into the differences between the two.

A nine-year-old may be asked to explain how these three are similar: snake, cow, and sparrow. The responses that would be considered correct and receive I.Q. credit are that (1) they are all animals; (2) they can eat in the fields; and (3) none of them can talk.

But a completely wrong answer, with no credit awarded, might be: A snake crawls, a cow walks, and a sparrow flies. They do. But the question asks for similarities, not differences. The child's I.Q. is lowered, it is obvious, if he *reads* or *hears* the question inaccurately. Perhaps if it were pointed out to the child that the question, as answered, is correct but does not correspond to the information sought, the child would readily give the accurate answer.

Further, the directions on the Stanford-Binet I.Q. Manual states: "Only if the standard meaning of the word can be given is the item scored plus. . . ." Doesn't that hurt blacks, Chicanos, rural, or disadvantaged children who may give different meanings and innuendos to their words or expressions?

In "Sanford and Son," the TV program, the visiting doctor looks as though he might be either black or white. Asks Fred Sanford innocently enough "Would you like some ripple?"

"What is that?" asks the doctor.

"Oh, just testing," answers Fred. "If you don't know ripple, you are not one of us. Thought you might be passing."

How many middle-class, white Americans (children) know that ripple is the slang name for wine?

Here are some of the activities that determine a child's I.Q. score:

Three-year-olds: Bead stringing, identifying a picture vocabulary, building block pictures, copying a circle, and drawing a vertical line.

Six-year-olds: Recognizing vocabulary, putting together mutilated pictures, understanding number concepts, knowing differences, recognizing opposite analogies, and maze tracing.

Ten-year-olds: Identifying vocabulary, block counting, defining abstract words such as pity or justice, finding reasons for problems, naming words, and repeating arithmetic figures up to six digits.

Fourteen-year-olds: Vocabulary recognition, inductive reasoning, ingenuity, orientation, direction, and reconciliation of opposites.

The Otis-Lennon Mental Ability Test, a popular group test, is designed to provide scores on a mass basis. It is similar to the Lorge-Thorndike group test. Obviously, it is cheaper to operate than the individual tests, but it is far less accurate. Both tests contain typical items: vocabulary, word opposites, analogies, arithmetical equations, drawings, and completions.

Examples include: Eye is to see as ear is to . . . head . . . hear . . . talk . . . nose . . . cheek. Children are instructed to place an X beside the answer they believe to be correct.

Or, in arithmetic, a sample question might be: A boy bought 3 pencils at 5¢ each. How much did the pencils cost? . . . 5¢ . . . 10¢ . . . 30¢ . . . 20¢ . . . 25¢ . . . none of these . . . The correct answer, of course, is 15¢. Since this answer is not given in the sample, the choice "none of these" is correct.

Children are not told that they are taking an I.Q. test. The Manual suggests that the examiners say: "This is a test to see how well you can solve different kinds of problems."

Still another, the Peabody Picture Vocabulary Test, is used for young children and has received recognition in the testing field as being valid and reliable. Only ten to fifteen minutes are usually required to administer this test.

With children eight years of age and above, the examiner giving the Peabody test says: "I have some pictures to show you. See, there are four pictures on this page. Each of them is numbered. I will say a word, then I want you to tell me the number of, or point to, the picture which best tells me the meaning of the word."

The examiner may point to a picture of a fish, a crib, a butterfly, or any one of the 150 plates containing pictures. The I.Q. is scored on the basis of right answers, compared with those made by children of the same age. The test is designed for any English-speaking person in the United States, between the ages of two and one half and eighteen years, who is able to hear words and see the drawings.

As for drawbacks found in the test, the child must be familiar with a wide variety of objects, such as tweezers, beehives, ambulances, casseroles, wasps, or observatories. He must be able to decode the pictures to determine which ones best represent such words as harvesting, soldering, astonishment, horror, or dissatisfaction. In some cases the words in the vocabulary list are not commonly used in spoken English, such as shears, chef, cobbler, or hydrant. At least, these words would not be commonly understood by underprivileged children or youngsters from inner-city areas.

The Wechsler Intelligence Scale for Children, already mentioned as one of the two most widely used I.Q. tests, consists of eleven subtests and is heavily loaded with academic material. Here is the way a child's I.Q. is determined through the WISC test, at various ages from six to sixteen:

Information Subtest—This consists of thirty questions which require a large English vocabulary to understand such words as rubies, C.O.D., barometer, average, hieroglyphic, lien, or turpentine. Information is asked about the Fourth of July, Labor Day, Romeo and Juliet, English weights and measures, United States and world geography, history, and biology.

Comprehension Subtest—This measures the extent to which a child has adopted certain American values. The series contain fourteen hypothetical situations in which the child is to tell why certain behavior patterns are better than others, or to describe what a person would do in various situations. Correct responses reflect a value system which holds that big children should not fight with smaller ones, brick houses are better than wooden ones, lives of women and children should be saved before those of men in case of a shipwreck or other accident, payment by check is better than payment by cash, and that it is better to give a person a job because of a high score made on a test even if he is competing with a member of your family.

Arithmetic subtest—This consists of a series of sixteen increasingly difficult, timed questions. The child is required to add, subtract, multiply, and divide rapidly in his head and must know such terms as half, one third, two thirds, a quarter, a dozen, or similar measures or fractions.

Similarities Subtest—This consists of twelve pairs of nouns. The child is asked to explain how the objects symbolized by these nouns are alike. The relationship between the pairs of nouns becomes increasingly more difficult to discern as the test progresses.

Vocabulary Subtest—This section contains forty English words, mostly nouns, which the child is asked to define. Typical among the words contained in the test are fur, diamond, sword, nitroglycerin, microscope, shilling, belfry, hara-kiri, catacomb, vesper, or chattel.

Digit Span Subtest—The child is asked to recall a series of numbers and repeat them after the examiner. The initial series contains three digits and this is increased, progressively, to a total of nine. The child is then asked to repeat the numbers backward.

On the basis of answers to the above six subtests, the child's I.Q. score is then computed.

This is followed with five subtests that are designed to provide the score on the *Performance* I.Q. of the child. These are all timed, with the emphasis placed on speed rather than power, as is the case in the *Verbal* section. These follow:

Picture Completion—This consists of a series of twenty drawings of objects which have some part missing. Many of the objects are familiar, such as a hand, human face, coat, door, or cat. Others are less known to some children, such as a rooster, fish, thermometer, umbrella, or cow. The child is given fifteen seconds to name, or to point to, the missing part of the object.

Picture Arrangement—Consists of a set of cards, which, when arranged in proper order, either makes a complete picture of an object or tells a story. The child receives an I.Q. bonus for fast performance. It appears, after viewing the cards used in this subtest, that the child who has read comic books, or seen movie cartoons, has an advantage over the ones who have not, but who may be just as alert.

Block Design—The child is expected to arrange colored blocks so that they duplicate various designs formed by blocks as arranged by the examiner. Again, I.Q. bonus points are given to the child for faster completions.

Object Assembly—This consists of four puzzles, increasing in difficulty from five to seven pieces. The objects depict a man, horse, human face, and a car. These are all familiar to most American children regardless of their cultural heritage. The performance is timed, speed being rewarded with higher I.Q. points.

Coding—This subject asks a child to fill in or to substitute one set of symbols for another set. Example: two lines to be filled in for each ball, one line for each star, and so forth. The children are scored according to the number of correct insertions or substitutions they can make within a given time limit.

Upon completion of the full test, the scores on the verbal and performance are added, to arrive at the total I.Q. of the child. What, then, does the I.Q. score mean? Evidently, a familiarity with the English language, a knowledge of the Anglo-Saxon culture, and acceptance of its social, moral, and ethical values.

A favorite group I.Q. test is the Lorge-Thorndike, widely used in many school systems. This test is nonverbal at the two lowest levels, verbal at later stages. Briefly, the tests cover items dealing with abstract and general concepts, interpretation and use of symbols, relationships among concepts and symbols, flexibility in the organization of concepts and symbols, and the utilization of one's experience in new patterns by utilizing power rather than speed in working with abstract materials.

Another commonly used group test is the Otis Group Intelligence Scale. It is designed for children from kindergarten through grades one to four. The test contains these eight separate subsections: following directions, picture association, picture completion, maze tracing, picture sequence, similarities in pictures, synonym-antonyms, and common-sense judgment.

Many other I.Q. tests, individual as well as group, could be mentioned here, but the above gives a sampling of what a child may expect to find when his I.Q. is tested. Most of the tests stress knowledge of arithmetic, verbal skills, reasoning, sentence completion, logical selection, synonym-antonym, and symbol-digit. In addition, emphasis is usually placed on computation, information, vocabulary, analogies, and comparisons.

Scores of tests have been devised to evaluate a child's potential almost from the day that he is born. I am convinced that it is a waste of money, time, and energy to measure a child's I.Q. before he can get out of his crib or toddle across the floor. However, these early-age tests are offered to schools and parents in all seriousness, as though they were the ultimate truth in detecting that spark, or lack of it, that will remain with a child for a lifetime.

I cannot accept the reasoning of psychologists that the I.Q is a measure of the ability of the child to learn. Rather, I accept the views of those authorities who maintain that the I.Q. tests do not measure the ability to learn, but what has been previously experienced and mastered by the child.

To accept the I.Q. as the measure of a child's intelligence is to agree with the assumption—entirely false in my opinion—that all children have had an equal opportunity to learn the material contained in the tests—symbols, similarities, sentence completions, and all the other items the tests stress.

When a child is asked to define the meaning of "justice" or "integrity," it is assumed that he has had an exposure to this abstract concept. An eleven-year-old in a suburban school undoubtedly has had greater opportunities to understand these and other abstractions than his eleven-year-old counterpart in downtown Detroit or the slums of Harlem.

Here is an illustration of what I mean. On the Stanford-Binet, one of the questions asked of the ten-year-olds is:

"Give two reasons why children should not be noisy in school."

The child is given a plus on his I.Q. score if he answers along this vein:

"Because they'll get a lickin'."

"They'll have to sit in a dunce chair."

These two reasons are acceptable. But the child will get a minus score, a point detracted from his I.Q., if he replies:

"Because they're supposed to sit down and be still."

"They should do their studying when the teacher tells them to."

Frankly, if I were the examiner administering the I.Q. test, I would mark both answers right, or both wrong, or question both of them. How does an item of this type measure intelligence? What makes the examiner so knowledgeable that he can discern between such fine, intangible answers?

I have seen I.Q. scores vary as much as thirty points in the same child during the same school year. I have also found that different examiners and psychologists who administer the tests have their own methods of arriving at the total I.Q. scores. Just as there are "hard" and "easy" markers in schools among teachers, as every student soon finds out, so there are hard and easy markers among psychologists who administer the I.Q. tests.

As the tests are rarely objective, the examiner has tremendous leeway in deciding whether to give a child a "plus" or a "minus" credit for a particular answer. In the WISC, the examiner has the option, on many questions, to give two, one, or zero points, depending on how he interprets the child's answer. On other questions, the examiner may give either one point, or no point at all. This may, and does, make a substantial difference in the final I.Q. score. It can end up as 100 or 130, from average to superior.

What a difference this makes to the child! As a parent, I would want my child tested by more than one psychologist—if I were to have any testing done at all. I have known examiners who "went by the Manual" and penalized the child for any infraction of the stated rules, whether fair or not. I have also met with psychologists who were humane, compassionate, dedicated, with a sense of empathy and who brought out the best in the children whom they tested.

At the request of a parent, whose twelve-year-old son tested 92 on the WISC, I recommended a retest on the Stanford-Binet with another examiner. The result? A score of 132. Which one was right? Fortunately, the child showed superior ability in school when placed in a high-level group. If he had not been retested, he might have been labeled for life as "slow," placed in a slow class, and overlooked by his teachers and guidance counselors.

I cannot blame parents or teachers for being cynical when it comes to accepting the I.Q. score as a sacrosanct objective test of measurement. The I.Q. manuals specifically warn examiners against bias, against the "halo" effect that comes when a child is known to be the son of a college professor, or on the opposite side, the son of a janitor.

Examiners are human, but some are ill-prepared and are as susceptible to human frailties as the rest of us. The only difference is that they often hold the professional life of a child in their hands. The child himself can react negatively, or positively, toward an examiner. For example: a black, timid ghetto child, confronted by a stern, unbending, white examiner, may find himself tongue-tied, resentful, or ill at ease—factors known to mitigate against an accurate I.Q. score, if such exists.

The world-famous geneticist, Dr. Theodosius Dobzhansky, writing in *Genetic Diversity and Human Equality,* warns that there is always a danger that the tests will be biased in favor of the race, social class, culture, and subculture to which the test constructors themselves belong. A fair comparison becomes less and less possible as the groups tested differ more and more in socioeconomic, linguistic, traditional, and attitudinal backgrounds. Attempts have been made to correct these sources of error, but with scant success.

A child's I.Q. is determined in various ways, through numerous tests, by human minds working in devious manners, to arrive at a numerical score. The I.Q. test is not the final word in his development. It measures, to some extent, the learning that he has received, the knowledge that he has garnered in the few years that he has been in school or at home. It may predict success in school or college.

But let's stop at that. It does not predict future success in business, in the professions, in the world outside the academic classroom. A child will know what a "silhouette" is if he has seen one, or read about one. This adds one point to his total I.Q. score, but what does that mean in his life?

The I.Q. cannot tell you anything about a child's curiosity, his motivation, his inner thoughts, his ability to get along with people, his chance to become an active, responsible member of society, his role as a community or national leader, his creative abilities, or his contributions to mankind.

At best, the I.Q. score provides an indication that a child, in this one test, at one point in time, shows promise of academic success and possibly high grades in school. At worse, it can prove a dangerous, self-destructive instrument that may place a child in a gigantic academic and social noose from which escape is difficult if at all possible.

4

How I.Q.'s are used in school

How are the I.Q. tests used in school? Usually to predict academic success, to place pupils in special scholastic tracks, to provide them with the books and other instructional materials deemed appropriate for their intelligence levels, to determine the rate at which they should progress in class, and to recommend them for entrance into general, commercial, or vocational courses rather than in a program that would lead toward college or university training.

It is tragic that millions of schoolchildren can be pushed ahead, held back, denied appropriate instruction, or otherwise handicapped on the basis of a set of numbers attached to their names, an I.Q. dog tag, always kept handy in an accumulative file for instant identification.

What do the numbers mean?

In most school systems, administrators keep a file for each child. This folder contains basic information, some of it valuable, much of it routine, and often harmful or misleading. Usually found in the accumulative record file is the child's name, then his date and place of birth, allergies or other physical defects, class assignment (superior, average, slow), behavior problems of the past, and scores received on various I.Q. and other standardized tests.

Conspicuously, a place of honor is reserved for the I.Q. score. This is a magic number of two or three digits—two for the "dumbbells," which means 99 or under; three is reserved for the average, superior, or talented, ranging from 100 upward. By this scale, 100 is average, 80 is considered retarded, and 150 is a genius, with all sorts of gradations and variations in between.

How did this magic number, which may plague the child for the rest of his school days and beyond, appear? Who put it there?

Not a sinister force, but a pair of human hands—a teacher, guidance counselor, educational psychologist, or professional examiner might have done so. And the score came from a group I.Q. test, as a rule, nothing more than a pencil and paper standardized test that presumably separates the sheep from the goats, the imbeciles from the Einsteins, the average child from the superman.

Depending on the city or state, the type of group test varies. But the most popular and the one your child is probably tagged with, if you take the trouble to look or are permitted to examine his accumulative record folder, will be found among the I.Q. scores from these widely used tests: the Otis-Lennon Mental Ability Test, the Lorge-Thorndike Intelligence Tests, the California Test of Mental Maturity, the Otis Quick-Scoring Mental Ability Test, the Henmon-Nelson Test of Mental Ability, or the Kuhlmann-Anderson Intelligence Test.

How reliable are these tests? Do they have validity? In any case, it is certain that whatever else they may measure, these group I.Q. tests certainly do not measure your child's intelligence, nor his potential capacity or ability.

To standardize the tests, identical questions are given to small groups of children of the same age. Some tests, for example, have been standardized on less than a hundred children in each age group. The test is then presumed to be an accurate gauge of what children everywhere in the United States should know at age six, based on the results of the hundred or less six-year-olds tested in one section of the country.

One erroneous assumption is made by the test makers: that all persons of the same age, whether six, seven, ten, or twelve, have had, substantially, the same opportunity to understand and appreciate the items found on the particular test being used.

It is stretching the imagination beyond bounds to assume that all children, eight years of age, have had the same type of educational or home experience in Georgia, the Appalachian Mountains, the farmlands of Kansas, the suburbs of Long Island, the fishing villages of Maine, or the inner cities of New York and East Boston.

To make matters even more devastating to the children, the tests now in use to measure the I.Q. have been standardized on native-born, white, middle-class Americans. These standards are vastly different from the children of the poorly nourished Chicanos in the migrant camps in various parts of the nation, the Indian children on their restricted reservation, or the blacks who only within the last twenty years have had access to schooling comparable to that received by white students.

Examine any of the group tests and you will find that they are heavily dependent on verbal knowledge. Seven- or eight-year-olds are presumed to know the meaning of words such as mechanic, hinge, funnel, banister, crouch, duet, silhouette, or portable. A test designed for third- and fourth-graders asks: "Which of the following words does not belong in this group: major . . . private . . . colonel . . . captain . . ." Would all children, from farmland to the cities, know that "private" does not belong, since the other three mentioned are army officers, and a private is not?

Or take another sample: "Which of these words does not belong in this group: foolhardy . . . cautious . . . reckless . . . daring . . . rash . . ." The student would have to know the meaning of all five of these words to recognize that "cautious" is out of place.

One of the items on an I.Q. test reads: "Velvet is a kind of deed . . . cloth . . . brush . . . picture . . . leather . . ." Will the answer provide a clue to a child's intelligence, native ability, or life experiences? Does it matter whether he knows that velvet is a kind of cloth rather than leather?

Often a child tabbed with an I.Q. of 85 at age seven may blossom mentally and at age ten have an I.Q. of 135. I have seen at firsthand how changeable the I.Q. can be, and often is. It has not been unusual for me to find a child with an I.Q. of 100, retested a month later by a different examiner, using another test, show a jump of 25 to 35 points, thus escaping from the normal category to a bright, superior class. What a difference it makes to the child, his teachers' attitude toward him, and the entire family atmosphere!

On the other hand, I have seen children with high I.Q. scores, in the 130 range, drop to 95 on retests. Which figure shall we accept? Or better still, what does the elusive magic number mean?

Is there an analogy between mental and physical achievement? A boxer who lets his muscles deteriorate, who gets flabby from lack of exercise or overconfidence, may be knocked out in the first round of his championship fight, while with training he may make a comeback and become a winner again.

Similarly, a bright child who permits his mind to become flabby may also find that he has deteriorated mentally. Much depends on whether the mind is used and how it is used, both at home and at school. I have seen so-called average children reach the top of the academic ladder once they became motivated, had the fortune to get good teachers, and were reared by understanding parents. I have also seen bright children lose interest in their schoolwork, drop out of the academic mainstream, and flunk out of school.

Unhappily, teachers, parents, and even students place far greater emphasis on the I.Q. concept than the tests deserve. The I.Q. scores are misused and abused in school, in industry, by guidance counselors, and in our everyday world, both in and out of the educational arena.

The noted Swiss educator Dr. Jean Piaget has never been impressed with the standard I.Q. tests. He does not believe that they lead to an understanding of how intelligence functions. He bases his belief on the presence, or absence, of the essential abilities related to intellectual functioning.

Items used on the I.Q. tests are largely drawn from the cultural experience of the middle-class group in our nation. That is why, says

Dr. Robert J. Havighurst of the University of Chicago, a giant in the field of education and testing, children of ethnic groups and of lower-than-middle socioeconomic groups—and these are the great majority of American children—are at a disadvantage and penalized by the existing I.Q. tests.

Many items on the tests are drawn from school experience. The child who spends more time in school prepares best for these tests and gets a higher score. But is this innate intelligence? Often, a child may be unable to go to school because of pressure or indifference at home, because he must get a job and help earn money to pay for family food, or because he is bored by the schooling he receives.

School is an important ingredient for middle-class children. Report cards are studied carefully by parents, often critically, but usually with constructive guidance. That, of course, is not the case with many underprivileged families. They do not have the time, patience, or understanding to show concern at their children's accomplishments or failures in school.

Moreover, middle- and lower-class children bring to the I.Q. tests widely disparate cultural experiences. If the test is to be reasonably accurate, its questions should be selected from experiences which are common to the majority of children to be tested. This does not take place at present.

Long known for his experiments in improving the I.Q. tests and removing the cultural bias from them, Professor Allison A. Davis of the University of Chicago points out that the lifelong process by which culture helps to guide, develop, and evaluate mental problem-solving has not received attention from either test makers or educators. They continually make the error of regarding middle-class culture, particularly school culture, as the true index of what constitutes education. Most of the items that appear on our hundreds of I.Q. tests are taken from those areas in which middle-class experience is greater.

For his Alpha nonverbal test, Dr. Arthur S. Otis, in his Otis Quick-Scoring Mental Ability Tests, divided pupils into two groups —an inferior and a superior one—according to whether the pupils were retarded or advanced for their ages. Only those items were retained which showed a distinct difference between the two groups. And this difference was in favor of the superior group of children.

Is this sound practice in preparing an I.Q. test?

No, says Dr. Davis, for we know that those groups of children in elementary schools who are retarded in grade placement are overwhelmingly from the lower socioeconomic groups. Thus, the Otis method, as is true with the other tests, rules out all problems on which the lower socioeconomic groups are equal or superior to the top socioeconomic groups.

Binet made it clear that he had become greatly concerned over the danger that large sections of his test measured chiefly the effects of cultural training rather than of mental capacity. He tested only children in the working-class neighborhood of a French community; the first standardized test was based entirely on the responses made by the children of working-class parents. Binet knew that children of high socioeconomic status had a much easier time with his type of tests.

What, then, is the answer to the use of I.Q. tests in school? The whole problem needs rethinking. Rather than validate the tests in terms of school marks, we should look for successful problem-solving in all aspects of life. This would hold true not only for middle-class children, but for the lower class as well. Dr. Davis recommends that we study the kinds of problems these children attack, the ways in which they attack them, the respect in which their solutions are appropriate, and the ways in which the problems are symbolized by different children.

We might evolve a battery of tests, each measuring problem-solving ability in a cultural or status area, with the pupil's score reported in profile form. It might show that the child has high ability to meet problems that are important in low-status culture, but only mediocre ability to meet middle-class problems. If we want to test a child's ability to do scholastic work of highly verbal and academic kind, tests will consist of material in that area. These tests would then be labeled as instruments for specific aptitudes, not general I.Q. tests.

Below are several examples of items found in our popular I.Q. tests which obviously do not measure innate intelligence. If anything, they measure knowledge gained through home or school experience. Children in the ten-year-old range are presumed able to answer these items:

1. Pick out the one word which does not belong with the others: priest . . . organist . . . minister . . . rabbi . . . bishop . . .

2. Find the three things that are alike in this list:

store . . . banana . . . basket . . . apple . . . seed . . . plum . . .

3. Find the two things that the first thing is never without:

cat . . . hair . . . owner . . . mouse . . . claws . . . milk . . .

4. Find the two opposites in this list:

old . . . rich . . . wide . . . poor . . . green . . . full . . .

5. Bird is to feathers as fish is to:

scales . . . tails . . . song . . . beak . . . mouth . . .

The thirteen- to fourteen-year-old group showed dramatically that the cultural experience of the children plays a major role in the I.Q. scores that they receive. Here is a comparison of the percentage of correct answers given by high-status and low-status groups on an I.Q. test. . . .

1. *Sonata* is a term used in:

drawing . . . drama . . . music . . . poetry . . . phonetics . . .

Seventy-four per cent of the high-status children knew the correct answer (music) while only 29 per cent of the low-socioeconomic-status children did.

2. A man who acquires the property of others by deceit is called:

traitor . . . swindler . . . burglar . . . prisoner . . . lawyer . . .

Here 67 per cent of the high-status children answered, while only 29 per cent of the low status knew the answer was *swindler*.

3. A wheel always has:

circumference . . . spokes . . . tire . . . wood . . . metal . . .

Forty-eight per cent of the high status knew that *circumference* was correct, compared with a tiny 6 per cent of the low-status ones. Actually, the question is tricky, as wheels usually have spokes—but not always, as look at the wheels on an automobile.

When the test item is expressed in strange, academic, or bookish words, children from middle- or upper-middle classes do much better than those from the lower groups. Those questions which show small cultural or economic differences either are nonverbal or are expressed in simple, easy to understand, or everyday vocabulary. For example, let us look at this I.Q. test item:

"A boy who often tells stories he knows are not true is said to:

brag . . . cheat . . . joke . . . lie . . . exaggerate . . ."

In this case 83 per cent of the high status and 78 per cent of the low status knew that the answer was "lie." The difference between the two groups was insignificant.

Nor was there much difference in response to this item:

"Herring is a kind of: wig . . . flower pattern . . . jewel . . . fish . . ." Most children, from poor or rich homes, knew that a herring belonged in the fish category.

What can we conclude from these brief examples? To me, the answer is obvious: the I.Q. tests are geared to the middle-class children, while the lower-class children, with not as much opportunity to experience the many facets of life enjoyed by their more fortunate classmates, are severely handicapped in their responses. By revising the I.Q. items and questions to meet the standards of the majority of children, black or white, rich or poor, rural or urban, we will be more likely to develop a test that is valid and fair.

The I.Q. scores might then reflect a truer picture of the abilities of all children, as measured by these tests. The vast differences in socioeconomic groups would disappear. Of course, bias, we know, will never fully disappear, but, at least, it could be contained to a much greater degree than is now the case.

A youngster who doesn't know what a "sonata" is may not be as "dumb" or "dull" as the I.Q. tests make him out to be. Fact of the matter is, he just has not had any musical experience.

As a result, the "norms" that the test makers have set are averages only for middle-class white children. Other classes, or groups of children, do not receive an even break in the academic scale of I.Q. values. We tend to strangle many children with the artificial self-imposed norms. How can we assess a child's capabilities in terms of norms when their rate of development varies so greatly? Dr. Lois Barclay Murphy, eminent psychologist who has carried out a series on long-range studies of normal children at the Menninger Foundation in Topeka, Kansas, issues this strong warning:

"Reliance on the I.Q. has stultified our thinking about potentialities of children."

We have various norms that combine to strangle the child's learning ability and stifle his motivation. Speed norms can be especially misleading, as has been shown from studies of American Indian children, as well as children who have been thrown unexpectedly into strange situations.

Age norms are a major culprit. Without exception, I.Q. tests are based on age versus mental ability. The stranglehold of the age norm has created more mischief and caused more academic disruption than any single factor in I.Q. testing, standardized achievements, or any of the measurements we now make that are based on age alone.

"To a large extent," Dr. Murphy's studies say, "each child's development is a mystery story whose outcome we cannot really predict. The complexity of the developmental process with the emerging capacities, drives, investments, conflicts is still far beyond our complete comprehension at our present primitive stage of understanding."

That little reliance can be placed on I.Q. tests is shown dramatically in studies at the University of California's Institute of Human Development. Conducted by psychologists Jones, Bayley, Macfarlane, and Henzik, the studies, which began at Berkeley in the 1920s, are still continuing.

In one of the studies, Dr. Macfarlane found that between the ages of six and eighteen, more than half the children showed a range of 20 I.Q. points difference during a series of tests that they took over a number of years. Ten per cent had a range of more than 30 I.Q. points.

Beyond this change in I.Q. scores, Macfarlane notes that a number of men, with poor records both on mental tests and school grades, had acquired positions as adults that required a high degree of intelligence and creativity. One man, who had an average I.Q. of 100, repeated three classes, and finally graduated from high school at age twenty-one without a college recommendation, suddenly "found" himself. He made up his school deficiencies, excelled in courses that he had formerly failed, went to college, and is now a highly talented and respected architect.

For years this "average" student thought of himself, in his term, as a "listless oddball." He was handcuffed by the I.Q. norms set for him at school. That he finally broke loose and found the key is miraculous. Too often the student forced into a mold is unable to escape academic, social, economic, or vocational handicaps.

We learn further that of the children studied by an experienced research staff, 50 per cent turned out to be more stable and effective adults than any staff member had predicted. Scarcely one third turned out as forecast. Among the 10 per cent who later became far better than predicted were two students who persistently spent their energies in defiance of regulations, who received marginal or failing grades throughout their school years, and finally were expelled at ages fifteen and sixteen. Both of them are now well-adjusted, confident, successful adults.

From these and numerous other controlled studies, we begin to recognize that the I.Q., personality, achievement, aptitude, and various other tests have limited predictive value. All that they show us is what a child is doing at a particular moment, whether in the classroom, at home, or in his community. However, tests cannot tell us what the child is capable of doing once he is stimulated, challenged, inspired, or freed of his anxieties. Furthermore, the tests give an "average" score. You do not know in which direction the child may be gifted, talented, or creative, or whether he is the one individual who will go above or below the average line.

Still another limitation in grouping young children on the basis of the I.Q. test is that we can only assess a restricted range of information. The child's physical and emotional state at the time he took the test might readily affect the results adversely, enough to invalidate the final score completely. Physical conditions, such as an uncomfortable room, noisy surroundings, an unhappy home experience just prior to taking the test, or a child suffering from a head cold, can have a direct bearing on the I.Q. test scores. The test may give us the final score, but it tells us nothing as to how the child arrived at it, or the significance it may have for his future.

Too few people realize that intelligence can be taught and that the primary business of schools is to teach it, not to rely on scores or man-made numbers. This, at any rate, is the view of one of the nation's leading authorities in the field of testing, Dr. Henry S. Dyer. For many years vice-president of the Educational Testing Service at Princeton, Dr. Dyer maintains that Binet's original plan consisted chiefly of two fundamental contributions to the measurement of children's cognitive functioning. These were the invention and development of a set of psychologically complex exercises that differentiated children who were doing well in school from those who were not, and the invention of a normative scale, the mental age, to measure children in accordance with their performance on a variety of these tasks.

The notion of a normative scale was a breakthrough in its time.

As it has become more widely used, however, its basic nature and its limitations have not been understood by those who use it.

"In my experience," reports Dr. Dyer, "most teachers and other school people fail to understand that the use of years and months to measure a child's cognitive behavior, or for that matter any kind of behavior, is a fundamentally different operation from the use of feet and inches to measure the child's height.

"The units in a normative scale are not additive. You, therefore, cannot in logic say, for instance, that the cognitive functioning of a child with a mental age of eight is twice that of a child with a mental age of four."

For better or worse—and mostly the latter—the I.Q. often tends to give teachers the belief that they can hide behind these numbers and thereby be relieved of any pressing obligation to understand and help their children develop to their fullest potential. Children should be observed, considered, treated as individuals, not as members of a "norm" to which they must adhere. Truly, the I.Q. can strangle the child if teachers abdicate their duties and rely on the biased score rather than their own professional judgment as to the abilities of the youngsters in their classrooms.

It has taken a long time, Dr. Dyer laments, for Piaget's ideas to percolate into the thinking of American education to the point where teachers may, hopefully, become perceptive child watchers and not just textbook watchers, or, worse still, I.Q. addicts.

Piaget began his investigations by simply watching young children at school and at play, observing the patterns of behavior that emerged as they interacted with the phenomena of their world. He was not at all concerned with the I.Q. score or any other test. He wanted to find out, if he possibly could, through observation, what was going on in the minds of young children.

It often is difficult to make some school people see that intelligence has many facets which can be observed and assessed if one pays close enough attention to the behavior, in or out of the classroom, of their pupils. The child is an individual. We should not use the I.Q. to place him into a slot in which he remains a virtual academic prisoner.

A tragic waste of human resources and of mental brain power has resulted, and they continue to be wasted. This will continue as long as we cling to the concept of a mental capacity that is enclosed by an I.Q. wall, a pencil-and-paper wall, a wall that does grave injustice to substantial segments of the American population.

More particularly, severe damage is done to the minority groups, the disadvantaged, the late bloomers, the timid, the poor test takers, and to those who do not measure up to an arbitrary, unscientific, unrealistic I.Q. norm.

5

I.Q. tests play a dominant role in nation's schools

The I.Q. and other standardized tests are a vital factor in American education. A survey of one hundred school systems, selected at random, that I made in the fall of 1973 showed that more than half of the systems used various forms of I.Q. testing. Virtually 100 per cent evaluated their students through achievement tests in reading or arithmetic, aptitude tests, college-board tests, and a host of other forms of evaluative materials.

For the most part, those who favored the continued use of the

I.Q. tests held that they helped to classify the mental ability of their pupils. Moreover, the scores were used to place students in certain groups or academic tracks, although it is known that the group I.Q. tests are highly unreliable.

The response from the Pittsburgh Board of Education testing bureau was typical of the others received. All children, except those classified as educationally mentally retarded, receive group scholastic-aptitude tests on a three-year cycle, beginning in grade two and repeated at grades five, eight, and eleven. In addition, children in the seventh and tenth grades are given aptitude tests to measure whatever specialized abilities they may possess.

The I.Q. tests are used to measure the child's school-learning ability. The educational officials are convinced that the scores correlate positively with academic progress. In addition to group I.Q. tests, the Metropolitan Achievement Test Batteries are used to get further data on the students' competencies.

Sponsors of the test hope that the information it reveals will provide teachers with data about the strengths and weaknesses of their children in specific skills, knowledge, and understanding. In this way, the teaching instruction can be directed and modified.

Detroit uses regularly scheduled standardized achievement tests on a city-wide basis. They are designed to help teachers diagnose individual and group-learning difficulties and accomplishments. The tests also provide guidance counselors with objective information that can be used when counseling students.

The Scranton, Pennsylvania, co-ordinator of pupil personnel services, in explaining why I.Q. tests are given to all the children in the school system, observes that the I.Q. tests are useful in determining the range of abilities within a single class, grade, or school population. The tests are also used as an aid to classify students for instruction, and to identify gifted, talented, or mentally retarded students.

Hundreds of teachers in the St. Paul, Minnesota, public schools asked for a moratorium on testing pending a complete appraisal of the existing testing programs. Teachers criticized the tests for their ambiguity, lack of relevancy, questionable validity, and the use of excessive administrative time.

Testing consultants were asked for their opinions on how to meet the objections of the St. Paul teachers. One specialist said that the testing program was a failure because it did not generate enough feedback to parents, teachers, and the general public. To get an adequate view of the value of the tests, it would be necessary to supply individual and group item analysis data, performance ratios, skill profiles, and decile bands comparing a student's performance with the national standardization group in the same grade, percentile limits, individual and average growth-scale values, predictions of growth, and combination listings of ability and achievement data.

All of this information is necessary, for this is the type of feedback data that makes testing relevant and useful.

Looking over the many areas that are deemed essential to the testing process, it is no wonder that the I.Q., achievement, and other standardized tests are losing their validity, value, and meaning. There are many ways in which the child's test scores can be invalidated, accidentally or deliberately.

Among the most common errors detected in the schools giving these tests were these: teachers do not copy the correct grade-equivalent scores and percentiles on class-record sheets; mistakes may be made in raw scores reported; wrong or outdated answer sheets were sometimes used; many tests now in use were found to be obsolete; up-to-date norms were not always available; the age of the child was sometimes inaccurate, placing the entire results into wrong focus; and some examiners were fatigued when they gave the test and did sloppy work in reporting the results.

Yet, a child's educational future, whether he is to be recommended as college material, placed in a slow or subnormal group, or permitted to take special courses often depends on the outcome of these I.Q. and achievement tests! Who is to know whether they have been accurately reported, effectively administered, or scored without error?

How many outmoded I.Q. tests are still being used as an economy measure? How valid are the tests used in thousands of school systems, placing millions of students in jeopardy and denying them adequate educational programs? How many children have been seriously, if not irreparably, damaged because of the error of an inexperienced teacher or an overworked clerk? How meaningful is it to either parents or students, and perhaps teachers as well, to discuss "stanines," "standard deviation errors," "percentiles," or "decile bands"?

One good bit of news: my survey shows that a number of cities have abolished the I.Q. tests, or are using them more sparingly than in the past. They agree that the tests have limited value in educational decision-making for the school system. Achievement tests, on the other hand, are universally used and are continuing to be used in school systems throughout the country.

Their value is still considered to be important, although here and there voices are heard in opposition. Teachers usually object to achievement tests because they are forced to "teach to the test." That is, they must be certain that the subject matter that they cover in the classroom is similar to the questions that will appear on the standardized tests. Otherwise, they will find that their students do poorly on the tests, and this, in turn, will generally reflect on the teachers themselves. At least, it will in the eyes of misinformed parents or school-board members who hold achievement tests, particularly in reading and arithmetic, to be the measurement of effective teaching.

Until the fall of 1973, California required that I.Q. tests be given to all public school pupils. The group Lorge-Thorndike test was used. However, because of vigorous parental opposition, including several law suits, the state limited these tests, making them optional rather than mandatory.

Many systems in California, as elsewhere, still use the I.Q. tests, even though they may not be state-mandated. The Sacramento City Unified School District, for example, uses the I.Q. test on an individual basis to diagnose the mentally handicapped child and to place children in groups according to their test scores.

Standardized achievement tests are universally used in California although the I.Q. test is no longer required. One of the testing co-ordinators explained that "the tests show how we compare with various norms across the country." Administrators find it difficult to get away from the stranglehold of the norm.

A survey of the testing programs used in the nation's hundred largest school districts, made by the Educational Division of the Houghton Mifflin Company in 1973, confirmed much of the data that I assembled in my study. More than 75 per cent of the school districts assess mental abilities through group I.Q. tests at one or more grades. Many school districts administer achievement tests to all children in each of the elementary grades.

Among the most frequent achievement-test batteries used in the nation's school systems are the Metropolitan Achievement Test, Iowa Tests of Basic Skills, Comprehensive Tests of Basic Skills, Stanford Achievement Test, SRA Achievement Test, California Achievement Tests, School and College Ability Test, Kuder Interest Inventory, Kuhlmann-Anderson Nelson Reading Test, and many, many others.

As can be seen there are quite a number of tests from which to choose. In fact, far too many are offered, frequently of unknown quality. Too often, as a result, the test scores are invalid or inaccurate. It costs money to conduct a competent testing program. In a school system with twenty or thirty thousand pupils, the cost of keeping the I.Q. achievement and other testing programs up to date becomes virtually prohibitive. It is easy, then, for the hard-pressed school superintendent, or the budget director, or the board of education to say:

"Oh, well, the tests used for the past four or five years are still good for one or two more years. We don't have enough money in our budget to buy new sets."

But pressure from the publishing houses cannot be discounted. Salesmen flock to the schools, urging administrators to change brands, try another test, revamp the entire testing system, sample a new test that will beat them all!

But that's only part of the story. The unhappy part belongs to unwary children and their parents who do not realize that they are being forced into artificial state or national norms, frequently developed on a minuscule ratio of our school population. The children that are used by the test makers to standardize the tests may, or may not, be representative of the entire school population. But once the test is standardized, as was the Stanford-Binet in its 1937 revision, or the WISC in 1949, psychologists who are involved in these tests are reluctant to make further changes. The process is time-consuming and costly. Besides, the stock answer I receive when I raise the issue with those responsible for this situation is:

"Standards don't change. What was true for children fifty years ago is basically the same today."

Thus, the stranglehold takes its toll and is hard to loosen. That is why a moratorium on all I.Q. testing is essential.

Usually, the test is given in the first grade, sometimes within a week or two after the youngster enters school. The score is then duly transcribed on the child's record. Unfortunately, many parents blindly and unquestioningly accept the word of the educators who say that their children are bright, average, dull, retarded, or mentally deficient.

But we know that the I.Q. tests do not measure motivation or the ability of a child to adjust, either in school or in the world at large. Nor do the tests measure leadership, character, ambition, creativity, common sense, curiosity, integrity, or native intelligence.

A psychologist who has worked with children related that a distraught parent came to him, upset that an I.Q. test had placed his young son at an I.Q. of 105—too low to enter the private school for which he had applied. The psychologist suggested a retest.

The result? The second test placed the boy in the upper ninety-seventh percentile, with an I.Q. of 135. Which test was accurate? Both. At the time the first test was taken, the child might have been uncomfortable, ill at ease, unable to concentrate. Or the examiner might have been tired and hurried the test along so that he could get home in time for dinner. On the retest, the child evidently had built a good rapport with a sympathetic examiner and was able to relate better, and thus up went his I.Q. score.

The examiner plays a greater part in the I.Q. testing process than is commonly realized. I found that to be true when I recommended children to various testing offices. In the case of one psychologist, the scores were invariably low. I later discovered that the examiner was unable to relate to minority-group children; moreover, he had a cold, hostile manner toward all children.

Often one test is not sufficient to determine whether a child is bright or dull. Sometimes even two tests are insufficient.

I simply cannot accept the premise of those who support the theory that I.Q. test scores reveal the amount of intelligence a child has. It may be possible to predict that a child with a high I.Q., if measured on a valid scale, will do well in school. The original Binet test was based on the assumption that children who made good grades would answer a greater proportion of questions on school subjects, such as reading or arithmetic, than would students who got poor marks.

Therefore, questions on the test that were answered equally well by children whom the teachers designated as bright or slow were discarded. Only those items were retained that showed a higher proportion of right answers by the supposedly bright children, who were classed as such on the basis of academic performance alone.

That is why it is possible to predict with accuracy, through high I.Q. scores, that, by and large, those pupils with the better I.Q. scores will have higher school grades than those with low scores.

How deeply is intelligence involved in I.Q. tests? If one considers school performance a mark of intelligence, it is highly relevant. However, we know that not all children have an equal opportunity to develop, since they do not have equal access to good schools or good educational facilities. They may attend inferior schools conducted by incompetent teachers, and thus be at a disadvantage when taking a school-oriented I.Q. test.

Often, I.Q. tests measure information that children are apt to pick up at home, on TV, at school, in the community, but rarely in the ghetto slums or tomato fields of southern Florida.

Here is an item in a popular I.Q. test that definitely suggests that I.Q. and intelligence are poorly related:

"A symphony is to a composer as a book is to: paper . . . sculptor . . . author . . . musician . . . man . . ."

Dr. Davis revised the question to read:

"A baker goes with bread the same way that a carpenter goes with: saw . . . spoon . . . house . . . nail . . . man . . ."

Eighty-two per cent of the children from the upper-income group knew that a symphony had the same relationship to a composer as a book had to an author . . . the composer wrote the symphony while the author wrote the book. But only 52 per cent of the lower-income group answered the question correctly. Probably many of them had never heard a symphony nor knew what a composer was and, therefore, could not relate an author to a book.

An equal percentage of each group, however, answered the revised question correctly. It was apparent that children from both groups, the lower- and upper-economic scale, knew that a carpenter used a saw and that a baker made bread.

Convinced by this response that the I.Q. tests merely measure acquired knowledge, not innate intelligence, Dr. Davis prepared a set of tests that he felt would probe the native mental alertness of the individual child. Problems were based on experiences common to all children, no matter in which environment they were reared.

Many children who did poorly on the existing tests registered higher scores on the revised I.Q. instruments, since the items on the newer tests dealt with material with which they were familiar.

The I.Q. tests cost millions of dollars annually. They create unhappiness, heartache, or unwarranted hope. One way to improve your child's I.Q. is not to give him one! That may sound like a paradox and maybe it is. However, if a child of six, seven, or eight has a below average I.Q., compared with other children of his age, it may mean, as often as not, that he has not as yet developed mentally or physically to the average "norm" of the six-, seven-, or eight-year-old child. Who is to say what the "average" is for him?

The dominant role now assumed by the I.Q. in our nation's schools must be eliminated. Only then will we go ahead with the job of providing our children with the best education based on their individual needs.

In a dynamic and constructive school system, there must be concentration on the potential ability of each child, rather than on acquired knowledge or information.

6

The I.Q.—is it inherited or acquired?

Ever since Binet developed his tests to measure the potential scholastic abilities of children, the question of inherited versus acquired intelligence has simmered, mostly on a low flame, on the back burner. But the issue has suddenly become violent and controversial. Psychologists, educators, geneticists, anthropologists, psychometricians, parents, teachers, experts in testing, and pseudoexperts have brought the controversy into the open, creating a storm that has rarely been equaled in the field of education. It has had a devastatingly dramatic impact upon American schools and colleges.

The question of nature versus nurture, inheritance versus environment, broke wide open with the publication of an article by Professor Jensen in the *Harvard Educational Review,* spring issue of 1969, entitled: "How Much Can We Boost I.Q. and Scholastic Achievement?" The article immediately drew the fire of critics who charged that Jensen had libeled the black race as well as other minority groups.

The reason? Dr. Jensen drew the conclusion, based, he said, on hundreds of studies made over the past quarter century, that the blacks, on the average, had I.Q. scores that were fifteen points lower than that of whites. No other inference was available, he said, than that, genetically, blacks were inferior to whites and therefore should not be made to compete with them in the typical school situation. A special type of schooling might be in order.

But Dr. Jensen went even further: he devised an elaborate formula by which he deduced that the I.Q. is an inherited trait. By his involved reckoning, at least 80 per cent of our intelligence is inherited, leaving only 20 per cent for the impact of environment on the human mind. According to the Jensen formula, four fifths of our intelligence is basically determined at birth, and little can be done to change that condition, no matter how we try.

Why, then, spend millions of dollars to improve programs for the inner-city or disadvantaged children, or indeed, seek ways to help the economically poor get out of their poverty-level groove? The disadvantaged will always be with us, since the I.Q. correlates highly with the economic level of our populace. And, proceeding further on the Jensenian thesis, since the I.Q. can rarely be increased and scholastic achievement cannot be boosted, the truck driver will always remain a truck driver, and so will his son. The farmer's son will remain a farmhand, while the professor's, or the banker's, son will land on top of the economic heap.

Dr. Jensen and his associates have added fuel to the I.Q. fire by postulating that environmental factors are relatively unimportant in determining the I.Q. score, or in attempting to raise it. Genetic influence is in; environment is out.

In his provocative article, followed by his book, *Educability and Group Differences,* Dr. Jensen presents what he purports to be evidence that social-class and racial variations in intelligence cannot be accounted for by environment, but must be attributed to genetic differences. According to him, prenatal influences may have greater influence on the I.Q. than the Head Start or other compensatory programs sponsored by the federal government during the past decade at the cost of billions of dollars. These projects, Dr. Jensen insists, do little to help disadvantaged or ghetto children "catch up" with children from more prosperous communities, or who come from professional-oriented families.

It is his view that the genotype—genetics—must take precedence over the phenotype—environment. The genetic factors are formed at conception, when sperm and ovum unite.

What really set the educational house on fire, or rather, that part of it that believes in social justice and equal opportunity for all, regardless of race or ethnic origin, was Dr. Jensen's conclusion that blacks had an inferior I.Q., and that nothing could be done, as far as schools or colleges were concerned, to make up the 15 point deficit. If nothing could be done, then why try?

This viewpoint was quickly, almost eagerly, embraced by Dr. Shockley of Stanford University, who went even further. He called for a complete re-evaluation of the schooling now being given to blacks or others with low I.Q.'s. Much to the chagrin and dismay of some of his colleagues at Stanford and psychologists elsewhere, Dr. Shockley proposed a "sterilization plan" for parents of low I.Q. children. He would have the state or government pay each person, white or black, who agreed to be sterilized, $1,000 for each I.Q. point they had below 100. Thus, if a person had an I.Q. of 90, he would receive a bonus of $10,000; if it registered 75, the subsidy would rise to $25,000.

Dr. Shockley based his plan on the theory that low I.Q. parents produced low I.Q. children, and that these children then became welfare cases, thus costing the government millions of dollars annually. In the long run, said Dr. Shockley, the nation would save money through his plan because an initial outlay of, say $15,000, would be less than it would cost to maintain the numerous children of the low I.Q. parent on welfare. No indication was made by Dr. Shockley as to who would give the I.Q. test, what test would be used, which score would be the determinant as to how much money the person would receive if he agreed to be sterilized, or how the damage could be rectified if at a later date the 90 I.Q. had changed to 115.

Fortunately, this proposal has not been taken seriously by the educational fraternity, nor by those engaged in the I.Q. fight. But it has deeply offended blacks, who are the main target of the Shockley thrust.

Professor Herrnstein then entered the fray, ready for battle but somewhat more subdued. Writing in the September, 1971, issue of the *Atlantic Monthly,* Dr. Herrnstein agreed that the I.Q. is, in large measure, up to 80 per cent inherited and that differences exist among various groups and races of our population.

Dr. Herrnstein, too, came in for severe academic reprisals from both students and teachers on the Harvard campus. He was banned from speaking at various campuses, as was Shockley, threatened with physical assault, called a racist, and found himself an outcast in his own university.

In his book, *I.Q. in the Meritocracy,* Dr. Herrnstein suggests that neither inheritance nor environment can claim complete responsibility for the I.Q. score. He wonders, though, why I.Q.'s usually stay about the same during most people's lives (my research shows that they don't) and why high or low I.Q.'s tend to run in families. (Do they?)

Dr. Herrnstein himself supplies an answer: while the hereditarian can call on the fixity of the germ plasm to uphold his theory of inherited intelligence, the environmentalist may argue that the I.Q.'s remain the same to the extent that their environment remains unchanged. Furthermore, if one is fortunate enough to be born to wealthy or middle-class parents, the I.Q. will show the benefits of both physical and mental nurturing, which in turn gives an advantage in the ongoing competition for social or financial success.

In meager, limited surroundings it is more than likely that mental growth will be stunted. We know that early training fixes the I.Q. more firmly than later experiences, in or out of school. Social barriers and economic factors keep the underprivileged and disadvantaged in a poor hopeless environment. On the other hand, the privileged may be able to enjoy a rich and varied cultural life.

In the 1930s, Nazi Germany, led by Hitler, showed how dangerous the philosophy of racial superiority could become. Perhaps that is why those psychologists who advocate the principle of inherited intelligence find themselves attacked and ostracized. We are opposed to any suggestion or belief in a "master race," nor do we accept the theory that whites are mentally superior to blacks, Jews to gentiles,

Orientals to Indians, middle-class Americans to the disadvantaged poor whites.

Studies show that a father's occupation is a fairly reliable index of the child's I.Q. One study lists the I.Q. range, in descending order, from a top of 116 to a low of 95, that goes this way, based on occupation: professional, semiprofessional and managerial, clerical and skilled trades, rural landowners and farmers, semiskilled minor clerical workers, slightly skilled workers, and urban day laborers.

Does this mean that if you have a high I.Q., you will be on "top" in the economic race, and if it is low, you will fall to the bottom? Not at all. The evidence merely suggests that the I.Q. tests, as currently constructed, conform to the professions, just as they relate to school grades. We know that if a person is able to improve his environment, he will have a better chance to succeed in many ways.

Most parents want their children to do better, to rise higher in educational, social, economic, or professional status than they have done. That is why so many families do everything possible to enable their children to go to college and to use their education as a ladder that leads from a lower economic level to a higher one.

It is here where environment plays an important role by encouraging children to aim for higher educational goals and improve their economic and social status. Their I.Q.'s can be raised through motivation. It is well to remember that the I.Q. is a label that can be applied at will, and not something that is stapled onto a child at birth.

The noted geneticist Dr. Theodosius Dobzhansky maintains that class and race differences may be ascribed to inequalities in educational opportunities and living standards. However, some of the differences may be genetic. This issue is not, actually, heredity versus environment, but how environment may affect genetic conditioning and thus change the genetic potential.

It is readily apparent, in viewing the literature available, that both heredity and environment play an important role in developing the child's I.Q. The primary argument boils down to whether the ratio is as high as 80–20 as Jensen, Herrnstein, Shockley, and others claim it to be. Or is it closer to a chance 50–50? That this is the case seems reasonable and it should make an extremely significant difference in our approach to learning. Professor Christopher Jencks of Harvard believes that it does.

It is quite evident that the level of intellectual growth is limited if only one fifth of it can be shaped by environment. If one accepts the 80–20 ratio, the child's intelligence cannot be substantially changed no matter how his living conditions, schooling, or economic status improve.

A long-range study, conducted by Dr. Robert B. McCall, psychologist at the Fels Research Institute (Yellow Springs, Ohio), indicates that the I.Q.'s of severely deprived children can be raised through stimulating educational programs. It would appear, then, that children are not "locked into" a given range of I.Q. performance. Thus, since childhood mental performance, caused by nongenetic factors, can change, the nature-nurture I.Q. controversy becomes somewhat academic.

Studies now show that the home, too, can affect the future academic achievement and I.Q. of children long before they enter school. The first three years of a child's life may often determine his later intellectual development. This is evident in a project with young children, conducted by Professor Burton L. White of Harvard. Over a ten-year period, Professor White has found definite growth in the I.Q. and the achievement of young children, brought about when teachers worked with parents in the homes of the children.

By working with both parents and children, Dr. White and his staff were able to discover the factors that were crucial for optimal growth. They found that changed home environment had a drastic effect on the child and subsequently improved his I.Q. score to a substantial extent.

Heredity did not have as much influence on the child's I.Q. as did a change in environment. Children from the poorest surroundings were able to do as well, and often better, than upper-class children once they were offered similar advantages.

The Harvard study suggests that a changed, improved environment has a drastic effect on heredity. Underprivileged children now doomed to the lowest rung of the educational ladder are able, when stimulated and encouraged, to reach the heights of the more favored children, whose genetic traits are presumably superior.

Going further, it has been shown that the better educated parents create experiences for their children that help make higher I.Q. scores possible. Writing in the Harvard Bulletin, *Inequality in Education,* Professor Jerome Kagan reports that working-class mothers issue more arbitrary prohibitions and are more likely to remind their children of their faults, holding out threats of punishment, than are college-trained mothers. As a result, self-confidence is frequently impaired, a self-image of failure develops, which subsequently affects performance on the I.Q. tests.

In a study of firstborn white children, Dr. Kagan traced their progress from their fourth through their twenty-seventh month of life. A remarkable difference was found among the four-month-old infants in their tendency to babble spontaneously. Some were extremely quiet while others cooed and made gurgling sounds almost continuously.

Observations made in the homes of these children revealed that college-educated mothers were much more responsive to their infants' babbling than mothers less educated. The college-bred or middle-class mothers talked to their infants and engaged in long, reciprocal, if unintelligible, dialogues.

At twenty-seven months of age, the children who were the most talkative and had the most extensive vocabularies, as well as the highest I.Q. scores, had been highly vocal infants reared by college-trained mothers. Those infants who had been raised by lower-middle-class and less-educated mothers were significantly less proficient verbally and had, probably as a direct result, lower I.Q.'s.

In raising doubts that heredity accounts for a major portion of the variation in I.Q. scores, the Harvard psychologist makes these points: the I.Q. test is a culturally biased instrument, the similar I.Q. scores of genetically related people can be simulated in genetically unrelated persons who live in comparable environments, and the correlation between heredity and environment is ignored in current interpretations of the projected 80–20 heritability ratio, as suggested by the study with the infants.

Of course, the I.Q. is, in part, inherited, or rather the tendency toward intelligence is. But, we do not know nor dare we say that an upper limit can be placed on the child born in a lowly environment. The child from a rural area or another culture may know different things, have had varying experiences, but he still may have the basic concept and capacity to remember, to symbolize, to reason, to categorize, and to understand abstractions.

Amazing as it may seem, Dr. Kagan found that in his work with children in Guatemala, ten-year-olds living in extremely isolated agricultural villages showed a capacity for symbolism, memory, and conceptual inference completely comparable to that displayed by middle-class American children.

True, the Guatemalan child knows less than his counterpart in the United States about airplanes, computers, fractions, radios, or television sets. But he knows much more about how to make rope and tortillas, how to tell the weather from cloud formations, and how to play in the forest without getting lost. The ghetto child knows how to play the "dozens," the intricacies of stickball, how to protect himself from harm, but does not know how to play tennis or use a library.

Each culture, and each group within the culture, knows what is necessary for its own existence.

Observes Dr. Kagan: "There are only a few incompetent children if you classify them from the perspective of the community of adaptation, but millions of incompetent children if you classify them from the perspective of another society."

An unusual project that shows once again that the environment plays a significant role in raising the I.Q. score is found in Israel. Here is what Professor Benjamin S. Bloom, University of Chicago psychologist, reports:

Children of European origin were found to have an average I.Q. of 105 when raised in their own homes. But if reared in a kibbutz for four or more years, with trained, experienced nurses and teachers, their average I.Q. scores jump to 115.

In contrast, the Middle-Eastern Jewish children from Yemen, Syria, Lebanon, or Egypt, raised in individual homes, have an average I.Q. of only 85—close to the mentally retarded range. However, when they migrated to Israel and were placed in the kibbutz programs, they also reached an average I.Q. of 115. They performed the same, intellectually, as the European children with whom they were matched for education, occupational level of parents, and the kibbutz groups in which they were raised. Through a drastic change of environment, from their backward, restricted lives in the Mid-Eastern countries, to the more enlightened environment in their new land, their I.Q.'s jumped an astounding average of 30 points in from two to four years. Had these children remained in Yemen, for example, they would have continued to be considered mentally inferior with their low 85 I.Q. score.

Here is yet another remarkable illustration of the effect of changed environment on the growth of the I.Q. score:

A small group of mentally retarded year-old orphans were taken out of the institution in which they had been placed and put under the individual care of feeble-minded women who were living in a wing of the hospital ward. The children had minimum individual attention in the small Iowa orphanage. But the women, although considered to be below average intelligence, adopted the retarded infants, fed them and played with them, talked to them, mothered them, and showered them with love. The infants responded.

In two years their average I.Q. jumped 30 or more points, going from the mentally retarded level of 60 I.Q. to the average range of 95. They made further gains, when later placed in adoptive homes; because of the attention and love they had received while away from the orphanage, they were now bright enough to be adopted by normal families. A retest, some years later, showed that the average I.Q. was now 105. Many of the previously listed retarded children married and had normal children of their own.

By comparison, the children who had remained in the orphanage and who were not placed under individual care did not increase their I.Q.'s. In fact, the children deteriorated and became, indeed, mentally retarded. If anything, their I.Q. scores were lower or at best remained static.

What can we deduce from this startling experiment? Change of environment, providing children with individual attention, giving them love and affection, had worked the same wonders with the Iowa children as it did with those from the Middle-Eastern lands.

Stimulation, special learning, affection, and personal acceptance combined to bring out the buried intelligence in both instances. And the number of such incidents can be multiplied many times.

To go a step further, let us examine the effect of schooling on the child's I.Q. By almost any standards one can wish to adopt as a measurement, the majority of urban and rural slum or ghetto schools fail their children. More than half of each age group do not complete high school. Fewer than 5 per cent enroll in college or pursue any other form of higher education, compared with 40 to 50 per cent of the total school population. In many of the disadvantaged schools the child's average I.Q. is measured at 85 or less, compared with 100 to 105 for the middle-class school—and the I.Q. scores of the lower-class children continue to drop as they grow older, while it is more likely to increase with the middle-class group.

But studies show that the I.Q. can be raised if the school program adjusts itself to meet the needs of the individual child. As an example, I.Q. scores were found to improve steadily and significantly when black children migrated from the South, where their schooling was woefully inadequate, to Philadelphia, where they enrolled in better than average schools.

Yet another example: two hundred students, both black and white, were admitted to Harvard on a special trial basis. They had been reared in poverty, were graduates of slum or unaccredited schools, and were entirely unqualified for acceptance by Harvard's high standards of admission. After receiving special tutoring and other scholastic help, 85 per cent of them graduated, some with honors; one received a Rhodes scholarship.

These were society's rejects, the genetically blighted children. A constructive environment made all the difference in the world and opened new worlds, a new vision, higher horizons, and unknown intellectual delights for these young men.

On reflection, that should not be surprising. Jean Piaget sees notions of space, time, matter, and causality as necessary to develop an early sensorimotor stage of intellective growth. Much depends upon the environment and the use made of it. For example, migrant workers travel with their children from Florida to Maine, from Texas to California, from New Mexico to Oregon, without learning anything about geography or history en route. There is little or no communication between parent and child. The parents are too harassed by poverty and worry to point out historical or geographical land marks. As a matter of fact, the parents have no idea that these exist, as they, too, were born to migrant workers.

On the other hand, most middle-class, white-American parents interact with their children. They call attention to events, ask questions, get their children to talk about their own experiences, major or minor as they may be. The child is motivated to become involved with places and people and is not surrounded by a confusion of stimuli that is difficult for him to assimilate or understand. Significant changes in infants' and children's I.Q. scores have been correlated with the different amounts of environmental stimulation that they receive and how their parents or peers react to these stimuli.

Another point to consider: children from disadvantaged areas find it difficult to postpone their desire for the gratification of their needs. They do not have the achievement drive that will help them get better jobs in the future. Their school behavior problems interfere with their learning. Everything is in the present, in the "here and now." The future does not exist, or at best, is a hazy, distant object that is beyond the child's comprehension or understanding. Since he does not get any encouragement from his parents at home, or his peer group in his own neighborhood, or from his teachers at school, he adopts a "what's the use" attitude, totally unconcerned with events that may take place a week, a month, or a year away.

Children are often reared in unspeakably poor surroundings, conditions that undoubtedly will affect them for life and will certainly show up in extremely low I.Q. scores. Here is a description of a child-rearing environment of a low-class socioeconomic family, believed to be fairly typical, contained in the *American Journal of Orthopsychiatry:*

"The youngest child usually was found in his crib in a back room. Diapers were changed infrequently. As often as not a partially full bottle was somewhere in the crib beyond the baby's reach.

"During our visits, crying often remained unheeded while the mother discussed her own worries and needs, or she would hold the baby with little attention to his comfort. Activities were impulse determined; consistency was totally absent.

"The mother might stay in bed until noon while the children also were kept in bed or ran around unsupervised—no pattern for anything. Until children learned not to mess with food, the mothers fed them and prevented them from holding the spoon."

Left in this type of deprived environment until he enters first grade, the child from the disadvantaged home has built habits of thought and action that may actually, and usually do, interfere with his school learning. He develops speech and thinking patterns that are at variance, and often in direct conflict, with what he needs to learn at home or at school.

The Head Start or Follow Through programs, initiated in the summer of 1965, and continuing to the present, were designed for the preschool child and were financed by the now defunct Office of Economic Opportunity. However, the programs were not planned to initiate experimental approaches to help the disadvantaged, but to provide experiences based upon a traditional nursery school curriculum. It is difficult for the traditional middle-class nursery school program to bring deprived children up to the development level of more privileged children.

However, some experimental programs, when their objectives were modified, have proved successful. One conducted at New York University exposed children to a special curriculum, beginning with two years of schooling prior to entrance into first grade, and continuing through the third grade. Three groups were studied over an eight-year span.

A varied and enriched program was offered. Changes were made in mathematics, language, science, reading skills, and concept formation. Language training was supplemented to expose children to acceptable verbal patterns. The vocabulary dealt with concepts of size, shape, color, number, space, time, and temperature. Music and art were an important part of the program.

Much of the language contributed to preparation for reading. It was found that children exposed to the enriched curriculum were able to maintain or increase their achievement level, while the performance of those left untutored and neglected in their unwholesome surroundings made no academic progress and even deteriorated.

Children who entered public school, without prior nursery help, scored significantly lower than those who had kindergarten or nursery experience. The longer a child remained in his culturally disadvantaged environment, the greater was his deficit in his I.Q. scores. For whatever it may mean, the children who received special help before entering first grade scored high I.Q.'s on the Peabody Picture Vocabulary Test, the Columbia Mental Maturity Scale, the Stanford-Binet, and the Illinois Test of Psycholinguistic Abilities.

Environment, an enriched school program, and special attention to the needs of the children paid off in higher I.Q. scores. Were the genes improved or changed, or was it a betterment of environment? Whatever the answer, this only confirms my dogmatic view that the I.Q. test is really an exercise in futility, that it holds little meaning and less promise, and that it is not a measure of inherited intelligence.

A position similar to mine is taken by Professor Edmund W. Gordon of Columbia University who stresses that children from disadvantaged backgrounds, in comparison with middle-class children, are less able to make use of conventional verbal symbols when they want to express their feelings or interpret their experiences.

Another study reported by Dr. Gordon concluded that children in lower economic groups take a year or more longer to reach essentially mature articulation, compared with those of upper groups. Disadvantaged children fail to develop a high degree of dependence on the verbal and written language forms necessary in the learning process. Many simply have not adopted the means of expression that are usually associated with school success. This has been seen in a study of disadvantaged children whose answers to questions have been given to them, by their overworked and inattentive parents, in monosyllables rather than complete sentences.

It is not uncommon for parents to bark at their children with such phrases as: "Sit down." "Shut up." "Don't bother me." "Uh-huh." "No." Or perhaps just a nod of the head in a disinterested manner. By contrast, children in middle-class homes will usually find their parents speaking to them in full, complete sentences, and encouraging a similiar response.

I believe enough evidence has accumulated to conclude, without reservation, that the I.Q. is not inherited but is an acquired trait. Many children with low I.Q.'s, we have shown, were not born that way. They merely failed to learn those aspects of learning so necessary in our traditional schools.

Lower-class children ignore difficult problems; they are not interested in mastering abstractions. Over a period of years, from first grade through twelve, if they get that far, the learning ability is decreased proportionately through neglect, indifference, lack of motivation and stimulation. If a child in fourth grade is reading at a first-grade level, he is not going to be inspired to try harder when he reaches the fifth grade. His frustrations will continue throughout the days of his schooling.

In turn, his I.Q. scores will continue to fall lower and lower, since he will be matched with children his own age who have had the advantages of a better environment, a richer home background, and continued emphasis on educational goals.

This does not necessarily mean that Jono, in the fourth grade, who reads on the sixth-grade level and scores an I.Q. of 135 is any brighter or more intelligent than Roger, also in the fourth grade, who reads on the second-grade level and has an I.Q. score of 85. It merely means that Roger needs additional help to compensate for his early failings, caused by his unfortunate circumstances of birth, not by genetic malfunction.

Jono and Roger may have equal intelligence. Genetically they may be on an equal basis. However, to make them truly equal, mentally and intellectually, we must equalize their environment and their school experiences.

7

Nature versus nurture—can the I.Q. be raised?

Intelligence cannot be equated with the I.Q. score. The two are not the same. There are many facets to intelligence, as studies on creativity, artistic talent, rote learning, and various phases of mental ability have shown. Intelligence Quotient is only the measurement of what the child has learned at school or at home.

John Locke, in the seventeenth century, noted that the minds of children are blank at birth and that all later differences between them are caused through the circumstances of environment. Locke was supported in his theory by the French philosopher C. A. Helvetius (1715–71) who said that the inequality of minds was caused by the difference in the amount of education each individual received.

Interestingly enough, the late psychologist, Dr. Irving Lorge, whose Lorge-Thorndike group I.Q. tests are widely used in our schools today, said virtually the same thing when he wrote, in the 1945 Teachers College record, that "schooling makes a difference." Education, he found, can increase mastery of abilities as measured by I.Q. tests. Increased educational advantages influenced the scores made on these tests.

Lorge tested a group of eighth-grade boys in 1921, and then retested them twenty years later. The I.Q. scores of the men who went to college, he found, were higher than those who stopped with a high school education, and still higher than those who did not go beyond the tenth grade. From these findings, Dr. Lorge made this observation:

"An intelligence test score obtained at age fourteen does not predict the extent of education a person will get. The score obtained at age thirty-four shows substantial relation to the extent of education he has received."

What are the implications of this revealing study? It suggests strongly that the amount of schooling makes a difference in the later intelligence test scores of adults. It indicates, also, that environment plays a major role in the I.Q. scores registered by children. Education is an important part of this environment.

A majority of children from disadvantaged areas do not go to college, often not more than 5 per cent as compared with 50 per cent for the advantaged or privileged. More than half drop out before completing high school. Factors such as money, motivation, poor training in the early grades, disinterest, or teacher neglect are in major part responsible for this unfair situation.

Various studies have found that the highest grade completed by a child is dependent upon the income level of the family, the geographic region in which a person lives, and the early training received in elementary or high school.

It would appear, then, that the I.Q. score represents the interaction between a child's, or adult's, basic ability and his environment. We are squandering our chief human resources, the mental power of our citizenry, by permitting extraneous circumstances to keep many of our children, regardless of race, color, or economic status, from getting their full share of educational opportunities. To make matters worse, we then find that eminent psychologists blame low I.Q. scores on inherited qualities, rather than on the disadvantaged environments which is the lot of so many of the nation's young boys and girls.

Followers of Professor B. F. Skinner of Harvard assume that nearly anyone, if given proper teaching methods, can learn almost anything. Even if genetic differences in ability exist, appropriate techniques can modify inborn ability and give the youngster an opportunity to overcome his handicaps.

The famous statement of psychologist John B. Watson, a behaviorist and stanch supporter of the environmentalist theory, is often quoted:

"Give me a dozen healthy infants, well-formed, and my own specified world to bring them up in, and I'll guarantee to take any one at random and train him to become any type of specialist I might select—doctor, lawyer, artist, merchant, chief, and yes, even begger-man and thief, regardless of his talents, penchants, tendencies, abilities, vocations, race of his ancestors."

Unfortunately, Dr. Watson never did get the opportunity to prove his contention, which has often been challenged. Probably he exaggerated, as he himself confessed when he said:

"I am going beyond my facts and I admit it, but so have the advocates of the contrary and they have been doing it for many thousands of years."

We should ask, as we delve into the issue of nature versus nurture, or the place of the I.Q. score in school, what do the tremendous number of tests really measure? What insight do these hundreds of I.Q., achievement, vocational, aptitude, creativity, and other tests add to the knowledge we want to acquire concerning our children?

It is apparent that a test devised to measure intelligence of children in Harlem is unsuitable for pupils in Grosse Point or Long Island. A test standardized on white, middle-class children can hardly be valid for inner-city children of Los Angeles. Since tests do not measure native intelligence, the current reliance placed upon them is both deceptive and unjust.

Changes in the social, educational, economic, and other environmental influences result in substantial changes in I.Q. scores. One example: 87,000 eleven-year-old children in Edinburgh were given I.Q.

tests in 1932. Fifteen years later similar tests were administered to 71,000 children in Edinburgh, also age eleven. The average I.Q. increased significantly. Why? It was found that during this decade and a half between tests, the economic and cultural conditions improved among the families whose children had been tested, and the children had received more schooling.

A marked rise in the average intellectual capacity of the British has taken place over the past hundred years, as has a similar spectacular rise in the Soviet Union during the past half century. This increase, too, in both instances, can be attributed to the higher economic levels of the populace, as well as the greater emphasis on education.

These examples bring to mind the statement made by the group of expert consultants to the United Nations Educational, Scientific, and Cultural Organization (UNESCO), when it delcared:

"According to present knowledge, there is no proof that the groups of mankind differ in their innate mental characteristics, whether in respect of intelligence or temperament. The scientific evidence indicates that the range of mental capacities in all ethnic groups is much the same."

This echoes the belief of Professor Hunt who holds that if we but apply Piaget's theories of child development we could raise the I.Q. score of the average Western child by 30 points. Piaget maintains that you cannot think of intelligence as a definite entity or power which simply matures as the child grows older. Rather, it is cumulative building of more complex and flexible "schemata." This takes place through the impact of the environment on the growing organism.

Now we come to another point: mental abilities are much too varied to be described in terms of a monolithic general intelligence "g" factor—a symbol devised by Professor Spearman in segregating intelligence, and useful if you believe that the I.Q. score represents a score of one's intelligence.

However, as we have noted, intelligence is not monolithic. You find such variations as verbal, numerical, spatial, perceptual, mechanical, imaginative, cognitive, memorization, or creative reasoning facets. A child, or adult, may be superior on two or three of these traits, but slow or inferior on others. Who can say which are the more important—verbal power or mechanical ability in a person's life career?

An early training project has been undertaken at George Peabody College, where it was found that children with deprived backgrounds were far behind in their reading-readiness tests. The college staff conducted a ten-week program for the disadvantaged children, prior to their entrance into first grade.

The program worked. Children were helped to overcome their reading difficulties. They showed an improved attitude in school and benefited greatly from the preschool help that they had received. Just as, or perhaps more, important from the long-range point of view is that the parents of these poor, disadvantaged children were also stimulated and challenged. They began to take greater interest in the educational, social, and physical development of their children.

Home visitors in the experiment brought toys, books, pencils, blocks, and assorted playthings for the children. In one case, a woman with a set of twins came daily to the preschool sessions. Although she was not in the program, she watched the teachers as they worked and played with the youngsters in the project. To the extent that she could, she followed the instructions given to the other children and their parents. When her children entered first grade, they too became competent students. Through interest and observation, this mother and others helped to improve their children's success in school.

A program of preschool help, extended and tailored to meet the needs of the deprived children, can have lasting effects. However, if the home environment remains the same, if motivation and learning patterns are not sufficiently supplemented and encouraged by home environment, the gains may be gradually lost. Educators who work with underprivileged children have found that it is virtually imperative that in each case the home must become involved. Teachers can show the way, but, without co-operation from the parents and the community, the final results may be nullified.

Inappropriate motivation, depressed levels of aspiration, academic disenchantment, and underdeveloped intellect are all too frequently the products of poverty, lack of opportunity, and discrimination. When these conditions are corrected, perhaps then would we be in a better position truly to compare the I.Q. scores of different groups within our communities. Nature and nurture cannot be treated as isolated aspects of a child's growth and intellectual development. Both are need to raise a child's I.Q. or better still to develop his intelligent potential to the fullest.

We do not confront an either/or situation—either the child is born with superior brains or he is born a dullard. That would be entirely fallacious. But it is being done in this country and many nations abroad. For example, in Great Britain the traditional method of separating the bright from the dull student was, and still is to a large extent, the scholarship system. British teachers and parents, in the early days of testing, thought of scholarships as a means for rewarding hard work rather than as a device for detecting talent.

The London County Council, in 1913, appointed a Dr. Cyril Burt as an official psychologist. Burt found that in the poorer districts of the London East End, there were three times as many defectives, eight times as many backward pupils, but only one tenth the number of scholarship winners as were reported in the well-to-do areas of the city.

Who and what were to blame? The teachers? The homes? Traditional examinations? Heredity? Environment? Two theories developed: one held that differences in intelligence could be corrected through improved surroundings; the other that the ability was due mainly to genetic endowment. Dr. Burt did not accept an either/or answer.

Analyzing the studies of siblings that he had made in London, Burt concluded that 88 per cent of the I.Q. variations were due to genetic factors and 12 per cent to nongenetic or environmental influences. This does not leave much room for the improvement of children—they were doomed to inferiority from birth.

However, going further, Burt found that based on tests alone, 77 per cent of the variations in intellect could be attributed to genetic factors, while a larger proportion, or 23 per cent, were nongenetic. From which Dr. Burt reached this conclusion:

"This of course means that the common practice of relying on tests alone—usually a group test applied only once—is by no means a satisfactory method of assessing a child's innate ability. Better assessments are obtained by submitting the test scores to the teachers for criticism or correction and, where necessary, adjust them. . . ."

Although Dr. Burt conceded that group I.Q. tests are not a satisfactory method to determine a child's intelligence, these tests are still widely used. The nongenetic factors are of primary importance and cannot be overlooked.

Environment appears to influence the I.Q. scores in three ways: the cultural amenities of the home and the educational opportunities provided by the school; the presence of an intellectual background to develop motivation and work habits; and illness or malnutrition during the prenatal or early postnatal stages.

We do not have sufficient information to determine the relative roles of heredity and environment, despite the efforts of some psychologists to evolve a magic formula. Even though he is a strong and ardent geneticist, Burt readily admits that much can be said for the environmentalists. The interaction that takes place between the two cannot be lightly dismissed as being of little relative value or importance.

Environment can influence the child's I.Q. score in a variety of ways, some of which have nothing whatsoever to do with inherited genes. In one extremely pertinent and revealing study, pregnant women in low-income groups whose normal diets were generally deficient were provided with a dietary supplement during pregnancy and lactation. A control group received placebos.

When tested at the age of three and four, children of the experimental group obtained significantly higher I.Q. scores than did those in the control group. This test showed that the I.Q. can be influenced, through proper nutrition, months before the child is born! Where did heredity come into this experiment? Both groups of parents were equal in every respect, with one exception: some of the mothers received a more wholesome diet, and this, in turn, reflected on the I.Q.'s of their as yet unborn children.

But let us continue with the effects of environment on growth and intellectual development. Viewing the reading-readiness scores of children who had entered the first grade, Dr. Esther A. Milner found that the lower-class children seemed to lack two advantages enjoyed by the middle class: first, a warm positive family atmosphere and, second, an extensive opportunity to interact verbally with adults in the family. Lower-class children perceived adults as predominantly hostile. Their parents discouraged or even prohibited mealtime conversation or, indeed, communication at almost any time of the day or evening.

Research demonstrates that children growing up under adverse circumstances may have their I.Q. scores lowered by as much as an average of 15 points—the difference in I.Q. attributed by some psychologists to that which exists between black and white children. The child in the middle-class home, unlike the one in the disadvantaged, gets instruction about the world in which he lives, uses language more effectively, understands the concepts of similarities, word differences, logical relationships—all basic items in the standard I.Q. tests.

Writing in *Compensatory Education for Cultural Deprivation,* Professors Bloom, Davis, and Hess considered the mental and physical deficiencies that exist in poverty-level homes. Physical handicaps, frequently observed, include dental problems, impaired hearing, defective vision, inadequate nutrition, or general lack of medical care. These operate to influence learning in a number of ways: the child is less able to concentrate on his school tasks or his learning assignments. He becomes easily fatigued, is restless, and all too often entirely unmotivated.

Ideally, early intellectual development should take place in the home. All later learning is likely to be influenced by the basic concepts that have evolved by the age of five or six. But if learning cannot be provided in the home, the school must assume the responsibility to provide the culturally deprived child with as good a set of skills and techniques as the child gets in the more advantaged and affluent home.

The child from the culturally privileged home is likely to begin school with a love of learning for its own sake. By contrast, the culturally deprived child has difficulty adopting this concept, or that of learning, for parental approval. Each year the deficit grows as the child suffers further frustration and failure. He becomes alienated from school. There is little likelihood that he will get any satisfaction or sense of accomplishment from his educational experience. That is why he leaves school as soon as he can, legally or otherwise.

Then, when the teacher does not recognize the vast gulf that separates the background of the children in her class, and she uses the conventional materials and methods of the school curriculum for all her pupils, she will often blame the listlessness, lack of discipline, and poor study habits on the failing disadvantaged child, rather than on the meaningless (to him) curriculum and school routine.

It has been found that the typical disadvantaged student, when he enters high school, is reading three to four years below his grade level. He is also considerably behind in arithmetic and other skill subjects. His problem-solving and abstract thinking are at a low level. He is often apathetic, hostile, rebellious, unmotivated, frustrated, and sees little relevance between his school life and the outside world which to him is dreary, grim, and without promise of success.

Is it any wonder that an I.Q. test given at this stage of his life, just as a test given to him much earlier in his school career, will find the scores far below that of his more privileged classmates who are reading at, or above, grade level, have a career in mind, are motivated, and, for the most part, have the support of their parents in seeking future goals?

The measured intelligence of the deprived child does not reflect his true learning ability. But when stimulated, challenged, and offered badly needed help, both intellectual and physical, his intelligence, as measured by even the biased I.Q. tests, shows a substantial increase. The higher I.Q. scores are meaningless and may even become dangerous, unless the schools recognize that their job is to go beyond numerical computations and into the daily living problems of their students.

Many children from poverty homes fail in school not only because of poor cultural background, but because the schools themselves are doing little to compensate for this lack. Unless the teachers are acutely aware of the child's home environment, and many are not or are indifferent to it, the child not only is tagged with a low I.Q., but soon becomes inattentive, frustrated, distracted, bored, and hostile. The poverty-level child is often tired and hungry and suffers from physical problems that need medical attention.

The apathetic, malnourished child cannot be expected to respond to school routine in a constructive way. Until we can equalize, to some degree at any rate, the same advantages for all children, correct physical defects, improve home conditions, and eliminate the vast cultural differences that now exist, we cannot blame genetic inferiority on variations in I.Q. scores among races, ethnic groups, or occupational pursuits.

A study was made with a group of South African Negro children, in which one group suffered from malnutrition while the other had an adequate diet. Both groups belonged to the same social stratum, that of unskilled laborers. It was found that the malnourished children had lower I.Q's., were shorter in height, weighed less, and had smaller heads than the well-nourished children.

The two groups of youngsters were observed and tested over a seven-year period. At the end of that time, a final I.Q. test was given to all the children. A difference of twenty-two points was found between the two groups, with the well-nourished children being on top. More recent tests, with the children now approaching adolescence, indicate that the I.Q. differences were sustained, and that the gap between the two remains undiminished and, if anything, will probably increase.

Can the I.Q. be raised? Indeed it can, as shown from this experiment. Proper food is one essential phase that must be considered. Cultural help, too, is vital.

However, such help, through special compensatory programs, will not suffice by itself. Children who have been excessively exposed to illnesses are unlikely to be helped by more schooling. To be effective, help for the children must take into account the many major difficulties that confront the disadvantaged and underprivileged in their homes or at school.

An antagonistic environment retards the child's mental development, a condition that may exist for many years or even a lifetime. Sometimes he is never able to regain this loss. Fortunately, the reverse process is also true. Once conditions are removed that caused retardation, mental growth may take place, often at ages when such growth is commonly assumed to have ceased. The Higher Horizons Program of New York City found that supposedly uneducable children and older adolescents from lower socioeconomic backgrounds could learn and succeed in a reorganized, meaningful, structured school environment.

Take the case of Ned. He lived in a ramshackle tenement in East Harlem. He went to school whenever he felt like it, which wasn't very often. He knew how to avoid the truant officer. At school he was troublesome, apathetic, and belligerent in turn. Living in a fatherless home with a mother too busy with day work to keep the family together and another brother and sister, Ned could not understand why he should go to school, why he should do his class assignments, what purpose there was in life for him, anyway.

"Don't need much schooling to be a bootblack," he once told me.

The New York Board of Education decided that something should be done to motivate and help Ned and the thousands of others like him. Higher Horizon programs were initiated to offer Ned and his classmates a better opportunity to succeed. Smaller classes, more stimulating teachers, relevant courses, and challenging instruction became part of Ned's new curriculum.

He accepted the challenge, came to school, and began to enjoy his education. From reading on a fifth-grade level, even though he was in the ninth grade, Ned quickly jumped to his normal grade, aided by supremely dedicated remedial-reading teachers. Spurred on by his teachers, encouraged by his mother, and showing a new and surprising aptitude for math and science, he applied and was accepted at the Bronx High School of Science, a school that admits only superior students. He finished in the upper quarter of his class despite the fierce competition of students who had had all the advantages that Ned lacked.

Upon graduation, he was offered a four-year scholarship at Harvard, on condition that he go to a private school for a year, to enable him to "catch-up" on the gaps in his education. Andover gave him a full scholarship, and at the end of an academically successful year, he enrolled at Harvard.

This true story has a happy ending. He finished his studies at Harvard with honors, was admitted to Yale Law School, graduated with above average grades, and passed his bar examination with little difficulty.

"If I hadn't received the help in school when I was floundering and ready to quit, I'd probably be in a reform school now," he told me, philosophically. "What can a black, poverty-stricken boy from Harlem hope to do in life, when all the odds are against him? But now I'm proud of myself and happy that my mother kept encouraging me to go higher and higher."

I might add, as a footnote, that an I.Q. test taken in elementary school placed Ned in the 90 range. He was definitely not college material at that percentile. But a discerning and sympathetic teacher sensed in Ned a tiny spark of curiosity and response and recommended him for the Higher Horizon Program despite his 90 I.Q. She thus created a fulfilled professional young man because she had the foresight and the humanity necessary to overlook the devastatingly low I.Q. score. A retest later found Ned's I.Q. to be 138.

We cannot brush aside the studies that show, vividly and force-fully, that the I.Q. can be raised, that disadvantaged children such as Ned can be helped, that environment can be a diabolical influence on a child, and that every effort must be made to provide help for those children who are on the bottom rung of the social and economic ladder. Genetics may have played a part in Ned's intellectual bloom-ing, but environment played a greater part. Whatever ability might have been present in Ned could never have been released if his envi-ronmental conditions had not been changed, nor his schooling re-vised to meet his needs.

It is apparent that environment makes a difference in helping to raise the child's I.Q., or to keep it from ever rising. Although this is contrary to Jensen's theories, he reports the classic case of Isabel, an illegitimate child whose disgraced grandparents kept her and her deaf-mute mother from the world. Isabel lived with her mother in a hidden attic until she was found at the age of six and one half years of age. She had been isolated with her mother and communicated largely through gestures. Not being able to speak, she made strange croaking sounds. Her mental age measured at one year and seven months, putting her I.Q. at 25, almost the lowest possible score, below that of an idiot or imbecile. After several years of treatment, with special help that enabled her to adjust to the new world in which she found herself for the first time, and able to hear voices that she had never heard before, Isabel became normal. Her I.Q. now came within normal range for her age level.

To which Dr. Jensen comments: "Extreme environmental depri-vation resulted, by the age of six, in a level of development that was commensurate with the lowest level of human ability to be found in institutions for the severely defective, and through intensive educa-tional therapy it was possible to ameliorate this condition, by the age of eight or nine, to a level of normal functioning."

Ghetto children, like Isabel, live in their own forsaken attics. Why can't Dr. Jensen and those who support his views on the I.Q. recognize this contradiction?

But going a step further, Dr. J. P. Guilford holds that the trou-ble with the traditional I.Q. tests is that they define an intelligence that is far too constricted. Not enough attention is given to the special abilities that children possess. It is almost impossible to give the same test—the Stanford-Binet, the WISC, or the others—to the differing age levels of children. Infant and preschool tests measured abilities other than those measured by the more common scales used as children grow older.

Moreover, youngsters who are shy, unmotivated or unco-operative will do poorly on the I.Q. tests. Children may be tested under unfavorable emotional conditions, or by overanxious examiners. A child's anxiety is known to interfere with the test. The personality of the examiner looms larger and more threatening to the test-anxious child.

Again we must ask what the objective of the I.Q. test is. If it is solely to predict future academic status and success in passing the school subjects, it may be fairly adequate. But if it is to determine situations that go beyond the classroom, these tests hold little value for the child or the teacher. As Dr. Kenncth B. Clark, noted psychologist, puts it:

"Don't say that the disadvantaged child has a low I.Q., but that he has not learned things that other children already know."

The evidence strongly suggests, in the opinion of Dr. Clark, that the socially deprived child will learn, if taught properly and accepted, respected, and approached as a human being. Under these circumstances, the performance of this child may readily reach the "norm" performance of all other children within his age group, regardless of economic status.

A revision of the I.Q. tests should be made to include the strengths of the inner-city, culturally below normal children: their insights, ways of coping, values, and life styles that fit them for their particular culture.

The various studies, reports, experiments, and projects that have been conducted during the past half century, and are now under way, suggest strongly that intelligence is not genetically determined at birth. It does not develop and spring forth in a predetermined manner. Environment, on the other hand, seems to be a key factor in the development of the mind. Optimum intellectual development is influenced by the student's self-concept, the influence of his peers, his attitude toward himself and his parents as well as his teachers.

The poorly prepared child is academically inferior because he has not learned many of the necessary aspects of schooling found in the traditional educational pattern. Then, when his deficits begin to pile higher, and the child drops one or more grades behind his classmates in reading, or arithmetic, or writing, the spark for learning may become extinguished before it is even lit. Unless society helps him, the way it helped Ned, he is lost.

The deficits cannot be removed overnight. This correction involves a long-range program and poses many as yet unsolved problems. We must recognize that schools and government agencies should take a more immediate interest in the child's physical, emotional, and mental needs.

When the child's environment improves, so will his I.Q. Through patience, money, a revised educational curriculum, and compassion, a child's I.Q. can be raised.

Millions of parents and their children who have been cowed by the powerful and threatening I.Q. concept should take comfort that the I.Q. is not a fixed and permanent part of one's life. Just as is the case with all of life's processes, it can be changed, enriched, fulfilled, or it can be neglected and made to wither.

One thing is certain, however: *No place exists in the schools of the United States for a class system based on the I.Q.*

8

The changing I.Q.—the
I.Q. is a yo-yo

Today we have enough evidence to convince all but the most skeptical that the I.Q. is not constant. Like a yo-yo, it can bounce up and down, depending on the skill and technique of the one who is pulling the string. But we know that normal, average children, unless genetically deformed, range higher or lower in their I.Q. performance during childhood, adolescence, and adulthood, many to a substantial and striking degree.

A long-range study conducted at the Fels Research Institute, begun in 1929, and continuing to the present, has found that the average individual's I.Q. could vary between two and one half and seventeen years of age by nearly 30 points. One of three children in the study displayed a progressive change of more than 30 points, while one in seven showed more than 40 points. In certain instances, increases as high as 74 I.Q. points were authentically recorded!

Changes in performance on standardized mental tests continue throughout life. But the changes are not inserted on the child's record cards, his accumulated file, nor noted by his teachers. Thus, a child, who is tested when he enters school at age six, may have an I.Q. of 105. This score, like Mary's lamb, follows him to school each day, year after year, stenciled on his accumulative record card. He is not likely to be retested.

Teacher after teacher, from grades one through twelve, looking over past records, will see the number 105 and will say: "Johnny is an average student. I won't expect a spectacular performance from him."

However, at age ten, Johnny's I.Q. may have risen to 125 and by age fourteen to 140. Of course, much will depend on what I.Q. test he takes, who does the scoring, how the lad feels when he is tested, how his parents feel about his education, where the family lives, how ambitious they are for their child's success, and the quality of his public school educators. Writing in *Inequality,* Dr. Christopher Jencks and seven colleagues point to the immeasurable influence that teachers have on the academic as well as social lives of their students.

In the meantime, the youngster, labeled as average, is denied the educational advantages and enrichment that are frequently given to students of superior rank. Schools tend to provide an enriched program for the so-called "bright" children, based on high I.Q.'s. The average or dull are neglected.

Also, let us remember, the I.Q. can go down as well as up. Decreases of 20 to 30 points are not unusual. Children whose I.Q. scores go down frequently come from homes which do not make any attempt to stimulate them, and where the parents are not sympathetic toward life goals for their children. In contrast, children who show increases in the I.Q. scores come from homes that emphasize learning, encourage success in school, and have a more communicative relationship with them.

Preschool children whose I.Q.'s rise dramatically are described by their teachers as independent and competitive. Elementary grade children, with I.Q. scores that tend to go higher as the youngsters grow older, are independent, scholastically competitive, self-initiating, and superior at problem-solving.

These conclusions are reached in the study, *Developmental Changes in Mental Performance,* conducted by Dr. Robert B. McCall and his associates. Much confusion, misunderstanding, and needless rancor have swirled around the question of the changing I.Q. in recent years. Dr. McCall and his coworkers point out that the failure to predict childhood I.Q. from scores found in infancy, plus the extent of systematic I.Q. changes during childhood, argue against the concept of I.Q. constancy.

Performance is variable within an individual. If the I.Q. tests are used at all, they should be given to the children periodically, not just once or twice, as is now too often the case. Nor should the group I.Q. test be used as the basis of determining the child's I.Q. These tests, widely used throughout the country, have proven to be notoriously inaccurate.

At the Fels Institute, during the past forty years, children were tested and retested as many as seventeen times between the ages of two and seventeen. The scores varied substantially, almost dramatically, during these years.

Probably the most impressive shift in I.Q. scores is for a boy who went from 78 at age three to 151 at age eight, or a change of 73 I.Q. points. The first test rated the child as being mentally retarded, a candidate for a school for morons. The second called him a genius, to be placed in a school for gifted children.

By contrast, a long-range study of children from predominantly disadvantaged environments has shown a progressive decline in I.Q. between the ages of five, ten, and beyond. Similarly, children from rural mountain villages or other isolated or disadvantaged areas have also shown declines in I.Q. performance as the children grew older. This may be further proof, if such is needed, that environment is more important then heredity in the intellectual development of children.

The data presented by the McCall study indicate that normal, middle- and upper-middle-class children change an average of 24 points on standardized I.Q. tests between the ages of three and twelve years. This finding should be encouraging to parents who are told that, at age six, Mary has an I.Q. of 98 and isn't it too bad, because she is such a sweet girl and will be handicapped all her school life, unable to keep up with the rest of her class.

It is unfair to label a child as "slow" or "below average" or even a "genius" at an early age, or at any age, inasmuch as the I.Q. score may readily increase or decrease when the child grows older and enters higher grades. An I.Q. increase is altogether likely if the home environment changes for the better, or the child is fortunate enough to be assigned to a compassionate, understanding teacher. As Dr. Jencks points out, teachers can, and do, make a difference in the lives of their students. They have a tremendous impact on the student's values, aspirations, attitudes, and desire to learn.

Take the case of Sonya, shy, retiring, frightened, ill at ease in the presence of others. When she entered school, a standard Otis Quick-Scoring test listed her I.Q. as a low 88. Her teacher felt sorry for the child, but as she told Sonya's parents, who lived in a small town in Massachusetts: "Let's not push her. She'll learn to read in time. But frankly, Mrs. Jenkins, you should know that Sonya will always be a dull child. She was born that way. Just look at her I.Q. score and you'll know what I mean."

But the parents, educated and well informed, in professional positions, did not accept the teacher's pessimistic and even fatalistic verdict. They paid more attention to their child, took her to the Boston museum, to exhibits, to zoos, to children's theaters. They showered her with affection and encouraged the youngster to speak out, to come out of her self-made shell, to become more confident of herself and of her abilities.

When Sonya entered the second grade she was placed in the slow track, because, after all, the I.Q. record of 88 followed the shy child. But now something happened: the teacher, a happy, well-informed, sympathetic, well-adjusted woman with three children of her own, took a personal interest in Sonya. After school, her teacher, Mrs. Knowlton, helped Sonya with her reading, taught the child how to form her numbers, and aided her in improving her writing.

Day by day the child became better adjusted. She began to like school, and her face lit up with a happy smile at the mention of her teacher's name.

The parents, at the close of the second grade, suggested a retest, to see if the first I.Q. test had been an accurate reflection of their daughter's true ability. An individual Stanford-Binet showed that Sonya was now registering an I.Q. of 122. When school reopened in the fall, and Sonya entered the third grade, she received a WISC—again at the insistence of her parents. Now her score, for total verbal and performance scale, came to 130.

"What does the score mean, anyway?" Sonya's mother asked Mrs. Knowlton. "In the first grade my child was below average with a group score of 88. A year ago it was 122. Now it has gone to 130. Is Sonya a dull child, a normal one, or a bright girl?"

Mrs. Knowlton looked a bit nervous, so I answered: "Your child is a healthy, normal, lovable girl. Don't worry about her I.Q. It doesn't mean a thing. It can be pushed up or down, as you have seen, and much depends on her teacher, her classmates, and more particularly her parents. Sonya is fortunate that she had both a good teacher and exceptionally fine parents. She'll find her way."

And she did!

Results even more striking than those found at the Fels Institute were reported at the Rehabilitation Research and Training Center in Mental Retardation at the University of Wisconsin. The design of the project, now in its ninth year (1975), is simple to understand and evaluate: Can a child's I.Q. be raised if parents get special help together with their young children? Will a program of family intervention, beginning in infancy, prevent mental retardation in low-income homes where the mother, or father, has a low I.Q. and the risk that the child may also have a low score is that much greater?

It differs from previous enrichment or other early childhood education projects in its focus on children who, identified as retarded, are a high risk.

The direct infant intervention program began at three months of age and continued to age six when the children entered public school. It was conducted on an all-day basis, five days a week, twelve months a year. The objective was to provide an environment and a set of experiences which would allow each child to develop to his potential intellectually as well as socially, emotionally, and physically. The child's feelings of self-worth were promoted by attentive teachers who not only attempted to plan activities within his capacity and ability, but who also provided support, encouragement, and positive feedback to the parents about the child's attempts to understand and to deal with his world.

The results were truly astounding. Those children who received help did remarkably better than those in the control group in almost every area of learning, particularly in the language skills. After the first year of testing, the experimental group was one year ahead of the control group. At the end of the second year, the children who had received help were one and a half years ahead in their performance, compared with those who had not had help and served as the controls.

All the language tests indicated that the program had a profound effect on the experimental group's ability to perform on structured tests of linguistic development. At five and a half years of age, or just about the time the children were ready to enter school, their group I.Q. had increased by 30 points. The only difference between these "special" children and those whose I.Q. and performance were lower was the help that had been given to one group, and not to the other. A 30-point spread is highly significant—twice the 15-point gap that blacks are presumed to have as compared with the white population, and which is considered in various quarters as an unchangeable inherited quality.

Children can do poorly on the I.Q. test for a variety of reasons. They are fortunate if they find co-operative teachers and parents who are able to understand their needs. Jim, for example, was a smallish, unhappy, frightened lad of twelve when I first met him. His parents brought him to see me, with the hope that he could enroll at a school for gifted children which I headed at the time. His academic record was poor—hardly a good omen for success. I sent him to a certified psychologist for an I.Q. test, and then received this discouraging report:

"Jim is definitely below average in intellectual ability. He scored 92 on the WISC, did not respond to the examiner's questions, was apathetic, definitely needs, psychiatric help. My recommendation is that he enter a school that caters to slow or below average ability children. He certainly does not belong at your school."

When Jim's parents came to see me, I told them that their son was not eligible. His I.Q. score did not warrant his admission. Jim's mother began to cry. The boy was terribly unhappy in public school, she said. He was teased because of his shyness; he didn't do his homework. He could not fight back, as he was slender and underweight and, I presume, afraid of the older boys as well, so he stayed home frequently. One day it might be a stomach-ache; the next, his eyes hurt; the third excuse would be a headache.

I listened intently while the mother spoke. Jim's father sat back, saying nothing, glum, obviously not the least bit interested in our discussion. During the interview, Jim fidgeted in his chair, half-listening, evidently not caring one way or the other. I asked the parents to leave the office, and turning to Jim, said:

"Why are you doing so poorly in school?"

"I hate school," he snapped, bitterness in his voice. "I just can't stand it."

"Why, what's the problem?" I persisted.

No response. Jim just glanced out of the window.

"Anything bothering you?" I asked.

"Everything," came the sharp answer. "The kids fight with me. The teachers don't like me. They think I'm stupid. And I hate them. They're always picking on me."

He explained further how he had to run the gauntlet each morning, chased by the other children down the school corridors. He was sent to the principal's office for disciplinary infractions almost daily, on the days that he came to school. His guidance counselor later told me that Jim just "didn't have it upstairs, nothing between the ears," that he was a social outcast, a failure, a troublemaker and, above all, stupid. She would be delighted, and so would the school, she said, if we could possibly take him off her hands.

"You should see his I.Q. score," she added, as though that took care of all the problems involved.

I turned to Jim, took a deep breath, as though I was getting ready to jump off the diving board into a deep pool, almost frightened at what I proposed to do, for at that stage I believed that the I.Q. score was all important.

"If I let you come here, would you behave?" I asked.

"I won't cause any trouble," was the answer.

"But what about coming to school every day," I continued. "And studying, too? You know, Jim, this is a school for bright kids who want to get good marks so they can get into college. They won't want you fooling around, wasting their time, being a nuisance."

"I'll study," he answered simply. "I'm not afraid to work. If the teachers treat me right, I'll treat them right, too."

I called in Jim's parents and said:

"Maybe I shouldn't do this, but I'll take a chance on Jim. I'll put him on probation. Our psychologist, I must tell you frankly, does not recommend that I accept your son. His I.Q. isn't high enough. But maybe if Jim likes it here and wants to stay, he'll settle down and work. You'll have to help, too, you know."

I took the psychologist's report, put it in my brief case, and, at the end of the day, took it home. I did not want it in Jim's file, where a teacher or supervisor might see it and immediately tab Jim as a slow learner, a troublemaker, someone to keep at arm's length. To me, Jim was just another student, on equal ground with his classmates. I expected him to succeed. And he did!

The first few months were rough. I had placed Jim on a three months' probation, just as I usually did when the I.Q. score did not quite measure up to our standards, and when I had reason to believe that if the youngster could be motivated by our teachers, he would succeed. At the end of three months I called Jim into my office. I had asked his parents to be there, too. Only his mother came.

"Jim," I said quietly, "I'm proud of you. I have a report from your teachers. They say you're still a bit behind, but they think you'll get there. I know you are having trouble with reading and math. And look at your awful spelling. Still, you do come to school every day. I know you're trying. That's what I really wanted to hear from your teachers. You can stay the rest of the year, and come back next year, too, if you keep plugging away. I've asked your teachers to give you whatever special or remedial help that you may need."

Jim did not let me down. He continued to improve. At the end of the year he was promoted to the eighth grade. When he entered high school he joined the athletic teams and became an outstanding soccer, baseball, and basketball player. He was voted the best athlete of the school three years in a row and won permanent possession of the athletic trophy. When he graduated, with good grades, he was accepted by an excellent college.

He came to see me in his senior year, getting ready to enter a graduate school as a science major. Confident, happy, at ease with himself and the world, he was no longer the diffident lad that I had known when he first came to see me.

"You had confidence in me," he said. "You thought I could do the work here. My teachers thought so, too. And that is when I knew that I would graduate, go to college, and work for my advanced degree, maybe go for my Ph.D. if I can get a fellowship. You gave me a chance. You didn't treat me as though I were stupid. More than anything else, you and the teachers made me see that I could be somebody if I tried. And that is when I decided that I'd try my best."

Jim, at twelve, with an I.Q. of 92, was now, at twenty, an honor student, planning to take his Ph.D. Instead of ending somewhere along the line as a school dropout or a juvenile delinquent, he is now a valued member of society and will, I am confident, make a lasting contribution in whatever profession he may enter.

I can parallel Jim's case with that of Ellen, admitted to a special school for the gifted, even though her WISC I.Q. score measured 101. She reminded me, in some ways, of Jim. She, too, did not like school, did not like her teachers, was not the least bit motivated to continue, but waited impatiently to reach her legal school-leaving age of sixteen, when she planned to drop out. She came from a broken home and lived with her mother, an older sister, and two younger brothers.

I struggled hard to make the right decision. Most of our pupils were in the 130 and over range. Would Ellen be able to compete with them on an equal footing, would she become discouraged, or would she be able to make the necessary adjustment?

The high I.Q. scores did not particularly impress me by this time. Nor did the low ones. I wanted to know how the students did in school. How much did they want to learn? Were they motivated to do their best work? How intelligent were they, or could they become, under challenging and stimulating conditions? Since I do not believe that the I.Q. measures intelligence, I looked beyond the report sent to me by the school psychologist.

By this time I had read *Inequality* and recalled that Dr. Jencks had written: "Standardized tests measure skills that are useful in getting through school, not skills that pay off once school is over."

I turned to Ellen and asked: "Why do you want to change schools and come to this one?"

"Because," she replied honestly, "I don't want to be treated as a number, as I now am in school. I hardly know my teacher's name, and she doesn't know mine, I'm sure. How can she, with thirty-nine of us in the classroom?"

At the end of the year, Ellen received the highest possible grades in all subjects. With an average intelligence, she could be expected to just about pass her subjects. But low I.Q. or not, she was far better than average. She led the class in every respect, both in curricular and extracurricular activities.

"Would you be willing to take another I.Q. test?" I asked, when I saw Ellen's final report card and knew that it did not in any way correlate with the score made on her previous test.

She was, and her parents agreed. She took the Stanford-Binet this time, since she had already taken the WISC and I did not want to have her score prejudiced in any way by previous knowledge of the test items, even though a year had passed between testing, and it would be extremely unlikely that she would have retained any memory of the items that were included. Besides, she was a year older.

On the Stanford-Binet she scored 138, a gain of 37 I.Q. points in one year. Nor was this unusual, as I found when I retested other students who had low I.Q. scores, were admitted on probation, and later increased their scores from 10 to 35 points.

On the other hand, I have seen the opposite take place, despite every effort on the part of the teachers. When I recommended Bill for admittance, I was elated to find that he had an I.Q. of 175, definitely placing him in the genius, one in a million, class. I confidently expected that Bill would lead all the rest, and for the first semester he did. He made high honors in every subject; his teachers were delighted to have him in their classes. He was an asset to his classmates and to the school.

But then the reverse took place. Bill became erratic. He rarely did his homework, skipped his classes, was found smoking marijuana in the bathroom, was threatened with expulsion, recommended for dismissal by his teachers, reprimanded for unruly behavior, and slowly sank into an apathetic, uninspired, rebellious lad of fourteen. What had happened? I tried to find out.

"What's the trouble, Bill?" I asked him, when he came into my office at my request.

"Nothing at all," he answered curtly. "Everything's okay."

"Come on, Bill," I entreated, "I want to help you. What's up?"

Gradually his story unfolded. Bill's parents, getting a divorce, had broken up the only home Bill had ever known. Unfortunately for Bill, neither his father nor mother wanted custody of the boy. He was placed in a foster home. Within four months he had three different homes. It seemed that no one wanted him.

The ending was dismal. Bill ran away from his fourth foster home and, when caught in another state, was returned and placed in a reform school, as an incorrigible minor.

The yo-yo effect of the changing I.Q. goes beyond schoolchildren and reaches into adult life. Dr. John Kangas, director of the University of Santa Clara Counseling Center, had evidence that the I.Q. changes as one grows older. In this study, Dr. Kangas found that the intelligence quotient of forty-eight persons went up 20 points between their first test at a preschool age and tests made in their middle age.

The forty-eight persons tested were among a group of 212 who resided in the San Francisco Bay area in 1931, when they were two to five years old. The children had a mean I.Q. of 110.7 points. Ten years later, another psychologist, Dr. Katherine Bradway, tested many of these children again. She found that their mean I.Q. had risen to 113.3, a small gain, not too significant.

In 1956, Dr. Bradway made a second retest and this time the mean I.Q. registered 124.1—highly significant. While he was studying for his doctorate at Washington State University, Dr. Kangas gave the test in 1968 to forty-eight persons, divided equally between men and women. This time they had an I.Q. of 130.1. The ages of those tested ranged from thirty-nine to forty-four.

It is the belief of Dr. Kangas that subsequent tests in later years would show a continuing increase. This finding would appear to contradict the view of psychologists that the I.Q. stops growing at age fifteen, or twenty, at most. Changes take place constantly, in young and old. The old cliché had validity: one is never too old to learn.

The discrepancy between group scores and individual scores increases as the intelligence level rises. The highly gifted are penalized most by the group tests. I would like to cite several instances, based on a study I made at a school for gifted children.

Take the case of a boy who had a score on both the Stanford-Binet and the WISC of 134 when he was admitted to school. On a group retest three years later, using the Otis-Lennon Mental Maturity Test, the score dropped to 101. Which is correct? Or is either? What would a group test two years from now show? Would significant changes be noted if he received another individual test in the morning, or in the late afternoon on a hot summer's day?

Generally speaking, an I.Q. of 101 would be brushed aside by teachers and psychologists as barely average. On the other hand, 134 is considered high enough to admit the student to a school catering to gifted children. The young boy did well in his studies, among the top 10 per cent of his class, and has been accepted to a college where, I predict, he will succeed with little difficulty.

Let us look at another pupil, a girl who scored 126 on the California Mental Maturity Test. A respectable score for those who believe in numbers. She fared extremely well in school, was praised by her teachers, and proved to be much above average in all her studies.

Two years later she, too, took a retest with the Otis-Lennon group instrument. Now she scored an unbelievably low 84 points! Not only was she classified as an inferior student, but, if the score is to be believed, she is a slow learner! Here we find a deficit of 43 points, but what is even more serious, this decrease placed her in the near-retarded category.

Had she enrolled in a public school where group tests are given to all children, she would have been placed in the slow-learning track. And, having been placed in it, she undoubtedly would have remained a slow-learning child, living up to the teachers' expectations of her. Certainly, she would not have had any of the advantages accorded to those students who get special attention because of their presumed giftedness.

A greater discrepancy, though, occurred in the case of a ten-year-old boy who when admitted to school scored 156 on the Stanford-Binet. The examiner reported that rarely had he found a child with such innate intelligence, with outstanding cognitive and deductive powers, and with the ability to perform brilliantly on every section of the test.

Now four years have passed. John is a bright fourteen-year-old, doing extremely well, liked by his teachers, encouraged by his parents, and headed for a brilliant future. He is given, along with the rest of his classmates, a group test to determine his current I.Q. score. If the psychologists are right, the I.Q. should again be in the 150s. But he scores 103 on the Otis-Lennon. Just an average child. Can't expect much from John. He is on the same level as other average children. Nothing special about him.

My observation: Did John drop 53 points in four years because he lost one third of his intelligence? Or because when he took his second test he was not motivated? Or because the group test is far less accurate than the individual Binet? Or because he did not really care and answered the items on the test at random?

Whatever the reason, certainly we find that the I.Q. is a yo-yo, which bounces up or down. It bounces around in zigzag fashion, meaningless and often destructive.

Children develop intellectually as they grow older, under proper stimulation, despite what the I.Q. scores may tell us.

The University of California undertook a longitudinal research on intelligence. At the twenty-five-year point, the noted psychologist, Dr. Nancy Bayley, summarized its findings. One of the primary objectives of the Berkeley Growth Study was to explore the development of intelligence as measured by tests.

Dr. Bayley cites sufficient reasons why educators would like to think that the I.Q. remains constant and accurately measures intelligence. If it is constant, we would be able to classify a child in infancy according to his intellectual potential. We could plan his education, make better foster home placement, determine his college future, or recommend suitable occupations or professions.

The Berkeley study upset many psychologists. It showed that the I.Q. did not have the predictive powers claimed for it. The children developed in their individual ways, without regard to the predictions of test scores. To which Dr. Bayley observes:

"It is now well established that we cannot predict later intelligence from the scores on tests made in infancy. Scores may be altered by such conditions as emotional climate, cultural milieu, and environmental deprivation, on the one hand, and by developmental changes in the nature and composition of the behaviors tested, on the other."

Dr. Bayley sees no reason why we should continue to think of intelligence as a simple entity or capacity which grows throughout childhood by steady accretions. Rather, she sees intelligence as a dynamic succession of developing functions. The intellectual growth of a child is the result of complex, varied factors that can include inherent capacities for growth. The amount and progress of such intellectual growth would depend upon the emotional climate in which the child is raised, whether he is encouraged or discouraged at home, whether he has had opportunities to learn, and the extent to which these opportunities are utilized.

The Berkeley study, just as did the Kangas project, found that children increased their I.Q. scores as they grew older. Fourteen out of fifteen children who have been followed for a quarter of a century show continued I.Q. improvement, and they have not reached their maximum intellectual growth.

Various other projects substantiate these findings. For example, a study of the adult intelligence of persons in the Terman Study of Gifted Children disclosed that scores on the difficult Concept Mastery Test increased on a second test. The persons retested ranged in age from twenty to fifty years. When grouped in five-year age intervals, the test-retest scores of all age groups increased.

Similar results were reported by W. A. Owens in his long-range study when he repeated the Army Alpha Test on 127 men, now fifty years of age, who had originally taken the similar test as nineteen-year-old freshmen at Iowa State College. Their average I.Q. scores increased significantly over the thirty-one-year period.

Intelligence can grow not only with superior children but with average or dull children, also. The below-normal I.Q. children of the Berkeley Growth Study, now adults, are still improving their I.Q. scores after a twenty-five-year interval.

An I.Q. retest for twenty adults who had been diagnosed in childhood as feeble-minded, with a Binet score of 58, showed a steady increase to an average of 81 on the Wechsler-Bellevue Scale, a growth of 21 points. Every individual improved on the retest. Their mental ability improved considerably. Although not in the superior or gifted category, they no longer belonged in a home for the mentally retarded.

Frequently the first question asked about a pupil by his teacher is : "What's his I.Q.?"

The answer, regardless of its relevancy, often determines the attitude of some, if not all, of his teachers toward him. It is almost an unconscious response on the part of the teacher as she reads the child's record to say: "Oh, Ted, an I.Q. of 127. He'll be a good student. I'll keep my eye on him." Or in another case: "Bob, gosh, an I.Q. of 86, awfully low. I'll have to keep that in mind."

This may be one of the reasons that the National Education Association, representing more than one million of the nation's teachers, called for a moratorium on all I.Q. testing. It may take another ten years and a better understanding, on the part of parents, of the implications of the I.Q. score before action is taken to implement this important resolution.

In his *The Tyranny of Testing,* Professor Banesh Hoffman had this to say concerning the I.Q. and the other mental-ability tests now in common use:

"There is a place for multiple-choice tests, but it is a limited one, and its bounds have long since been overstepped. All methods of evaluating people have their defects, and grave defects they are. But let us not, therefore, allow one particular method to play the usurper. Let us not seek to replace informed judgment with all its frailty by some inexpensive statistical substitute."

It is not unusual to find teachers who believe that lower-class children are uneducable. This attitude rubs off on these children and depresses their already low self-esteem. The deficit in learning and achievement gets progressively worse. The more unsuccessful in school a child becomes, the more defeatist, apathetic, and rebellious is his attitude. Ultimately he simply gives up and drops out of school.

What is the answer? Compensatory education is one method by which children are helped. Several examples may be cited here:

Some 127,000 children in Michigan received special attention. They were one and a half years behind their classmates in either language or math skills. Through the help offered them, the children improved dramatically and erased their deficits.

And in Detroit, where 60,000 children enrolled in the state compensatory programs, educators speak glowingly of the results. New techniques are used, such as programmed learning, audiovisual tools, bright-colored books—almost anything that can motivate the children to better learning. If higher I.Q. scores are a criteria, the project has worked.

California has an $82-million state program to help educationally disadvantaged youths, with more than 50 per cent of the effort centered in kindergarten and the first three grades. Students are now scoring above the national average in reading. The program has reached 400,000 children, but another 600,000 are in need of special help in California alone. Funds are not available to provide it.

Disadvantaged children who gain in education today are the educated parents of the next generation. Their children will not suffer the same handicaps that they have encountered. But without an adequate program for educating today's disadvantaged, there seems little likelihood that there will be fewer mentally handicapped children in the next generation.

"An adequate program reaching the 20 per cent of American children who are disadvantaged and are distributed among thousands of local schools," reports Dr. Ralph W. Tyler, eminent University of Chicago educator, "requires a long term commitment to furnish funds and to develop programs and the professional competence needed to guide them. An entire generation of children is involved, which means a twenty-year effort."

The solution seems to be, therefore, less I.Q. testing and more emphasis on constructive educational programs for both child and parents. This is essential not only for disadvantaged areas, but for all children everywhere.

9

"I don't care what the I.Q. says—my child is not mentally retarded!"

Thousands of children are in mentally retarded classes today who do not belong there. Cries from parents echo across the land:

"My child is not mentally retarded. I don't care what the I.Q. score says."

However, because educators place such fantastic faith in the myth of the infallible I.Q. test, children are often labeled and frequently libeled for life.

Often their futures are shattered, their education clouded, their professional and academic growth stunted because an I.Q. score has become the all-important factor in educational evaluation.

Various states or even school systems have their own cut-off point at which they place children in the mentally retarded category. In some it may be 70, in others, 79, in still others, 84. A child with an I.Q. score of 69, for example, may be placed in a school for mentally retarded children in one school system, whereas his classmate with an I.Q. of 70 will be listed as having low-average intelligence and remain in a regular classroom.

Ironically, we know that the I.Q. tests do not measure accurately, not even within a five- to ten-point range; the standard deviation error can go up to fifteen points. Thus, a child with an I.Q. score of 69, the basis for segregating him in a mentally retarded class, statistically may just as readily have a score of 59 or 79. The latter would be a normal score.

A number of law suits have been brought by parents who object to this placement. They violently oppose having their children placed in mentally retarded classes. Their cause is now being championed by a number of noted psychologists who are convinced that one cannot label a child on the basis of an I.Q. test.

The child may be oriented to a non-Anglo culture, and thus be unable to answer the unintelligible (to him) questions on the test. Or he may be unable to speak English, as is the case with many Chicanos or recent arrivals from Cuba or Puerto Rico. Blacks are at a disadvantage, since the standardization and validity of the tests were based on a middle-class white culture.

A striking demonstration of how biased I.Q. tests operate to the disadvantage of black children can be found in San Francisco. Sixty per cent of the students in educably mentally retarded classes (EMRC) are black, while whites constitute 20 per cent. The blacks constitute only 28.5 per cent of the total school population. This racial imbalance of students in special education exists throughout the state of California, as it does elsewhere. Although blacks comprise only 9 per cent of the total student enrollment in the state, they comprise 27 per cent of the students in educably mentally retarded classes.

A report by Professor Mercer states that 75 per cent of the children in these retarded classes would not be diagnosed as retarded if appropriate assessment measures, which take into account socioculture background, had been used. In one county in California, 108 black children per 1,000 were in special retarded classes, as compared to sixteen white children. Many of the children, placed in mentally retarded classes, function normally when they are not in the classroom, when they are at home or with their friends. Their low I.Q. scores are usually caused by their inability to respond adequately to the two major items of an I.Q. test—language and mathematics.

The case of John, a sixteen-year-old boy, is fairly typical and most disheartening. He has a measured I.Q. of 83—with 85 being the cut-off for retardation—and has been in retarded classes for several years. John's mother complains, with understandable bitterness.

"John works on weekends down at the service station as an attendant. He is a good mechanic. He likes to work on cars, changes the oil, helps with overhauling autos, and works on motorcycles. Sometimes he irons, washes, cuts the lawn, goes to the store, runs errands, and things like that. He likes to be outdoors, play basketball and football on Saturdays and play with his friends."

He neither sounds nor acts like a retarded child, yet he is so labeled. Why? Because he did not hit the magic number of 85 in an I.Q. test, just two points shy, and is thus forever doomed, it would appear, to be tagged as a mentally dull, second-rate citizen.

Or there is the case of another boy, Dick, with an I.Q. of 66 measured by the Lorge-Thorndike group test, who has been in retarded classes for the last six years. His mother is upset, bitter, angry, but does not know to whom to turn for help. She explains how it all began:

"They told me Dick needed help in reading and if he was put in a special class he would get help because the class was smaller. Dick doesn't like being called retarded. It's affecting him. He begs us to have him removed from that class. They do the same thing over and over. He does not like school. The only reason he goes is because we have promised that he'll be taken out of that retarded class next year."

In a court action brought against the California State Board of Education, requesting that the use of group I.Q. tests be outlawed, and not used to place children in slow or retarded classes, a case was reported of an eight-year-old Mexican-American girl who earned an I.Q. score of 30 on the Stanford-Binet, placing her in the lowest possible mentally defective range. At her mother's insistence, Diana was retested by a Spanish-speaking psychologist, who translated the test into Spanish. Diana's I.Q. increased 40 points in this one retest. It is expected to go higher as Diana learns more of the cultural values of the American way of life. Her family recently came from Mexico. Even though her I.Q. is still low, it certainly is not in the range in which imbeciles are found.

Nine other children in the retarded classes were retested in Spanish, and, with one exception, all placed above the cut-off score of 79 used to place children in mentally retarded classes.

Many instances can be cited in which serious errors have been made in labeling children. Unfortunately, right or wrong, if a child scores below 80, or in some states, 70, on an I.Q. test, he is rigidly imprisoned in the educational system. Placed in special classes, he receives inferior schooling, and each year falls further behind the educational levels of his age peers.

The 79 I.Q. child, in a "slow" class, will be treated as retarded by his teachers. He will not have the same textbooks nor the same opportunities to advance educationally.

Louis, thirteen, one of nine children, attends a small junior high school. His family speaks only Spanish, as do the other families who live together in the migrant camp. As a result, Louis speaks little English and understands less.

In bringing suit against the school system, this is part of the deposition made by Louis's mother, through her lawyer:

"Last year Louis was required to take the Lorge-Thorndike group test. He could not understand the written instructions, nor many of the words in the verbal portion of the test. He achieved a composite score of 79, barely above the level used to classify persons as mentally retarded.

"I am afraid that teachers and counselors who see this score in Louis's file, in the years to come, will not know why it is low. Louis will be considered dumb and be expected to do poorly in school. As a result he probably will do poorly. Louis enjoys school and we hope he will graduate, but labeling him as borderline retarded will only hurt his chances."

There is also the case of Henrico, placed in the "dumb" class when his I.Q. was listed as 79. After considerable pressure from his father, the boy was removed from the retarded group and put in a higher level in the same grade. He has since improved both academically and emotionally. After his transfer his grades improved and he now enjoys going to school. He is more alert and has greater confidence in himself.

Comments Henrico's father: "These tests give the teacher a bad picture of my boy. If a test is to be given, it should take into account our culture, our language, the way we live. Otherwise how can the test be true?"

A classroom teacher recounts his experience in working with children who were caught in the I.Q. web:

"If a child scored low on an I.Q. test, he would be placed with slow learners, even though he might be very bright. No one paid attention to the language problems that the child might have, or whether he came from the same kind of background as the others in school.

"At the beginning of each school year we are given the accumulative file for all our new students and do not question the I.Q. score that is in the student's folder."

On one occasion a young girl, having scored low on her I.Q. test, was placed in a class for the mentally retarded. Her teacher soon found that the youngster did well in her studies, showed remarkable insight, and evidently could do more advanced work than that offered in a retarded class. When told about this child, the school psychologist shrugged off any suggestion that a change was necessary or even desirable.

"How can she do well in her studies if her I.Q. score is so low?" the counselor said, in challenging the teacher. "I'm not going to recommend anything further."

The counselor did not think it was necessary to retest the girl. After all, she said, a low score tells us that the child is dull mentally. Fortunately, the teacher was both resourceful and sympathetic and was able to have the girl transferred to an average class. She kept up with her classmates and had little difficulty in getting promoted to a higher grade at the end of the school year.

Many children would do far better work if their teachers did not have the I.Q. scores to prejudge them. Without the I.Q. numbers, the teachers would soon enough find out what the child could do, how fast he could learn, what his rate of reading was, what his strengths or weaknesses were, and in this way, discover his potential through actual observation, with encouragement thrown in along the way.

A teacher reports that she administered the group I.Q. test to her sixth-grade classes. Ninety per cent of her pupils in one class were of Mexican-American descent. Although the children appeared to be normal, were bright enough when they talked among themselves or co-operated with their parents at home, half of them received I.Q. scores below 70, qualifying them for the stigmatic mentally retarded classes.

"The experience of taking the I.Q. test was a frustrating and frightening one for the children," the teacher, distressed at the implications of the test scores, protested. "Over half the students could not read English well, as they had Spanish culture values and backgrounds. They could not understand more than two or three of the numerous items on the test. Most of the children simply put down answers at random.

"I cannot accept the validity of a test which supposedly measures intelligence but takes for granted a normal reading ability in English, which many children do not have. In my opinion, the I.Q. tests should not be given to children who come from minority cultural backgrounds, or have not acquired the opportunity to learn English. The test scores should not be placed on the student's cumulative record where it can influence the student's placement in the school system."

Sometimes the I.Q. test becomes a farce, yet it is potentially dynamite-filled for the child. A teacher recounts what happened when she gave a required group I.Q. test to her students. Many read English with difficulty. Their cultural backgrounds differed widely from the norm on which the test was based. But the law made no exception. All public-school children were involved.

Describing the dilemma in which she found herself, the teacher, experienced, sympathetic, in the school system for thirty-five years, put her feelings this way:

"My children can't possibly do well on a biased test. A number of my pupils were unable to read the instructions, let alone the questions. They put the test aside and began to do their regular work. A substantial number, unable to read or understand the items on the test, simply marked their answer sheet at random. Others became so discouraged that they, too, soon began the guessing game of marking answers without any references whatsoever to the questions that meant nothing to them."

Then the teacher added indignantly:

"These tests should be abolished immediately. The risk of irreparable injury to the child, when test results are based upon this mockery, is too great to permit testing to continue. We should not subject students to this type of grotesque experience where the consequences can be so damaging."

Because of the I.Q. tests, the educational system is producing what has been called "six-hour mental retardates." Low I.Q. children are placed in special retarded classes from nine in the morning until three in the afternoon. The other eighteen hours they are able to function normally. Many care for younger brothers and sisters, help prepare meals, clean house, and perform normal duties at home or in school. In no way does their behavior suggest that they are mentally retarded. Many of the children so labeled are independent, responsible, and able to act competently in virtually all situations that require sensible judgment or everyday decisions.

A struggle to eliminate the stigma of the "mentally retarded" label, because of low I.Q. scores, is now taking place in many parts of the country, but the fight has not as yet been won. One of the prime movers, Professor Mercer, cites actual incidents to show the injustice done to many children through this labeling process.

Her study of the use of I.Q. scores to place children in classes where they do not belong shows a shocking abuse of the I.Q. tests that create "six-hour retardees." These children are retarded while in school for six hours, but the rest of the time they are normal, healthy, active members of society.

Pete, a thirteen-year-old boy with an I.Q. listed as 79, has been in retarded classes since he was ten years old. His mother, seeking to get him placed in a normal class, explains:

"The school wanted to put Pete in a special class because he was not learning. They thought he was mentally retarded. I took him to a doctor; he gave him tests and said as far as he could see there was nothing wrong with my boy. He likes school and would like to learn more but is discouraged.

"At school, all he learns is to play, paint, make ceramics, paste, and, once in a while, spend a little time on reading. Pete is always active at home, always doing something. He built a two-room tree house that is just beautiful. He makes cars from old boxes, tires, wood, or anything he can find. He makes cages for animals. He is very helpful.

"Sometimes, when I am trying to fix things around the sink but can't, he just seems to know what to do. He is good at figuring things out, but he does not get a chance to be good at school because he doesn't get anything to do."

Often parents do not know what is meant by "special education" classes. They do not realize that in some schools it is a euphemism for mentally retarded classes. Maria, twelve years old, has been in special education groups since she was eight years old. When she took her I.Q. test, she could not read English, as Spanish was the language used in her home. As a result her I.Q. score tumbled to a devastating 62. At home her brothers and sisters tease her, calling her a "dummy." Maria's mother says sadly:

"I wish her teacher could see her at home. She is curious and loves to read. Many times I have to take books away from her. Sometimes she reads so much that her eyes hurt. She is good at sewing, too, and plays many different kinds of games. She baby-sits to earn spending money and helps me with my ironing and washing, or other things around the house."

What is mental retardation? Are Maria, Pete, and the other children retarded because the I.Q. score says they are? No, it goes beyond that. The Group for the Advancement of Psychiatry defines it this way:

"A chronic condition present from birth or early childhood and characterized by impaired intellectual functioning as measured by standardized tests. It manifests itself in impaired adaptation to the daily demands of the individual's own social environment.

Those persons who actually are mental retardates have subnormal intelligence and subnormal adaptive behavior. They cannot adjust either to their schoolwork, to their home environment, or to society in general.

More than the I.Q. is required, yet public schools rely primarily on I.Q. tests to designate children as retarded. Ninety-nine per cent of those designated as retarded were placed in this category entirely as the result of I.Q. tests. Very few received a medical diagnosis or other tests.

The stigma of being called a "retardee" weighs heavily on both parents and children. Parents report that their children are ashamed to be seen entering the "MR" (mentally retarded) room because they are teased by the other children in the school and are subjected to ridicule.

Parents also ask why their children are not taught to read as are the children in the regular classes. Many see the mentally retarded program as a sentence of academic and social death. Often parents resist vigorously the efforts of the schools to place their children in the special education classes. They know it to be an inescapable dead end, a crushing of all hope for educational achievement, for continued schooling, or for any kind of economic advancement that education might bring.

Only about one in five children who are placed in a mentally retarded class ever returns to regular classes. The rest either drop out of school or are sent to other institutions where they receive special training. Few, if any, ever receive an adequate education, commensurate with their mental ability, as compared with other children.

Black and Mexican-American children with the highest I.Q. scores come from families that have characteristics similar to those of the white, middle-class community. They live in a family where the head of the household has a white-collar job, with five or fewer members, where the father was reared in an urban environment and is living at home to maintain an intact family.

Thus, the more the family resembles the sociocultural average of the community, the higher the I.Q. scores made by the children. This adds to the contention that, to a significant degree, the I.Q. measures the sociocultural and economic traits of the individual, not intelligence or the progress that can be expected from the child in school.

This brings up a rather disturbing thought. If the I.Q. scores can be raised when socioeconomic and cultural differences are eliminated among the various groups of children who are tested, are we not then condemning vast numbers of children to mentally retarded classes because they come from poverty-stricken, substandard homes, rather than because they are actually mentally or intellectually deficient and are unable to maintain the standards arbitrarily set for them?

Another pertinent issue cannot be ignored or swept aside: What cut-off point should be used to determine whether a child is retarded? The American Association for Mental Deficiency recommends that those with I.Q. scores that fall below 85 should be considered to be mentally retarded. Educational usage ordinarily defines persons with I.Q. scores below 80 as being retarded.

The designers of the two major I.Q. tests, Wechsler (WISC) and Terman (Stanford-Binet), advocate the figure 69 as being the score at which a child can be called mentally retarded. Therefore, which score can be considered the valid one?

Another controversial question not to be overlooked in our discussion of I.Q. testing: On which I.Q. test shall the child be judged? *The Sixth Mental Measurement Yearbook* describes eighty group tests of intelligence, twenty-eight individual tests, twenty tests of specific aspects of intelligence, and fifteen multiaptitude batteries. More are currently being devised and are sold to schools and colleges.

In almost every case, the norms used to standardize these tests are based on the majority white, middle-class populace. Items and procedures used in intelligence tests inevitably reflect the abilities and skills consisting of the cultural patterns of our white population from predominantly middle and upper classes.

Measures of general intelligence tests are all loaded with verbal skills and knowledge. Most of the tests emphasize language, vocabulary, mathematical computations or spatial relations, reasoning or logic. To score high on the I.Q. test, or at least to be in the average range, the child must be adept in English, vocabulary, mathematical concepts and in abstract conceptualization, but little credit is given for musical, artistic, or mechanical abilities or knowledge.

Intangibles such as the ability to understand and respect people receive no credit whatsoever on the I.Q. scores. These are not considered when a child is pushed over the vague line that tags him as a retardate. Often, the same type of behavior may be found in two different children, yet one will be officially listed as retarded, the other as normal. The norms of the public schools in Riverside, California, for example, where Dr. Mercer made her studies on retarded children, considered a child with an I.Q. score of 79 as mentally retarded. However, the California Department of Mental Hygiene placed the cut-off point for retardation at 69.

Moreover, regulations of the school system that a child attends make a difference whether he will be listed as mentally retarded. When she gave I.Q. tests to children in Catholic schools in Riverside, Dr. Mercer found twenty-seven who had scores below 79. Had these children been attending public schools, they would have been placed in classes for the mentally retarded. However, in the Catholic schools, without a rigid cut-off point, they were regarded as normal and were working in regular classes and did not appear to suffer from undue competition or excessive school pressure.

In some public schools, also, not all children with I.Q. scores of 79 or below are sent to retarded sections. Most of those who are able to escape the "disgrace" of the mentally retarded classrooms are likely to be white children from higher socioeconomic homes and to have teachers who did not refer them to the special classes.

To point up the unfairness and injustice of the whole I.Q. charade, 20 per cent of those not recommended for placement in retarded sections had I.Q. scores below 64.

It is a frightening yet valid conclusion to state that children from low-status homes run twice the risk of being labeled mentally retarded as those from wealthier or more privileged homes. If the I.Q. test score alone is used to diagnose mental retardation, then it is grossly unfair to the many persons from minority groups and lower socioeconomic status who are performing successfully at home and in their community but are classified as mentally retarded in their schools.

Ironically, 8 per cent of those selected as mentally retarded had an I.Q. above 85, and a few above 100, well in the average category. They were in the mentally retarded classes because they were boisterous in the classroom, misbehaved in school, and irked the teachers or principals.

A struggle to eliminate the I.Q. scores as the basis for placing children in mentally retarded classes has developed in Boston, Massachusetts, where a committee of parents has gone to court to have this practice abolished. They have set up the battle cry, "My child may have a low I.Q., but he is not a moron!" Action by the parents challenged the arbitrary, irrational, and discriminatory manner in which students in the Boston public schools were classified as mentally retarded and placed in "special classes."

Children who got I.Q. scores below 80 were placed in the mentally retarded classes in Boston, just as they were in California schools. But in some instances, it was learned, the children were not at all retarded, but had become behavioral problems. Evidently the easiest way for a teacher to handle a troublemaker, an emotionally disturbed child, was to shunt him into the retarded group where he could be kept out of the teacher's classroom, even though what the child might have needed was psychological help, not punitive measures so extreme that they might ruin the child for life.

In its legal action, the brief filed by the committee attorneys held that the I.Q. tests are not sensitive enough to distinguish among a wide range of learning disabilities, only one of which might be mental retardation. Other traits, they maintained, can lower the I.Q. score, such as emotional disturbance, perceptual handicap, lack of facility with the English language, and cultural differences.

Further charges were made by the parents, and they summarize succinctly the damage caused by placing children in wrong categories, especially in classes for mentally retarded:

"Individually, the misclassified student's self-esteem goes down; his ability to succeed even at the level at which he is placed drops, thus lessening the chance of catching up, even if he is returned to the appropriate level. He is exposed to the stigma of mental retardation when the term is not applicable at all."

In addition, the parents pointed out, their children must also submit to the wider teacher community prejudice about mental retardation, which makes it significantly more difficult for them to secure higher educational options and peer-group respect. At the same time, they do not receive any of the offsetting benefits of an educational program responsive only to the needs of students who are actually retarded.

Psychologists from the Douglas Thom Clinic and the Boston University Division of Psychiatry undertook an extensive diagnostic evaluation of children placed in mentally retarded classes. They observed the children in the classroom, gave them additional intelligence tests, examined their perceptual-motor functioning and held clinical conferences on their findings. They concluded:

"Our findings indicate that over half of the children labeled as retarded had I.Q.'s in the normal range. Some had evidence of perceptual-motor handicaps. Some were emotionally disturbed. These children occupy a peculiar position in the school society. They know they are considered 'bad,' the 'dumb ones,' the ones nobody wants. These children are even denied access to certain activities such as field trips and physical education."

Responsible psychologists and informed educators know that a child must not only receive an I.Q. test, he must be evaluated through a number of other methods. Before a child is given the label "retarded," he should receive a psychiatric evaluation, a physical examination, a psychological analysis, a test of his perceptual-motor functioning, a report from his teachers on his school achievement, and a conference with the parents to find out what the child is able to accomplish in his own home environment.

This seems as though it is an involved process—and it is. But, after all, the child's entire future is at stake. It is not a matter that can be dismissed lightly. Even bright children may score a lowly 75 on an I.Q. test, as I have found out, when they are emotionally or physically incapable of doing their best.

What is even more alarming, the Boston Task Force arrived at the incredible conclusion that children are often put into mentally retarded classes because they "act up" in class, do not conform to the standards set by the teacher, and are unable to sit through the school routine during the day in an orderly, disciplined manner expected of well-behaved children. Moreover, parents are often not told that their children are placed in retarded classes. The test scores are kept in folders marked "confidential" with the notation "not to be shown to parents."

A survey team from the Massachusetts Institute of Technology found that special classes for the retarded are sometimes used as a "dumping ground" for children who cause trouble in their regular classes. They do not have low I.Q.'s nor are they mentally inferior. It was not unusual to find that the results of the Stanford-Binet tests were deliberately "rigged," so that the teacher could get rid of a troublesome child in the class. What an incredible, vicious reprisal against these children!

Fortunately, in Massachusetts at any rate, the illicit labeling will now become more difficult. The Department of Mental Health and of Education adopted a new set of regulations covering this area. Before a child can be labeled as being mentally retarded, he must be given a thorough examination and an evaluation not alone by the teacher, but by a physician, a certified psychologist, and a social worker. This will be followed by home visits, with conferences with the child's parents.

The child's behavior at home, in the neighborhood, and in his local peer group will be taken into consideration in making the evaluation. The psychologists will explore the child's mental, social, and cultural condition as well as other factors that may be pertinent to his learning capacity.

To the degree possible, the child will be permitted to remain within the regular class system. Unless there is drastic mental deficiency, the youngster will not be stigmatized by being placed in a mentally retarded group and isolated from his friends and classmates. He will receive every opportunity to function with other children, in a normal setting.

Even more important, and extremely helpful, the use of labels will now be avoided. Children will not be listed as educable, trainable, or custodial, based on I.Q. scores, as they had been in the past. The Special Education Act of 1972 abolished the old system of categories and labels in Massachusetts. The new law has only one category—child with special needs. This defines a child from three to twenty-one, without a high school diploma, who is unable to progress effectively in a regular school program and requires special educational services.

Not only will each child be evaluated individually and offered a program to meet his needs, but a periodic evaluation will be made to see if it benefits the child. The I.Q. score has been erased as the determining factor in labeling children as being superior, average, slow, or dull.

Thousands of children, now recorded as mentally retarded and separated from their fellow classmates, may be returned to their regular classes and lose the social stigma of a retardate.

Some children are retarded and need special help. However, it is appalling to see the heartlessness used in many school systems to destroy a child's future, based on the flimsy evidence of the I.Q. test or unmanageable behavior problems.

Let us recall Alfred Binet's warning in 1905 that it will never be to anyone's credit to have attended a special school. We should at the least, he said, spare from this mark those who do not deserve it.

It is an especially cruel and unjust act toward a child. The retardee label becomes a shameful burden and a stigma. It deprives him of his rightful opportunity to get an adequate education. It plagues him as he strives to find a productive place for himself in an adult society.

Fortunately, the California Education Department, just as the

Massachusetts department, has amended its regulations dealing with the labeling of mentally retarded children. It took court cases, in both instances, to effect the changes. Now better criteria are required before the label can be applied.

The I.Q. tests, now used extensively to determine the mental and intellectual abilities of schoolchildren, should not be applied equally to those who come from different ethnic or racial backgrounds, lower socioeconomic levels, or who simply are not prepared to take tests of the type now prevalent in our educational world. Other more valid criteria should be used.

No child should be designated as mentally incompetent until he is carefully assessed and evaluated by psychologists and psychiatrists, medical authorities, and experienced clinicians, and provided with a series of tests suitable to his educational, social, and ethnic background.

A child who can achieve a score of 75 on an I.Q. test when he comes from an overcrowded, Spanish-speaking, or poor white, home, in which the father or mother has less than an eighth-grade education, was never motivated to succeed, who does not want or expect the child to go beyond high school, and who does not communicate with the youngster, may well be within the normal range of children who have had little exposure to social experiences needed to pass our present culture-biased I.Q. tests.

We can assume that he is a person with normal learning ability who needs special help, perhaps, in English, math, or in our accepted standards of ethics and social living. Before an I.Q. test is administered, the examiner should have a thorough knowledge of the child's social and economic background and make the necessary allowances in the final scores.

In some instances, the arbitrary I.Q. score has been deemphasized as a measure of intelligence. For example, the New York State Department of Education now specifically states that a child may not be placed in a class for mentally retarded children solely on the basis of an I.Q. test. It is now possible that a child with an I.Q. score of 65 may be retained in his regular classroom. This is a farsighted step in the right direction.

However, examples of I.Q. testing misuse abound. When Juan entered first grade in Chicago, his I.Q. score was low, and he was classified as mentally retarded. After attending the retarded classes for nine years, at the nagging insistence of his parents, he was re-tested. An embarrassed school social worker said:

"We made a mistake. Your child was never retarded."

Yes, but who is going to give Juan back the first nine years of his school life? How is he ever going to "catch up" and join his age-group classmates, after these many years? Why didn't the child get a retest somewhere along the line? Why was he, like Isabel, placed in an attic and the key thrown away?

Following an investigation of a number of schools in Chicago, in which the placement procedure was under scrutiny, it was found that many children were labeled retarded because someone had made a mistake.

"Lives are being destroyed because of misplacement," frankly admitted the Illinois Superintendent of Public Instruction.

Similarly, studies have shown that in many New York City classes for children with retarded mental development, Puerto Rican children had twice the frequency of Puerto Rican representation in the city's population. The majority of these children had arrived in the United States after the age at which children begin school. They were seven years or older when they arrived here.

Particularly striking in its social implications, reports Dr. Herman A. Witkin of the Educational Testing Service, is the fact that 42 per cent of a group of students, retested three to six years after leaving the retarded classes, now had I.Q. scores that placed them in the normal range.

The most obvious explanation of the change from mentally retarded to normal appeared to be in the improvement in the English language of the Puerto Rican children, greater ability to deal with the intelligence tests used, and particularly the verbal subtests. This challenging change from retarded to normal took place even though the children continued to live in an underprivileged community and attended public schools that were inferior to those found in the better sections of the city or in the suburbs.

How many normal children are still languishing in classes for the retarded, based on I.Q. testing, is not known. But their number is large enough to cause concern to all who are interested in helping children receive a good education.

10

The tyranny of I.Q. tracking

Billy is an eager, lively eight-year-old boy, good at running bases in the Little League, or helping Dad fix the motor of his 1968 Chevy. He is slow in reading and arithmetic and has trouble writing. Still, he is only eight, his parents are poor, the neighborhood is run-down, and comics are about the only reading material found in the house.

But Billy is already labeled. There are three groups in his third grade: the Bluebirds, with high I.Q. scores; the Sparrows, with average scores; and the Crows, with low scores, around 85 to 95.

Of course, the children know that they are set apart in rows, but they do not know why. Nor do their parents. But the teachers know. They know, by looking at the I.Q scores, that the Bluebirds are bright; the Sparrows, average; and the Crows, slow and dull. After all, isn't that what I.Q. scores are supposed to tell you?

Children in the other sections have it all figured out. They greet Billy with a twist-of-the-knife jab: "Hi, Bill, hear you're a crow, sitting in the pumpkin-head row."

Neither the children nor their parents realize that the rows and groups to which the youngsters have been assigned have "tags" on them and that these tags, in the form of I.Q. scores, will follow them for most their school life.

Teachers, principals, and school officials generally rely on unfair, inaccurate tests to label children, often in the first few weeks or months of their school life. It is likely that a child who sits in the Crow row will remain there for months or even years. He's the dumb one, "can't expect much from him, might be good with his hands in the woodworking or vocational classes in junior high, but he just doesn't have it between the ears."

Schools call this arrangement ability grouping, or tracking. It is also referred to as homogeneous grouping. In England, it is called "streaming." Many spokesmen for minority groups, or even parents of average children, call it biased and unjust.

Whatever the name, the principle is the same: separate the bright children from the average, the average from the slow, the slow from the retarded. Keep them in separate rows within a class, in separate classes within a school, or in separate schools within the educational system.

The theory behind this practice apparently makes sense. If all bright children are kept together, their teachers could give them the type of education best suited to their needs. Similarly, if the slow ones were all in one room, they, too, could get special attention and a curriculum geared to their needs.

It sounds good in theory, but has it worked in practice? Much of the evidence points the other way. It has worked to the advantage of the teacher, who finds her job made easier, but it has not always been in the best interest of the students. Dr. Jencks found, in his massive study, that when you put children from different social classes and abilities together in the same classroom, you help the slow learners without in any way harming the superior ones. It is important that children of all groups from society work and rub shoulders together in the classroom.

"Every elementary school," writes Dr. Jencks, "is nearly a microcosm of the larger society as far as cognitive inequality is concerned."

If schools did away with tracking, and mixed children at random, forgetting about I.Q. scores, it would be possible to get a representation of different ability levels, and different ethnic, racial, and minority groups, in each class.

Unfortunately for those who believe in social justice, some school systems use the grouping, or tracking, method to continue the segregation policies outlawed by the United States Supreme Court. Since it is well known that blacks, Chicanos, and other minority groups have received an inferior education for many years, and as a result do poorly on the I.Q. or achievement tests, tracking invariably places them in separate rows, classes, schools, or vocational courses. Once a child is tested and placed in the slow group it is difficult for him to get out of this category.

The effects of testing, tracking, and ability grouping cut across race, socioeconomic class, or neighborhood. They touch all children, whether black or white, upper or lower class, rich or poor. But the children from disadvantaged districts suffer the most. Grouping may have its merits, but for children it is a stigma, almost as much as being placed in a mentally retarded class. They are referred to as the dumb ones, the slow kids, the morons who can't read, the clowns, or the pumpkin heads. The meaning is clear.

The Director of the Southeastern Public Education Program of the American Friends Service Committee, in opposing the I.Q. tyranny of testing, explained how she came to realize that class distinctions existed in her school:

"I was educated in an all-white public school in the South. In my school we had the redbirds and the bluebirds. It took until the second year before I figured out that the redbirds were all like me. We all lived in the same neighborhood, had nicer clothes, and were the ones called on by the teacher to erase the board or run the errands. By the third or fourth grade, these classifications had come to mean that we, the redbirds, were the smart ones, and the bluebirds, whose folks worked in the mill, were just plain dumb."

An extensive study on ability grouping has been made by Dr.

Warren G. Findley of the University of Georgia, principal investigator of a Task Force, financed by the U. S. Office of Education, to consider the issue of homogeneous versus heterogeneous grouping, or tracking, in our public schools. Dr. Findley defines ability grouping as the practice of organizing classroom groups in a graded school to put together children of a given age and grade who have most nearly the same standing on measures of judgments, of learning achievement or capability.

Ability grouping may be based on a single I.Q. test, on teacher judgment, or on a composite of several tests and evaluations. A nationwide study made by Dr. Findley and his associates during 1970 disclosed that ability grouping is widely practiced in our American schools. This confirms the results of the survey that I made of one hundred school systems in 1973. I found, as did Dr. Findley, that grouping is characteristic of our school system and is found in both the elementary and the high school years.

The effect of ability grouping on the achievement and development of children is to reinforce or inflate favorable self-concepts of those assigned to the higher groups, the redbirds, but, in turn, it also reinforces unfavorable self-concepts in those who are placed in the low I.Q. groups. Most children who are labeled as "slow learners" quickly lose all incentive to work or to be concerned in any responsible way about their scholastic achievement.

The teacher, too, in many cases, looks down upon them as barely educable and not worth her best efforts of teaching. She longs for the stimulation and higher honor of being a teacher of "advanced classes."

The Task Force reached the conclusion that ability grouping, or tracking, is an unsound educational policy. Children from unfavorable socioeconomic backgrounds tend to score lower on the I.Q. or achievement tests and are then judged unfavorably by their teachers, in comparison with children from middle-class homes who have higher I.Q. scores. This discrepancy increases as the children grow older and approach adolescence.

The effect of grouping is to put low achievers together and deprive them of the stimulation of brighter children. Disadvantaged children, especially boys, it was found, often have to learn how to become more responsive and participate in the classroom with their teachers and classmates.

Test scores play a major role in group assignments, whether by themselves or in combination with other criteria. More than fifty different standardized tests are now used for this purpose. A frequent review of each individual's grouping status should take place. Whenever possible, heterogeneous grouping should be the rule, not the exception. At present 75 per cent of all school districts continue the policy of ability grouping.

School districts that employ homogeneous grouping insist that this practice improves the teacher's ability to meet with the child's individual needs, permits students, also, to progress at their own learning rate and, further, allows the students to compete on a more equitable scholastic basis.

But there are disadvantages, the educators concede. Leadership and stimulation are reduced, a stigma is placed on slow learners, and self-confidence is destroyed. Tracking often results in the separation of students by race and socioeconomic status and is frequently based on invalid criteria, offering the slow learner little challenge or stimulation to succeed.

Ability grouping in itself does not help improve the child's scholastic achievement. Indeed, it is often detrimental to children in the average and lower educational levels. Moreover, ability grouping, when started in the elementary grades, undoubtedly favors children from the higher socioeconomic class. The policy to separate students on the basis of the I.Q. or other standardized tests reduces the likelihood that students will be exposed to a wide range of cultural and ethnic differences.

In the opinion of Dr. A. Harry Passow of Columbia's Teachers College, ability grouping is simply a ruse to place pupils from lower socioeconomic, racial-, or ethnic-minority groups into slower and nonacademic programs. This, in essence, results in segregation within the school and provides the children who need the best educational program with an inferior one. It is painfully evident that low-ability groups have a disproportionate number of children from lower-class origins. The educational caste system, as well as class stratification, is encouraged.

In their review of the numerous studies made of ability grouping, Drs. Findley and Miriam M. Bryan, writing in *Ability Grouping: 1970,* conclude that assignment to low-achievement groups carries a stigma that is more harmful than any possible benefits that might accrue from homogeneous grouping.

Teachers use various plans to group children within their classrooms. This is especially true in the elementary grades, where teachers often create three or more groups to teach reading, arithmetic, or other subjects. This intraclassroom grouping is, presumably, used to permit the teacher to work with pupils of comparable ability. The teacher thus modifies her procedures to allow for differences among the robins, bluebirds, sparrows, clowns or pumpkinheads.

Reading and arithmetic are the most frequently used subjects that determine which groups the children will enter. Where heterogeneous grouping is used, emphasis is now placed on individualized instruction, team teaching, enrichment programs, and compensatory help as may be necessary to meet the needs of the children.

When ability grouping is applied to all grades and used throughout the school system, it is known as "tracking." Children are assigned to clearly labeled tracks, such as college preparatory, commercial, vocational, technical, or general. Depending on the track in which he is enrolled, a ninth-grade student, when selecting a mathematics course, may be assigned to college algebra, business math, or basic arithmetic. Only the course in algebra would be accepted by the college admissions office as a satisfactory subject.

Further, students enrolled in the college track would be permitted to select such courses as biology, chemistry, physics, geometry, advanced English, or a foreign language. On the other hand, those in the vocational or general tracks would be limited to general science or would not take any science course or foreign language course at all.

Ability and tracking arrangements divide students for instructional purposes. Their paths rarely cross, except perhaps on the football field or basketball court. A student enrolled in a vocational track is not prepared to enter college, when or if he completes his high school program. He does not have the required courses. The sad part of this arrangement is that, based on what may be an erroneous I.Q. or achievement test score, the student is arbitrarily placed in a terminal educational program. By the time he arrives at his full intellectual ability, or when it is found that the I.Q. score is inaccurate, the damage has been done. College doors are closed to him.

This danger is foreseen in a nationwide survey conducted by the National Education Association. It stated that despite its increasing popularity, there is a notable lack of evidence to support the policy of tracking or ability grouping in our schools today.

Ability grouping and the tracking system can be legally challenged by parents everywhere. And they would probably win. At least, that is indicated in the now famous decision in the United States District Court for the District of Columbia, where Judge J. Skelly Wright issued a decision banning the tracking system in the case of Hobson *versus* Hanson. Dr. Hanson was at that time superintendent of the Washington, D.C., school system.

The track system had been introduced by the superintendent in the Washington schools. Children were grouped in the classroom and within the schools on the basis of the I.Q. and other test scores. Black children were found to a disproportionate larger extent in the lower tracks. In a sweeping order, Judge Wright outlawed the track system. He pointed out that pupils were placed in tracks based on such tests as the Stanford-Binet and the WISC. It was difficult to know, he said, whether these I.Q. tests reflected lack of ability or lack of opportunity.

Citing the damages that could result when children were placed in the bottom educational tracks, thus being denied equal opportunity for schooling, the judge said:

"By consigning students to specifically designed curricula, the track system makes highly visible the student's status within the school structure. To the unlearned, tracks can become pejorative labels, symptomatic of which is the recent abandonment of the suggestive 'Basic' for the more euphemistic 'Special Academic' as the nomenclature of the lowest track.

"A system that presumes to tell a student what his ability is and what he can successfully learn incurs an obligation to take account of the psychological damage that can come from such an encounter between the student and the school, and to be certain that it is in a position to decide whether the student's deficiencies are true, or only apparent. The District of Columbia School System has not shown that it is in such a position."

In his summation, Judge Wright made this momentous decision, one which may well affect ability grouping and break the I.Q. tyranny of tracking in schools throughout the United States:

"As to the remedy with respect to the track system, the track system simply must be abolished. . . . Even in concept the track system is undemocratic and discriminatory. Its creator admits it is designed to prepare some children for white-collar and other children for blue-collar jobs; the danger of children completing their education wearing the wrong collar is far too great for this democracy."

An analysis of the Washington system showed that, similar to the track systems found elsewhere, the tracks correlated with race and with socioeconomic status. Poor blacks were predominantly found in the lower tracks, while middle-class whites were disproportionately assigned to the higher tracks. This disparity, the court said, resulted from ability tests which were culturally biased and measured children according to their socioeconomic status and racial background, rather than their ability.

Most children were placed in tracks as early as the fourth grade. Children rarely were able to escape from a low track because the instruction differed substantially and the educational gap between the two groups widened year by year. Children in the lower tracks had virtually no chance to acquire the skills and backgrounds necessary to qualify for college.

Because the tracking system had its basis in culturally biased I.Q. tests, was operated in a rigid manner, and offered no compensatory education to help those children who needed extra attention, it placed poor whites and blacks into classes that offered them an education that was inferior to that received by the other children. This, the judge said, violated the Fifth Amendment's due process clause, and was therefore unconstitutional. He added further that any system of ability grouping, which fails to bring the great majority of children into the mainstream of public education, denies those excluded equal educational opportunity and "thus encounters the constitutional bar."

Commenting on the legal implications of this decision, Merle McClung, staff attorney at the Harvard University Center for Law and Education, said that even if a tracking system could meet the objections raised by Judge Wright, the practice should be abolished as a matter of policy. The separation of children into groups limits interaction and creates a stigma, with adverse effects on low-achieving students. Officially sanctioned segregation gives formal school support to the sense of inferiority of children who are regarded as "dumb" and a sense of superiority to those who believe they are selected to the upper tracks because they have all the brains. The danger of becoming conceited is all too apparent among bright children who are placed in the upper tracks. The opposite is also true.

"This homework is too hard for us," one child told his teacher. "Don't you know we are in the stupid group?"

The examiner himself can play a crucial role in testing children, and thus determine where they are to be placed in the school's tracks. If we are to practice ability grouping in our schools, and a majority do despite the clear-cut ruling of Judge Wright, the least we can do is make certain that the tests are properly used. Often tests are used inappropriately, comparisons are made between children even though the tests measure different capacities, and examiners read into the tests scores more than the author or publisher ever intended.

The Peabody Picture Vocabulary Test has been particularly misused. This easy-to-give test is widely accepted as a reliable measure of general intelligence, rather than what it was designed by its author to be—only an estimate of verbal intelligence. It is often used to test culturally deprived children who have limited vocabularies. Moreover, it frequently fails to take into consideration the fact that even some pictures are foreign to children of a definite culture. Eight-year-old José, the son of migrant workers, has never seen a tennis racquet or a bathtub. He does, however, know the difference between a tomato field and a strawberry patch.

Among numerous instances of the misuse or abuse of the I.Q. tests, found by Dr. Findley and his associates, are these: the assumption that a test designed for gifted children of one age is suitable for use with older children with limited backgrounds, the assumption that a test constructed and standardized for children of a given age or school experience is equally valid for children of different ages and school experiences, and the treatment of different measures of learning ability as though their results were comparable, with little attention to exactly what the test measures or the effect the measurement will have on the children.

A common error, which results in invalid test scores, is to test too early in preschool programs. When a child has never handled a pencil or crayon, has never held a book or booklet, has never turned pages, never followed group directions, never worked steadily in a self-directed situation, it is evident that group tests such as the Metropolitan Readiness Tests, or I.Q. tests such as the Lorge-Thorndike or Otis-Lennon, cannot be a valid measure of the child's ability.

When I talk with teachers about abolishing homogeneous grouping, or discontinuing the tracking sytem, I get the smug, offhand, superficial reply:

"Sure, but what would you put in its place? You can't teach effectively a bunch of kids in the same class who have different I.Q. scores, can you?"

Yes, you can. Studies have shown that you do not improve the quality of the children's education by keeping them together on the basis of their I.Q.'s, or keeping them apart for the same reason. Children of different abilities can be taught in the same classroom. Often, the results are better than by keeping them apart.

Alternative methods, successful as a substitute for the current group or track systems, are suggested by Drs. Findley and Bryan, following their ability-growing study. Among the more readily available practices, found to be successful and used in a number of school systems, are included:

Individualized Instruction. After the teacher has established a rapport with, and gained a knowledge of, her students, she is in a position to discuss their programs with them on an individual basis. The student progresses at his own rate in the mastery of content. If the student is not able to keep up with his classmates, he is not failed but continues to study the topic until he masters it. The bright child can receive extra work if he is ready for an advanced program.

Heterogeneous Grouping. An important part of what children learn is obtained directly from other children who know things that they do not know. The teacher can plan lessons for her heterogeneous group by bringing together students who deviate extensively in various areas. The key is to stimulate the desire to share novel information, rather than promote headlong competition.

Stratified Heterogeneous Grouping. The so-called Baltimore Plan may serve as an alternative to homogeneous grouping. Under this arrangement, if three classes of thirty are to be assigned, consisting of a group of ninety children who are ready to start the fifth grade, the children are ranked in order of excellence on a standardized test battery, and then subdivided into nine groups of ten students each.

Teacher A will receive a class consisting of the first ten students, the fourth ten, and the seventh ten, based on their standing on the testing scores. Teacher B will get the second, fifth, and eighth ten students, while Teacher C is allotted the third, sixth, and ninth ten students. There is no top or bottom section; invidious comparisons are minimized or avoided. Each class has a narrower range of groups or ranks. Teachers can now give special attention where it is needed. This does not do away with the use of the I.Q. testing tyranny completely, but it is a first step toward its final elimination.

Student Tutoring. Tutoring, by older children, of children who are deficient in academic skills has been widely adopted. Those tutored show more than normal gains. What is perhaps somewhat more satisfying, when older children, themselves deficient in basic skills, are paid to tutor younger children, both those being tutored and the tutors themselves gain academically.

One of the most persistent arguments for homogeneous grouping is that it will stimulate the highly intelligent or gifted children to greater effort and, at the same time, reduce the frustrations of the "slow" children.

What about the child of average ability? Where does he fit into this pattern? In many schools, especially on the junior high or high school level, the widest tracks and the largest classes are for those pupils whose I.Q. scores have tested to be average, between 100 and 120. Even within this group, there are wide variations and the teacher must adjust her teaching skills to these differences.

In reverse, the slower average child must gear all his resources to keep up with the brighter average; he is often motivated and stimulated to work to his full potential. Sometimes, however, he shrugs his shoulders and refuses to keep up with the "brains" of the class. Whatever the situation, he learns from the experiences and reactions of the students who are quicker, better read, and more informed than he is, just as the "brainy" students learn from him, perhaps, skills and know-how at which he is adept and at which he is working after school. It may be such activities as the mechanics of fixing a car or making hamburgers and french fries in a quick-food stand.

A high school teacher of English used a "slow average" student's ability as a surfer, at which he was superb, as a central point for a lesson on poetry about the beauty and power of the ocean. The whole class was involved as the surfer described his exhilaration and sense of conquest in riding huge waves. In this way, too, an imaginative and creative teacher can handle heterogeneous grouping without depriving the brighter students of stimulation and the slower ones of self-confidence.

Calling a child dull will not stimulate him toward greater intellectual effort. Nor will it motivate him to continue with his education toward any form of higher schooling. Actually, the way the levels are stratified in ability grouping or in tracking, the child will not be eligible to go beyond high school. When teachers confront a class that is described to them as "fast," "average," "slow," or "retarded," their tendency is to regard all children as being in these categories. The youngsters lose their individualities—the teacher sees them as a group of twenty-five, thirty, thirty-five children, or whatever the number may be.

No plan of grouping, Dr. J. Wayne Wrightstone of the New York City Board of Education research office reports, makes teaching and learning a simple matter. Any group of thirty or more pupils, no matter how alike they seem, has enough individual differences to challenge the ingenuity of the most competent and imaginative teacher. Classification by ability cannot remove individual differences or the need to adapt instruction to meet their needs. Even though children may register identical achievement in reading, for example, at the beginning of the school year, within a month or two, vastly different rates of progress will have widened the range of achievement.

In Dr. Wrightstone's opinion, ability grouping is dangerous when it leads teachers to underestimate the learning capacities of pupils at the average-ability levels. It can also be harmful when it does not provide flexible channels to enable children to move from group to group, either from subject to subject, or within any one subject, as their performance at various times in their school careers indicates.

In recognition of the unreliability of the I.Q. and standardized tests to segregate children into ability groups, the California State Legislature passed two bills designed to restrict their use. One law, which took effect in 1973, eliminates all state-mandated group intelligence tests that had previously been given to children in grades six and twelve. Fifty per cent of the local school districts continue to administer these tests, but this practice has been challenged in the state courts.

In another law, the California policy on testing was amended to require the translation of tests into the native language of the children, in this case, for the most part, Spanish. But even this has not met with success because of gaps in experience among different cultures. Even where alternate wording was utilized, problems arose in the interpretation and use of the I.Q. test scores.

Ability grouping, whether based on racial or ethnic origin, or on I.Q. scores, is equally unjustified. A suit brought against the California State Board of Education by a number of Mexican-American schoolchildren, through their parents, objected to the forced taking of I.Q. tests, pointing to the unfairness this inevitably fostered. Several cases were cited in the court suit that challenged the validity of the I.Q. tests for the Spanish-speaking children.

On the basis of the I.Q. scores, the child is placed in either the rapid track, where he gets more advanced work, or the slow track, where he gets little encouragement and is discouraged from the very start. Because children with low I.Q. scores are funneled into vocational or general classes, while the others are encouraged to take college-bound courses, few of the low-track students can expect to become doctors, lawyers, teachers, scientists, or business executives. Rather, they will be relegated to the jobs and occupations reserved for unskilled laborers.

Many school officials recognize the injustice of the I.Q. score as a determinant in placing children into groups or tracks. The misuse of these test scores is documented by the firsthand experience of numerous teachers and administrators. One Superintendent of Schools in a fairly large school district wrote in an affidavit presented on behalf of children suing to have their I.Q. scores removed from their accumulate record files:

"Before coming to Delano my teaching experience was limited to working with lower-middle-class Anglo-Americans. . . . I belonged to that school of educators for whom the I.Q. score was all important, revealing, and unchangeable. Over the past twenty-five years I have experienced a radical change in my feelings and point of view regarding school testing.

"As I first began to come face to face with the learning problems experienced by youngsters having language barriers as well as cultural and environmental differences, when compared to traditional middle-class mores, I was shocked at the injustices that were, in many instances, unconsciously invoked upon them. Teachers, in all good conscience, coming from a 'Puritan ethic' value culture and being taught in professional courses to respect the near infallibility of the I.Q. score as a predictor of school success, would immediately attach labels.

"So we have the genius, the fast learner, the accelerated program, the average, the slow learner, the mentally retarded, and so on. The most tragic effect of this labeling was the fact that it more often than not reflected the teacher's expectation from the learner—how she valued him as a person, what she expected from him, to what extent she tried to help him, and how she went about it."

In another school system a guidance counselor points out the unfair reliance by school counselors on I.Q. scores:

"In my capacity as counselor at Fresno City College, I worked with, and attempted to assist, minority students who have average or below average high school scores. I have access to these students' files, and I have noticed that many of our Chicano sudents have low I.Q.'s, usually based on the Lorge-Thorndike examination, especially in the verbal area.

"Many of the students with whom I and other counselors work were considered noncollege material, and told that because of their low I.Q. scores they should not go to college. But most of the students, some with I.Q.'s below 80, are doing well above average work in college.

"It is a shame that we have lost so many students to the welfare rolls because a junior or senior high school counselor indicated that he or she was not college material, an assumption based on low I.Q. scores on the Thorndike and similar exams."

Another counselor, working with various types of children of different ethnic and racial origins, as well as socioeconomic status, says succinctly:

"I am particularly disturbed at the use of the group I.Q. test to assess intelligence and place children in tracks. The individual I.Q. tests, unreliable as they are, at least have the advantage of allowing the examiner to have personal contact with the child, and determine from the child's background why he or she is unable to answer certain questions."

Binet recognized this crucial element in intelligence testing when he warned against recording the gross results without making psychological observations, without noticing such facts as permit one to give to the gross results their true value.

The Lorge-Thorndike test, used in many instances to group children, consists of two sections—verbal and nonverbal. The verbal portion has five parts. In the first, each question gives a word in bold print, followed by five other words. The child is told to mark the word with the meaning most like the word in italic print. Here a few typical examples:

Conviction: surmise . . . release . . . hope . . . trial . . . firm belief . . .

In the second portion, the test offers a series of sentences with a word missing from each. The child is asked to choose from a list of words the one which makes the sentence truest or more sensible:

"The vanquished never yet spoke——————of the Conqueror."

ill . . . well . . . little . . . nastily . . . often . . .

The third section deals with arithmetic. It gives the child various examples to do, ranging from "easy" to difficult. How well he does depends on what he has been taught, not what he is able to learn in school.

In the fourth section each question contains a list of four words in italic type, followed by a list of five words. The child is asked to determine how the bold-type words are alike so that he may then choose from the five words the word which belongs with the other four.

crest . . . insignia . . . escutcheon . . . shield

favor . . . genealogy . . . uniform . . . steel . . . coat of arms . . .

The final section of the tests gives a pair of words and a third word, which is to be paired with another word chosen from a given list. The two words of the first pair are related in some way and the word to be chosen from the list is to be related to the third word in the same way.

jeopardy . . . security . . .——————*hazard . . .*——————

quarantine . . . safeguard . . . custodian . . . peril . . . convey . . .

Obviously, children from homes with greater cultural experiences will score higher than those from underprivileged neighborhoods since all correct answers depend on a rich and fluent vocabulary.

The nonverbal sections of the test are not as clearly tests of learned language and culture as are the verbal sections. However, if the child cannot understand the written instructions, is unable to read well enough to grasp the meaning of the questions, he will do as poorly on the nonverbal as on the verbal.

The Examiner's Manual stresses that the verbal battery, with its emphasis on English, is the important and significant score to be used in grouping or tracking children.

Homogeneous grouping is no longer tenable and should be abolished. The stranglehold of the I.Q. would be broken if teachers objected more strenuously, and if they realized that there are so many better alternatives available.

The pity of it is that three quarters of our school systems, large or small, city or rural, privileged or impoverished, still cling tenaciously to the practice of placing children in tyrannical tracks.

Parent concern can, probably, gradually eliminate tracking. Just as the proud mother lets slip the information at the bridge game that "my Jimmy is in three advanced or honor classes" so another mother may remember that her Jimmy or Joanie is in a slow class and she would rather not talk or think about it because of certain stigma attached to slow classes.

In a democratic society, there should be a form of democracy in American schools and classrooms, where superior ability is recognized, as well as encouraged, but where the potential of every student, regardless of social and economic background, and regardless of mental ability, should be cherished and brought to its greatest fulfillment.

11

What are standardized tests testing?

Not only the I.Q. tests, but virtually all other commonly used standardized tests should be abolished. They too often are inaccurate, invalid, and misleading. The so-called achievement, aptitude, vocational, personality, spatial relations, reading, math, and science tests have flooded our schools and are threatening to engulf them in a tidal wave of computerized scores.

School authorities, teachers, guidance counselors, legislators, and even parents look upon the massive outpouring of standardized testing not as big business running to hundreds of millions of dollars annually, but as valid documents that predict whether Milly can read on the fifth-grade level as she is supposed to do, or whether Michael should be in advanced history classes.

Millions of children in every city, rural or urban, in every state, in every school system, public or private, take an ever-growing variety of achievement tests plus I.Q. tests. These are tests that are given to children annually, semiannually, or sometimes monthly, and which often end up with bold front-page headlines: Local Schools Show Improvement in Reading Skills, or Drop in Math Ability Found in Inner-City Schools.

Teachers are often called to task, belabored, and told:

"You are responsible for the lower scores that your children received this year in the Basic Iowa tests."

Accountability has become the "in" thing in education. An experienced Iowa elementary teacher, with ten years of effective teaching behind her, was summarily dismissed from her position because her students measured "low" on the Iowa Test of Basic Skills. The case went to the United States Supreme Court, but the Court was not willing to hear the case, thus letting the dismissal verdict of the Iowa courts stand.

Disagreeing vigorously with the use of standardized tests to measure a teacher's ability in the classroom, the nation's foremost testing authority, Dr. Henry Dyer, declared:

"Any achievement testing program that is limited to measuring performance in the basic skills and mastery of academic subject matter . . . is almost certain to do more harm than good."

Even the federal government has entered into the act and threatens to withhold funds from school districts if they do not give standardized tests to their children. The U. S. Office of Education revoked nearly $1 million in grants to a Brooklyn school district which refused, on the grounds that they were racially biased, to administer math and reading tests in two of its elementary schools.

The purpose of the tests, Washington officials explained, was to monitor the results of the federal aid that had been allocated under the Emergency School Aid Act. This is a huge $258-million fund, used to help needy schools improve the instruction of disadvantaged or underprivileged children.

To determine whether this money is well spent, the Office of Education undertook the testing of 31,000 third-, fourth-, and fifth-graders in ninety school districts across the country. Before the tests began, the Office selected, at random, one hundred schools in sixty-five districts for preliminary testing designed to help evaluate the tests themselves.

It was taken for granted, by our highest educational authorities, that you can measure achievement through standardized tests.

Tests that are used need far more study and adaptation to our present-day society than they now possess. Standardized achievement and I.Q. tests have strangled the creative talents of many of our best teachers, forcing them to "teach to the test." If a teacher knows that the achievement test is going to ask a series of questions on graphs in the section on math, she will emphasize the use and construction of graphs. After all, she doesn't want her class to be dubbed "below average" and thus, in turn, be considered by her superiors as a poor teacher.

And worse still, she doesn't want to lose her job, as the unfortunate, yet fully qualified, teacher in Iowa did. That is a lesson that will be long remembered by her colleagues and teachers elsewhere, who know that they will be judged by results on an achievement test that most often does not measure their ability as teachers.

That is why the Tenth National Conference on Civil and Human Rights in Education has recommended an immediate moratorium on standardized testing. It stated that the testing of children whose language is other than standard English violates the norm and standardization of these tests and makes the results questionable.

The Conference charged that the currently used standardized tests do not measure either the potential nor the ability of bilingual or bicultural children. Yet the tests are used and relied upon to place and track these children.

It would seem that the primary use of I.Q. and other tests should be the development of individualized instruction for all students. These tests should not be used to stigmatize children as candidates for slow classes or to select students for "honor" classes, but they should be given with the primary aim of finding students' academic weaknesses and strengths, and then shaping the school curriculum to encompass them.

Differences in pupil motivation are not adequately compensated in standardized or in I.Q. tests. Usually, the meaning of test scores is misunderstood by teachers, administrators, and the general public.

The teachers, as a rule, are opposed to standardized tests and do not believe they are necessary for them to evaluate and assess their pupils adequately.

Having been on the "inside" of the testing game for many years, as vice-president of the Educational Testing Service, Dr. Dyer is afraid that educational testing has now become an instrument, if not a weapon, in the political process. If teachers are to be held accountable for scores made by their children on the achievement tests, then their position becomes untenable.

State testing programs have been transformed into state assessment programs, with a shift in emphasis from student guidance to school evaluation. This may well mean that the mishandling of tests and the misuse of test scores concern not only teachers and school officials, but have become a growing concern of the politicians and the pluralistic constituencies that they serve.

If properly conceived and interpreted, testing can improve classroom instruction. It is not the test itself, but the use to which the I.Q. and other tests are put that alarms many educators. Too much is expected from these tests. You cannot obtain information that is not available. Nor can you, or should you, dismiss a teacher or transfer a principal because the standardized test scores did not meet the unrealistic expectations of the lawmakers or of school boards.

If this trend toward accountability based on testing continues, education, and our children, will be in serious straits. Typical of the thinking that has taken place in this area is this nonsensical bill, introduced in the Kansas State Senate:

"If the performance of any school district on any test approved by the State Board of Education does not equal or exceed the national performance average for such a test for two successive years, said school district shall not receive any further state financial assistance until such time as said school district has achieved such national performance average."

Although the bill, fortunately, was not enacted into law, it typifies the confusion regarding the nature of testing and the proper use of test scores. To me it is meaningless to talk about "national performance average in tested achievement." And, even if the tests were valid indicators of the students' achievement, how can you improve this achievement by withholding funds from the schools whose very students are evidently not doing as well as expected? Will it help the academic program to cut off needed funds?

An NEA report held that group test results should not be used as a basis for allocation of state or federal funds. In some states, funds are distributed to schools on the basis of student scores on standardized tests. Often when applying for federal funds, school systems must agree to system-wide testing programs. But, since stand-dardized as well as I.Q. tests apply so unevenly to different groups and individuals and often inaccurately predict the potential learning ability, it would appear that their use for determining which educational program should be funded and what students should not get financial help may well result in unfair treatment and a serious injustice to both the schools who seek financial help and the students who need special assistance.

Because of this pressure on teachers to get their students to the "norms" set by the tests, many resort to the practice of "fudging" or seeking means to improve the scores of their students by dubious means. They get questions from previous tests, such as the Metropolitan Achievement, the Basic Iowa, the Stanford Achievement, the Otis-Lennon, or the Lorge-Thorndike, and then drill their pupils on the contents of these tests.

That is what many teachers have been doing for years in New York State where high school students still take the Board of Regents examinations. The teachers make certain, as far as they can, that the areas covered in the examinations are crammed into their classroom curriculum. The last six weeks of the school year are often just a "cramming" session, in preparation for the Regents. It is common practice to follow the same procedure to improve achievement scores and "prime" the students for the test.

One teacher, in explaining her attitude on testing, told me what she planned to do about it: "My students didn't do too well on their social studies achievement test this year. I didn't know that the test included graphs and charts about the weather, crops, and census figures. But wait till next year! My class will be right there among the top scorers."

The teacher examined a number of the Stanford Achievement Tests of previous years, found that a pattern existed in the kinds of questions used, and concentrated on these items. She didn't exactly "cheat," because she didn't use the actual 1974 Stanford tests, but the 1972 and 1973 were close enough. Later she said:

"Look at the scores my tenth-graders made! If the school wants high achievement scores, from now on I know how to do it."

Later I found out that the other teachers, who gave achievements in language arts, math, science, and other subjects, also used past tests to prepare their students for current examinations.

As a result, creative teaching is necessarily curtailed when the "teaching to the test" procedure permeates the classroom. This is done everywhere, on all levels. As a result, the teachers, as well as the students, find themselves in a tense "testing" state of mind and attitude that does little for meaningful learning and teaching in the classroom.

Now we find that teachers, school administrators, guidance counselors, parents, public officials, and even legislators use test scores to determine whether Johnny or Marion can read at grade level, whether they should be promoted or retained in their class for another year. Often, many of those people in this decision-making do not understand what the tests are actually designated to do.

The majority of persons who give and evaluate the tests do not have the time nor the ability to keep up with the enormous number that have descended upon the schools. The dimensions of the test-making explosion are indicated by the fact that the Princeton Educational Testing Service currently has 680 different tests in the one category of reading. The 1972 issue on testing, *The Seventh Mental Measurement Yearbook,* had to be expanded to two enormous volumes to accommodate the description of the tests and the literature in the field of measurement. Yearly, the mountain of tests grows higher.

It is essential that teachers, parents, and students, too, recognize that achievement or I.Q. tests are not sacrosanct, that they merely indicate directions to follow, and that they should not become overwhelmed or dismayed with the vague yet potent term "norm." It is necessary to eliminate the insistent demand that each of the standardized achievement or I.Q. tests be compared to national "norms." There should be no questions that insist on knowing:

"What did the Briggs Corner elementary school do in reading? How does it compare with Perryville? What did Mrs. Lillybridge's fifth-graders do? Why did the sixth-grade class under Miss Merry do poorer than Miss Carleton's children?"

Rather, we should ask: "What does this test show? Does David need any special help in reading? Do the math problems bother John? If so, how can we help him to understand fractions? How can Suzy be helped with her vocabulary usage?"

Another question to ask: "Does the reliability of the test depend on the examiner and under the conditions in which the test was given?"

In large city school districts, it is difficult to monitor accurately a testing program in reading or arithmetic in which 25,000 pupils are tested by 600 teachers in 250 schools, ranging from urban to rural to suburban. The chance for human error among the 600 teachers and their assistants, who are conducting the tests, cannot be overlooked.

Until we find a way to eliminate errors or minimize variations, we will never get a true standardized score or an acceptable "norm." The test itself may be valid, but human error cannot easily be eliminated. Thus the reliability factor remains questionable and unresolved.

Beyond human error, it is essential to recognize that in the study of reading and math—the two skill subjects most frequently used to determine whether a child is bright or dull—methods of teaching differ from school to school, the content covered is drastically different, as is the emphasis placed on these subjects.

Too many counselors accept the test score as a valid measure of the child's ability and achievement, disregarding such intangible qualities as motivation, desire, ambition, curiosity, and personality quirks. Children are victimized by being viewed as identical individuals within each grade level and are expected to reach the "norm" for this grade, regardless of personality differences.

"The best of our tests," warns Dr. Buros, "are still highly fallible instruments which are extremely difficult to interpret with assurance in individual cases."

Many would agree that the major use of tests should be for the improvement of instruction, diagnosis of learning difficulties, and prescription for learning activities in response to learning needs. They must not be used for tracking into homogeneous groups as the major determinants to educational programs, to perpetuate an elitism, or to maintain static learning, year after year. Tests must not be used in ways that will deny any student full access to equal educational opportunity. There definitely is an overkill in the use of I.Q. and achievement tests.

Criticisms of standardized testing and the problems they bring are examined by Professors Milton G. Holmen and Richard F. Doctor, both California educators. Writing in the 1974 winter issue of the NEA's *Today's Education,* they point out that the case for objective assessment of educational achievement through standardized ability testing is based upon the theory that we should try our best to measure accurately what children are able to do in school. This information should be of value to everyone who is genuinely concerned with the continuing development and improvement of educational practices.

But despite these worthwhile goals, which, incidentally, have not been attained, the testing process has come under attack from civil rights spokesmen, educators, critics of American education, sociologists, psychologists, philosophers, politicians, journalists, public administrators, and authors. To warrant this barrage of criticism, I.Q. and achievement tests obviously must have numerous flaws built within them.

Listed among these flaws are: Tests discriminate against many individuals; they predict imperfectly; the scores are rigidly interpreted; they are assumed to measure innate characteristics that cannot be evaluated; and they influence teacher expectation regarding the student's ability and his potential to succeed with classroom work.

Criticisms that go beyond the invalidity of the tests and testing procedure are cited by Professors Holmen and Doctor in their book, *Educational and Psychological Testing.* They say that:

Tests have a harmful effect on the shaping of cognitive styles. The widespread use of multiple-choice test items, matching items, and other test components with a single correct answer may contribute to undesirable styles of thinking. Frequently the more intelligent students are penalized. They go beyond the one answer expected of them and see logical alternatives.

Tests shape school curricula and restrict educational change. When teachers know that the evaluation of their students will be based on a particular kind of test of predictable content, they assist their students to perform well on these tests. Since the teachers know that they, too, are evaluated on the results, it is to their advantage to make extensive efforts to help them get higher scores.

Tests distort the individual's self-concept and level of aspiration. A student who has a low concept of himself to begin with will feel even less confident when he is shown his low test scores. Parents, too, may become discouraged when they learn that their child is below the state or national "norm" in reading, math, or science. Unfortunately, both students and their parents are likely to accept the verdict of the pencil-and-paper test without an understanding of its actual meaning.

Tests select homogeneous educational groups. Achievement tests are frequently used to determine to which group or class a student should be assigned. When based on invalid I.Q. or achievement scores, the consequences can be damaging. To be misplaced can be a heartbreaking experience and one to which a child should not be subjected.

Distrust of the I.Q. and achievement tests is voiced by Professor Leon Kamin, chairman of the Princeton University psychology department. Standardized tests, he says, are "peddled" by the very people who produce them. They have a product to sell.

State-sponsored assessment of student knowledge is springing up in the wake of the studies made by the National Assessment for Educational Progress. In the past, there has been considerable information about the number of school buildings in a state, the number of teachers, the amount and kind of equipment, and similar data. Increasingly, there is a demand for some measurement of what the pupils actually know. A question that is being asked more often and with greater insistence is:

"How much and what kinds of measurable pupil learning is the state educational dollar buying?"

But we will not get this information through existing I.Q., achievement, or aptitude tests. Other methods are necessary and should be developed.

One step toward the introduction of a valid measurement program has been taken by the Oregon Board of Education. It has asked the Science Research Associates to conduct a statewide assessment of its students. A battery of tests has been prepared to sample students in various grades.

The battery consists of a standardized primary-communication-skills test; a criterion-referenced, career-awareness test; and a criterion-reference test covering knowledge and attitudes toward social responsibility. Results are expected to provide baseline data for planning curricula and for future assessments progress.

The Educational Testing Service has brought together data from states that are using achievement and other standardized tests. The most frequently used results of the tests are for instructional evaluation, guidance, and identification of individual problems and talents. Most states provide assistance to local schools to help them with the interpretation of test results. The most common subjects tested are reading and mathematics, with language skills, aptitude, and social science following in that order.

A variety of recognized test instruments are used in the statewide programs. No single test occupies a dominant position. Some of the tests are purchased "as is" from the test publisher. Others are developed by the schools, specifically for use in a particular program. Among the most common tests used by the states are: Differential Aptitude Tests, Comprehensive Tests of Basic Skills, Iowa Tests of Educational Development, Iowa Tests of Basic Skills, SRA Achievement Series, California Achievement Tests, and School and College Ability Tests.

The state education department is most frequently mentioned as being responsible for the selection of the tests used. Some states seek advice from professionals in the field, or from their local college or university personnel. The testing program is administered, for the most part, by classroom teachers, guidance counselors, or the school administrative staff. Usually the tests are scored by the test publisher, outside contractors, or the state education agency.

State norms are used by the majority of states, while national norms, local, regional, and county norms are also frequently utilized. Class or school summaries are prepared, either by the state or the test publisher. Reports are usually sent to the schools, principals, teachers, and newspapers.

Little assistance in the interpretation and use of the test results is provided for nonprofessional members of the community. Only seven states report that parents get the results of the tests, while only six distribute the reports to the general public, most often only upon request.

When the New York City school system raises its reading scores on the Metropolitan Achievement tests, it is front page news. The New York *Times,* in a glowing editorial, congratulated the school officials for the improvement in the reading scores.

A short time later, however, news leaked out, again front page in the *Times,* that "cheating" had taken place in some of the schools. Teachers were accused of "teaching to the test," of having used questions similar to those on the actual test in practice sessions, in order to raise the scores of the children. In some instances, principals were accused of dropping the lowest five scores in each class, thus raising the total percentage made by that class. The school superintendent ordered an investigation, principals and teachers were disciplined, transfers arranged, and a retest ordered by the school authorities.

Why all this excitement? If a teacher knows that she is to be held accountable for the score made by her children, of course she is going to try to do her best to keep the score high.

But still this charade goes on. When the children at Miami's Charles R. Drew Junior High School raised their math score, based on the national achievement test scores, the Miami *Herald* crowed jubilantly:

"School Boosts Score With Contests, Computers." Congratulations were in order all around.

This continues, despite the fact that the National Education Association as well as school psychologists, educators, and organizations have urged that standardized testing be abolished as not being valid or relevant. Or, at the very least, that the test results not be overdramatized to suggest that some children are better or poorer readers because they score high or low on the Stanford or Iowa or Metropolitan achievement tests.

The mushrooming influence of the standardized test on the present and future lives of students provoked constant debate during the 1974 convention of the National Council of Teachers of English. Dr. Alan C. Purves, chairman of the NCTE Task Force on Measurement and Evaluation, warned that economic and social pressures encouraged misuse of standardized tests.

As a result, today teachers are faced by an increasing demand from the public to be accountable for what they do. Dr. Purves said that English teachers are challenged to preserve the ideals and aims of their profession. The most immediate threat comes from standardized achievement tests in English and the language arts. These tests often do not reflect the school curriculum, measure only a limited part of English, and are designed to show the difference among children, rather than what they have learned in school.

According to Dr. Purves, who teaches English at the University of Illinois, children are measured and teachers and schools are evaluated on the basis of tests that deal with literary selections no longer taught, grammatical principles and habits of usage that are no longer current.

"The public needs to be informed of the difference between the tests and the curriculum," Professor Purves stressed. "The public also needs to be informed of the failure of scores on standardized achievement tests to reflect the true academic growth of the children."

Standardized tests are available for almost every subject. Basically the tests seek to measure a child's knowledge and skill in a specific subject as compared with the achievement of other children of his age level and class grade.

Various tests, other than subject-skill instruments, have grown in recent years. For example:

The diagnostic achievement test presumably helps the teacher locate particular strengths and weaknesses that the child may have in a given subject.

Aptitude tests, usually given at the junior or senior high school levels, help to estimate special interests and abilities not revealed by achievement and intelligence tests. The results suggest a child's possible success in college or in employment. I say presumably because, from what I have seen, the aptitude tests should be taken with a grain of salt. It depends on who takes them, who gives them, who interprets them, what type of test is used, and how they are interpreted. Too many imponderables exist and too much margin for errors provides pitfalls.

Inventory tests are of two basic types. One asks a youngster to indicate his likes and dislikes, or preferences. For instance, does he like a specific occupation? In which activities is he interested? The interests revealed may be compared with those of successful people in various occupations.

The other type of inventory test seeks to explore an individual's personality, his attitudes, biases, and emotional stability. Both types of inventories are expected to give clues to a child's behavior, his deep interests, or his special talents which might otherwise go unnoticed.

Literally hundreds of achievement, aptitude, inventory, and other tests are now on the market. The Educational Testing Service has developed measurement tests used for such educational purposes as admission to college, placement, evaluation, and guidance. They are administered across a wide range, including tests for elementary and secondary schools, colleges, graduate schools, and various professions and occupations.

The Test Development Division plays a major role in the construction of instruments designed to aid in the assessment and evaluation of specifically defined program objectives. Specialists at ETS work closely with committees of outstanding teachers in drawing up test specifications, writing questions, and conducting critical reviews. Tryouts of examinations are administered to appropriate groups; detailed analyses supply the statistical data deemed necessary to insure technical adequacy of final forms.

Cooperative Tests and Services of ETS makes available to participating institutions an integrated and continuous program of testing in important academic areas from grade four through the second year of college. The score scale is continuous from level to level, making possible the measurement of group progress from year to year in the abilities and subject areas covered by the tests.

The battery of tests includes the School and College Ability Tests and the Sequential Tests of Educational Progress in reading, writing, listening, mathematics, science, and social studies. Another series includes reading, English expression, mechanics of writing, mathematics, basic concepts, mathematics computation, science, and social studies. The tests emphasize the measurement of the general outcomes of education which are central in a variety of curricula.

The Academic Education Council Placement Testing Program consists of tests for eighth- and ninth-grade students, for use in placement in secondary schools, and for general administrative purposes. Scores are reported to high schools, elementary schools, and central offices. These include General Aptitude, English Achievement, Mathematics Achievement, and Reading Comprehension.

The Secondary School Admission Test provides standard measures of scholastic ability for use in helping to select students for admission to grades seven through eleven in independent schools.

The schools, as well as the candidates' parents, receive a report of the scores.

Testing is big business, and growing bigger day by day. This practice, per se, cannot be condemned, but much evidence exists that the results of all standardized tests, whether achievement or I.Q., are too often misused, so that it is difficult to be complacent about their fantastic growth and their use and application in our schools and colleges. Until their objectives and goals are more clearly defined, and verified, a total moratorium is in order.

Because of pressure from various sources, particularly minority groups who have, in many instances, been shortchanged educationally, a few states have begun the laborious, yet necessary, task of revising their testing procedures.

California may be cited as a good example, one that may soon be followed by other states. Effective in 1973, the California testing program was drastically altered. The new law permits the state to develop its own tests rather than adopt a specific standardized national test. Although testing still continues in grades one, two, three, six, and twelve, significant innovations have been initiated.

Testing in the first grade will change from an assessment of reading achievement at the end of the year to an assessment of prereading or readiness skills to be made at the beginning of the school year. Designed to help teachers assess the skills children possess when they enter school, this evaluation will provide a basis to judge the progress made on the state achievement tests.

In the past, the scores for each school and district were compared with the state average regardless of initial differences in pupils' readiness to learn, or of differences in school resources for instructional programs. In the future, reports of test results will also reflect demographic characteristics such as poverty index, financial characteristics such as assessed valuation, and pupil characteristics to include socioeconomic level and mobility. As a measure of basic skills, the tests are expected to indicate initial reading readiness.

Reading achievement will be assessed in grades two and three with state-developed tests. Pupils in grades six and twelve will be tested in reading, basic mathematics, spelling, and effectiveness of written expression. These tests will also be state developed.

Moreover, the testing of scholastic aptitude of all pupils in grades six and twelve is no longer mandated by state law. Districts are free, however, to administer such tests at any grade level to meet local program needs.

Reporting on the number of months of achievement that each pupil in the second and third grades has progressed in reading has been eliminated.

In the past, California administered the tests to provide information for a wide range of audiences: state legislators, district administrators, program planners, classroom teachers, and the general public. In trying to meet the needs of such a diverse audience, ranging from the need of teachers for specific diagnostic information about students to the more general needs for an indication of education's attainment statewide, the testing program was unable to do its job adequately.

Now state testing will be directed toward broad program evaluation rather than the diagnostic assessment of individual students. A state testing program can best be used to identify strengths and weaknesses of educational programs. It cannot meet the classroom need for individual pupil diagnoses, which now becomes the responsibility of each local district.

The self-devised state tests are designed to make them more relevant to local needs than are the commercially prepared tests. Questions used will be reviewed by representatives of ethnic and economic minorities to eliminate those items that appear to be culturally biased. For example, reading passages in which the vocabulary appears to be more familiar to one cultural group than another will be modified or eliminated. Although it is difficult to construct "culture free" tests, considerable effort will be devoted to developing "culturally fair" tests.

Why make comparisons at all? Why use achievement tests, even those prepared on a state-wide, rather than national, basis? Why compare local schools and districts when each one has its own special problems and unique curriculum objective?

Answering these questions, officials of the new testing program indicate that by using criterion-referenced tests, districts can gain significant information about how well they have covered the objectives they set for themselves. Comparative information of a more general nature is expected to be useful for program improvement.

State legislation requires the reporting of test scores for every school and district. It is thus possible to meet the requirements of the state assessment law without interpreting results or making comparisons. Past experience has shown, however, that comparisons are inevitably made, especially by the lay public and the media. This is often done without sufficient background for valid interpretation.

California's revised law calls for the new state testing program to be fully operational during the 1974–75 school year. The development of new tests that appropriately parallel the curricula in California's schools, and possess the requisite statistical properties, appears to be a long and difficult, but important, task.

The scores of the I.Q. and standardized tests are powerful determinants of a child's academic future. One of the most controversial of these is the reading-readiness test, usually administered in the first grade. The tests may have a profound effect on the child's education. On the basis of an arbitrary score, which is often meaningless and without value, the child is put in a fast, normal, or slow group. He may not be allowed to begin formal reading at all if the test shows that he is not "ready," based on the scores that he receives.

For nearly half a century, the *Bulletin of the Council for Basic Education* points out, school people have held that a mental age of six and one half is the desirable, or even the ideal, time to begin a child's formal reading instruction. The result has been that those children, deemed to be "ready" as based on the tests given in the first grade, begin their reading instruction at that time. However, others, also based on test scores, which describe them as "not ready to read," do not get any instruction for most, if not all, of their first grade in school.

The results are often disastrous. Many children now enter the second grade unable to read, because they have not been taught, while those more fortunate, who are deemed to be ready, finish their first-grade readers and even go beyond that. This means that the children who do not get reading instruction in the first grade are academically handicapped from the very first day that they enter school. Unless a teacher or a worried parent objects strenuously, the child who is said to lack "readiness" skills will find himself a year or more behind his more fortunate classmates at the end of the first year, and this lag usually continues to grow greater each year.

What does a reading-readiness test consist of? It is designed to measure the child's development in attention skills, direction following, alphabet recognition, symbol-sound recognition, visual discrimination, recognition of similarities and differences in shapes or letters, the ability to choose the appropriate picture in response to single word or sentence cues, and language meaning.

It is obvious that "readiness" will naturally come faster to a child who has had the cultural advantages of a solid, middle-class home, rather than the deprivation of a ghetto or an economically disadvantaged upbringing.

If a child is not taught to read in the first grade, while his classmates are, because he has not had the necessary cultural background and is not "ready" to read, when will he be able to develop skills so that he can compete on equal terms with his more fortunate classmates? Here we have the vicious cycle again: a child enters first grade, is not taught to read because of a dubious I.Q. or other test, falls behind his classmates who are taught to read, then is advanced to the second grade, still unable to read, and is once again tested and found to be even further behind his age group. Unless he gets special help to overcome whatever handicaps he may have, and is enabled to join his age-level peers on an equal basis with them academically, he will consistently be the "slow" child, neglected and swept aside.

The time has come to abolish the usual I.Q. tests and standardized achievement, reading-readiness and other tests, starting with the first grade, and to replace them with a more equitable and more relevant system of measurement.

Laws exist that attempt to insure the American public that it will get truth in advertising. Now we need another law: truth in testing. The National Council of Teachers of English has expressed concern about the effects of testing on school programs, students, and teachers. Teachers, the Council found, place considerable faith in test scores, feel powerless to resist poorly conceived tests, and frequently do not know how to report test results. Most I.Q. or standardized tests are constructed by professional concerns that are far removed from the classroom.

Substantial and probing research about the curriculum and its topics should be completed before tests are constructed and used. As an example, there has been little agreement about English, language arts, literature, and other subjects in the general curriculum.

Our pluralistic society subscribes to a variety of learning goals. Standardized tests touch only a few of these. People use a variety of learning and living styles, and standardized tests gauge only a narrow range of these styles. Perhaps the public should also be aware of the great number and variety of tests in use, the costliness of the testing process, and the lack of feasible data that evolve from the testing programs.

Nationwide, testing has increased with the desire, even the anxiety, to verify student gains in basic skills each year, to evaluate programs within a state and to see which schools achieve the "best" results.

Every spring and fall in New York City, standardized reading achievement tests are administered in the elementary grades. Since group I.Q. tests have been abolished, reading test scores have become synonymous in the public mind with educational success or failure. These scores tend to blot out any other evaluative criteria that may relate to either the cognitive or the affective areas of the curriculum.

Within the thirty-two school districts, the schools are ranked on the basis of the reading scores. Those rated among the lowest 45 per cent are permitted to use an alternative method of hiring teachers. The teachers do not have to be certified by the school's Board of Examiners but may be hired on the basis of the National Teachers Examination and state certification. No data is provided about the schools; such factors as pupil mobility, bilingualism, cultural differences, or socioeconomic status are not made available in evaluating test results. The public gets only a "number" by which to judge each school and consequently deems it "good" or "bad."

The inference to be made from such ranking is obvious: schools with high reading scores are considered good and their teachers get a "gold star" for competency. Those rated low on the reading scores are considered poor and presumably have inferior or inexperienced teachers. Is this a valid assumption? What would happen if the professional staff of a school rated high was transplanted into a school with a low rating? Would the results change? It is obvious that misuse of reading test scores has become dangerous and educationally unsound.

Objecting to this practice, Jerome Green, principal of the Ochs School in New York City, asserts:

"We who work with children directly, we who consider ourselves teachers of the language and literature of English, teachers of humane values, cannot continue to accept the kind of simplistic thinking that reduces a child, an educational process, a class, a school environment, or a professional staff to a statistic."

Unless teachers and parents draw attention to the real issues, such as the inadequacy of the tests, reading scores, just as I.Q. scores, can be used as weapons against better schooling for our children, rather than as a means to strengthen and enhance the learning process.

Comparing the quality of education provided by schools on the reading test scores, or the I.Q. test scores, is as feasible as comparing the nutritional values in the diets of four different families on the basis of the size of their grocery bills. Test experts themselves disagree on the actual meaning and validity of the existing tests and how to interpret the scores made on them.

In a critical review of the misuses that have been found in the testing process, Dr. Richard L. Venezky of the University of Wisconsin, writing in *Testing in Reading,* charges that parents are generally not informed of the significance and utility of their children's test scores, teachers are often inundated with test results for which they have no use, and administrators often invest large sums of money in testing programs without having clearly defined plans for using the test results.

In some situations, a test adds nothing of significance to what is already known, and, further, two tests are not necessarily better than one and are rarely, if ever, twice as good as one.

If we are to use standardized or I.Q. tests in school, what kind of tests should be used, and how are the results to be properly evaluated? This is the question raised by Dr. Venezky. Take the case of a reading test: Should it be an oral reading test? A test for silent reading comprehension? A test of word-attack skills? Much depends on the content of the instruction. If the instruction is concentrated primarily upon word-attack skills and oral reading, then an assessment of silent-reading ability would probably be inappropriate. No information would be available as to why students failed on this test.

Educators, not test designers, should decide on the content of instruction. At present the tests are designed by those whose main concern is the salability, not the usefulness, of the tests. Assessment, through standardized tests, is secondary to instruction. That is why the teachers and other educators who plan their school programs and develop the curricula should be the ones to plan the assessments. Although testing specialists may be needed for aid in analyzing results, *Testing in Reading* points out, the more basic questions related to the specification of the forms and contents of the tests must be assumed by those who conduct the programs in the classroom.

Another question frequently arises in connection with I.Q. scores and standardized tests. Should parents and the news media generally know the results? I.Q. scores should be kept on a confidential basis, to be released only to the parents or guidance counselors, not to teachers or the general public. But on the issue of standardized reading, arithmetic, or other skills that are tested, the issue is not clear-cut. Schools are accountable for their actions. It is doubtful, however, that accountability is served by the release to parents and to news media of test scores alone.

Perhaps the most flagrant abuse of educational responsibility in this regard is the release to news media of standardized test scores which rank schools according to the reading, mathematical, or social studies, abilities of their students. Says Dr. Venezky:

"The immediate—and seldom contested—implication of such scores is that the schools on the bottom of the list do a poor job of teaching reading while those on the top do a good job. In fact, just the opposite is true—but this, of course, could never be demonstrated from the scores alone." Schools on the bottom of the list, Dr. Venezky implies, are usually in underprivileged areas, with overworked teachers and substantially lower budgets than the more affluent schools. Hence, the poor-ranking scores may be indicative of much better teaching, though the results are poorer.

There are sensible ways to make the information public, without stigmatizing any school or student within the school that is rated "low" or "poor." In California, for example, test scores are accompanied by the following information for each district: minimum, maximum, and media teacher salary, average class size, pupil-teacher ratio, nonteaching personnel, general tax refund rate, general purpose tax rate, assessed valuation per unit of average daily attendance, minority enrollment, scholastic ability such as the average I.Q. score, pupil mobility, rate of staff turnover, instructional expenditures per unit of average daily attendance and regular average daily attendance. The public could then get a far better insight as to the effectiveness of the teaching program in the individual school if a standardized test is to be the criterion. It would be grossly unfair to compare a school district that has poorly paid teachers, large rate of pupil mobility, and high minority enrollment, with a school that has a larger instructional expenditure and is in a more privileged community.

In Virginia the superintendent of schools usually holds a news conference, with the first release of test scores, to explain the testing procedures and the limitations of the test scores. Similarly, in Columbus, Ohio, and Tulsa, Oklahoma, extensive explanations accompany all test scores when they are released. The multitude of factors which might affect achievement is strongly emphasized. Through these methods, it may be possible to overcome much of the misunderstanding which usually accompanies the release of comparative test scores.

Test results should not be used as a weapon of power that often proves more harmful than helpful to the parent, the student, or the teacher. Standardized and I.Q. tests should be structured so that they give a relevant and meaningful direction to education. At the least, we should know what standardized tests are testing and if the results attained are worth the efforts engaged in this ubiquitous process.

12

Still more standardized tests—college boards and career testing

Standardized tests, together with I.Q. tests, are being used for all purposes. Among those used, and in my opinion unfairly, is the National Teachers Examination, offered by the Educational Testing Service. Particularly in some sections of the country, this is one method for eliminating unwanted teachers.

These examinations are used for teacher certification, selection, assignment, retention, salary determination, promotion, transfer, tenure, or dismissal. No single objective instrument is developed fine enough, or sensitive enough, for these purposes.

Recent court and legal actions have placed limitations on the use of the teacher examinations. A number of teachers were ordered rehired with back pay by the courts after they were discharged because of relatively low scores in the NTE. In Mississippi, a federal judge ruled that the school district had misused results of these tests when making teacher retention and selection decisions. In addition to enjoining the schools from using the teacher examination scores for re-employment or new hiring, the court further forbade schools to use standardized tests for employment purposes without its permission.

It ordered that the school district must first present to the court evidence of test validity, the pattern of test results by race of candidates, and the recommendations for test use by the developer of the test. The court's actions in various cases conforms with the stand taken by the National Education Association. It held that the National Teachers Examinations must not be used as a condition of employment or a method to evaluate teachers.

The Graduate Record Examination has also been used to determine the qualifications of teachers, although there is no known correlation between good teaching and a high GRE score. In fact, this examination, usually used to screen candidates for the master's degree, is inaccurate even for that purpose.

Here, too, the courts have ruled that the Graduate Record Examination is an invalid test to determine employment and retention of schoolteachers. In some instances, school officials equated competence in the classroom with scores on both the Graduate Exam as well as the National Teachers Examination. Both these tests have been described by school authorities, testing agencies, and the courts as being invalid as a measurement of teacher competency.

I am not opposed to all I.Q. or standardized tests, if used for the limited purpose for which they were designed. They can serve as diagnostic tools to identify areas of strength or weakness in an individual student, and then provide the student with appropriate remedial action.

The "Item Response Analysis" used by the Cleveland public schools appears promising. Clusters of item responses are used to develop educational prescriptions in response to identifiable learning problems. Teachers are treated as professionals. They are encouraged to select and try alternate teaching resources.

A key question asked by the teachers, when utilizing the responses of the children, is this:

"Is this something that should be reasonably attained by the child?"

In this approach, we get a meaningful goal for the conscientious teachers.

Without question, the most massive testing program in the United States, if not the world, is conducted by the Educational Testing Service. The ETS provides the tests for the College Entrance Examination Board, known generally as "College Boards." Mention College Boards to a high school student who is taking a college-bound preparatory course and he will usually tremble. They are an ordeal and worry to these high school students. The traumatic effect of the College Boards can be found wherever high school students sit, pencil poised, hearts beating rapidly, eyes blinking nervously, waiting for the word "go" from their proctor.

"I know that you've been following my progress through high school in anticipation of my acceptance to a high-quality university," Leah writes to her English teacher, airing her frustrations in which one morning's performance can outweigh four years of high school achievement. "Just recently I received my scores and thought you would be interested in the outcome.

"I regret to say they weren't very good. Just looking at them made me feel disappointed in my achievement in high school. Four years of hard work seemed to be compressed in these two tests which seem totally unrelated. You know how much I want to go to Stanford, but now it seems to me almost certain I won't get accepted. Maybe I won't get accepted at any of the places to which I want to go.

"But that doesn't make any sense. I have a 4.0 grade-point average. You know I'm involved in school athletics, hold a seat in the School Senate, and belong to a number of extracurricular organizations, but all that doesn't seem to matter. After four years of praise from my high school teachers in the form of grades and letters of recommendation I feel these tests have evaluated me as a near failure.

"It seems to me a test should be a learning experience. It should be a way to apply the fundamentals taught to the student. The college entrance tests don't do that at all. If a concept hasn't been shown to you or certain vocabulary words aren't familiar, how can you be judged on them? How does this sort of testing evaluate your potential for learning?

"All that hard work, studying hours on end for tests, doing homework, writing papers, and reading books may not seem important to the college officials, but I know that they are to me. Perhaps other students are better test takers than I am."

Another student vents his feelings this way:

"I have always been terrible at taking tests and, really, I see no use for them. To me, learning is a personal experience. When I sit down to a standardized test, whether it is I.Q. or College Board, I feel upset because I know I am taking it for someone else, not for me. Either my teacher or the college admissions officer will see the test and then decide if I'm bright enough to go to college. Don't my teachers know, since they've been with me every school day for four years?

"To me, the Scholastic Aptitude Test is a barricade that effectively narrows my learning experience. I know that if I am sufficiently motivated, no matter what the teacher expects, there is no way to hold me back. Precollege tests, in my opinion, are the most damaging of all the tests we have to take. The whole idea of mandatory testing seems wrong to me."

Presumably, the College Boards establish a student's scholastic ability as compared with his classmates of similar grade and experience. Two major sections has been included in the SAT: verbal and math, each of which are sixty minutes in length. In 1974, a thirty-minute Test of Standard Written English became part of the SAT. Most colleges and universities, notably the prestigious ones, require the College Boards and demand a high score on them.

The language usage test consists of fifty items in which students are expected to identify certain parts of sentences that contain errors.

For example: "I have just took my book home."

Students would indicate the part of the sentence that is incorrect; in this case, it is the verb form "took." To receive credit, they would rewrite the sentence correctly to read:

"I have just *taken* my book home."

A vigorous attack on this addition to the College Boards has been made by Professor Harvey Daniels of Northwestern University. He calls the testing a regressive, backward-looking, and muddle-headed innovation. It will, in Professor Daniels' opinion, endorse linguistic prejudice, downgrade the natural speech styles of normal adolescents, and penalize those who come from nonmainstream backgrounds. The test will put a premium on precise speech patterns. Dialects are not deficits but differences.

In addition to the SATs, the College Boards consist of a series of Achievement Tests, each one an hour in length. Frequently, students are required to take three achievements, either of their own choice or recommended by the college. Almost all require the English Achievement, while certain colleges may require a foreign language, math, science, or any of the thirteen subjects available.

Advanced Placement Examinations are also offered. Those getting a score considered adequate by the college admissions director may receive college credit, sometimes eliminating college freshmen courses. In English, for instance, a student receiving a predetermined score will be permitted to omit the demanding, but often dull, freshman composition from his program.

Other examinations for professional or graduate students, offered through the Educational Testing Service, include the Architectural School Aptitude Test, the College-level Examination Program, the Admissions Test for Graduate Study in Business, Law School Admission Test, Fundamentals of Engineering Examination, and the proficiency Examination for Clinical Laboratory Personnel.

Of all the tests offered the SAT is the most important for college-bound students. It often makes or breaks a student's chance of getting into the college of his choice, or indeed, of any college. For many, planning to enter college, the SAT can mean long hours of testing, anxiety, pressures, as well as physical and emotional strain, as we saw in Leah's comments after receiving her scores.

A test one or two hours can often determine a lifetime career or loss of it. Low scores carry with them frustration, disappointment, disapproval of adults and peers, and a lowering of self-concept. High scores can create a feeling of complacency and smugness, with the result that, not infrequently, the student finds that college is not as easy as he was led to believe by his standing on the test.

Measured are the learned skills, almost exclusively math and vocabulary. Not measured are those human relationships that are so important in today's society.

A side effect not often mentioned, but which is important, deals with the curriculum. Hundreds of coaching classes, all commercial, which capitalize on both parents' and students' fears of getting low scores on the SAT, have been formed in various parts of the country. Much money, time, and energy go into these agencies. Moreover, in a number of schools the curriculum is often geared to meet the type of questions that may be found on the SAT and the Achievement tests.

Even though some college admission directors admit privately that they place little faith in these tests and would like to see them abolished, they, too, are bound to abide by the results. After all, a student with a score of 600—the range is from a low of 200 to a high of 800—is usually given preference over another applicant with a score of 500, where 450 is about average.

Whether or not the students took the tests under similar emotional and physical conditions is of course unknown to the admissions office. If the student is rejected and angry parent wants to know why, answer is readily available:

"Your son, or daughter, did poorly on the College Boards."

It is hard to believe that an admissions director can determine on the basis of a one- or two-hour test that Bill will be a better college student than Jim, that Emma is a poorer school risk than Harriet. The test does not indicate in any way the student's ability to adjust to a new way of life, to accept a new type of discipline and self-responsibility, nor does the test give any clue as to the student's awareness of the political scene, social conditions, or interpersonal relations.

To get a high score on the verbal section of the test, the student must possess great facility in reading, writing, and vocabulary. In the sections on "comprehension," he is given long passages to read and then must answer significant, as well as insignificant, questions about minute items found in the passage. A good memory, rather than brains, helps. The verbal section is similar to the I.Q. tests. Both concentrate on verbal ability. With poor background in this area, the SAT score will be low, just as it will be in the I.Q. test. The questions are all multiple choice, leaving little if any room for cognitive reasoning.

Also, there are good "test takers" as well as poor ones. If Mary is happy and cheerful and unafraid, she is likely to score high. By the same token, if Bob is depressed, had a sleepless night, is emotionally upset, worried, and tense, he is already defeated before he opens his all-important SAT booklet.

Presumably, the SAT is an indication of what a student can do in college, as far as his grades are concerned. The College Entrance Examination Board, which is associated with ETS, was formed in 1900 when Harvard, Yale, Princeton, and a few other prestigious colleges considered the problem of testing for college admission. But it wasn't until 1924 that the College Board set up a commission to develop a series of tests, to be used by all students and acceptable to the colleges within the Board organization. There are some one thousand colleges today that use the Board scores as a guideline for their admissions program.

The commission, headed by Dr. Carl C. Brigham, a Princeton psychologist, devised the first SAT tests in 1926. They were the essay type then, but later, as the number of students taking the tests grew, and the cost of evaluating them became almost prohibitive, the current multiple-choice type of question was introduced.

Although a correlation between high SAT scores and high college grades has been found, there are so many individual differences and variants that a low-scoring student might still be successful in college.

I have known students in the upper 10 per cent of their class on the College Boards who dropped out of college at the end of a year. They either got in with a "wrong" crowd, became hooked on drugs, "freaked out," neglected their studies, or just did not have the motivation to succeed. College Boards cannot measure or predict these imponderables.

On the other hand, I recall a student who received a lowly 315 in the SAT verbal section and only 425 in math. He did not rate as college material based on his scores. The admission director of a Long Island college was persuaded to take a chance and admit him on probation. He floundered a bit the first six months, then adjusted to college life. He majored in English, was elected editor of the literary journal, and in his senior year received a prize for his excellence in English. On the basis of a 315 verbal score, the outlook for his success in college was extremely dim. Yet he succeeded and is on the road toward becoming an outstanding editor.

At no time can we presume that College Boards measure motivation, which we know is a key factor in learning. Yet we find that many colleges will only accept the higher scorers. But the colleges have an excuse. They, too, are under subtle pressure. The accrediting agencies look at the admissions figures, the SAT scores of those admitted, and may admonish the colleges, which admit more than a certain proportion of "low scorers," that they must change their policy or suffer loss of accreditation. High scores may be impressive statistically, but of what value are they when you do not know the student's work habits, his values, his attitudes, his curiosity, his integrity, or his willingness to work hard at his academic tasks?

Perhaps colleges should re-evaluate the College Boards and determine whether they should be the determining factor in the admission of students. Colleges should re-evaluate the significance of College Board scores and adjust admissions requirements accordingly.

Bowdoin College in Maine has abolished the SAT and is still able to attract and hold exceptionally fine students. The college has found that more important than SAT scores is the student's level of development, his personality traits, or his growth pattern in high school.

Even though they still retain their prestige, the College Boards have recently been challenged and their influence has dropped, slowly to be sure. Colleges need students now more than they did a decade ago. Even the top-ranking colleges that prided themselves on being intensely selective are gradually lowering their SAT, and other testing, requirements.

Moreover, a trend toward open admissions has developed. A number of colleges now accept all high school graduates, regardless of their grade average. Since it adopted its open-admissions policy, the City University of New York, with one of the largest enrollments in the nation, has dropped its SAT requirements. The trend toward community and two-year junior colleges has grown phenomenally during recent years. These colleges are more lenient in the admissions policies than the four-year institutions. They do not place their emphasis on College Boards.

In addition to the College Entrance Examination Board tests, high school students, seeking admission to college, may take the tests offered by the American College Testing Program, with headquarters in Iowa City. About half the high school graduates who go to college take the ACT rather than the SAT. Most of those students are from the Midwest and Far West and are enrolled in state universities. The ACT gives four separate scores, rather than two, as is the case with the SAT. They are in social studies, English, math, and science.

The question of how fair either the SAT or the ACT is remains unanswered. It is known that the black student gets a lower score, on the average, than his white counterpart. Many colleges have two standards of admission: one for whites, and the other for blacks. Whereas a white student might have to score in the upper 500s to be accepted, a black, with a score of 400 or less, will be offered admission in many institutions.

"We're working hard to identify unfair questions and to study those that minority students find hard," said Dr. William W. Turnbull, President of the ETS, the test-making arm of the CEEB. "The problem is that the tests are miniatures of what people are called upon to do in college. On the other hand, many minority students are handicapped by an impoverished educational background."

The ETS has brought in an increasing amount of black content into the SAT questions. Black educators have been asked to help write test questions. Whether this will help raise the SAT scores of minority candidates remains to be seen.

The CEEB suggests that the best way to regard test scores from a poor family, and that may include blacks, Chicanos, American Indians, and Puerto Ricans, is as a floor under his abilities, not as a ceiling. Because of the debilitating effects of limited incomes and substandard schools in poor neighborhoods, a low-income student's scores do not indicate how much he could have achieved, and may achieve later, under more favorable circumstances.

Low scores may augur poor academic performance the first year, but college administrators report that many minority or disadvantaged students, after struggling during their first year, go on to earn better grades and do well during their remaining stay in college, especially if they receive help.

Changes in both admissions philosophy and administration are essential if our minority and underprivileged children are to achieve educational skills in such fields as medicine, law, engineering, and teaching. The director of ETS's Minority Affairs Section urges a thorough re-examination of the logic and the consequences of an admissions process that perpetuates a separate and unequal education for minority groups. He claims that the SAT or ACT is the college admissions officer's security blanket, and the cut-off score is his pacifier.

The College Entrance Examination Board has been under attack and is now in the process of correcting the various abuses charged to it and to the testing it gives. A Commission on Tests, formed by the CEEB, and headed by Professor David V. Tiedeman of Harvard, made a comprehensive study of the College Board. In a two-volume report, *Righting the Balance,* it concluded that the existing tests do not meet the needs of the majority of students who want to go to college.

The twenty-one man commission held that the Board's current tests need considerable modification and improvement if they are to provide an equitable access to American colleges. Drastic reform was urged. In the views of some of the Commission members, the tests corrupt the process of education itself. The secondary school can always say of an unsuccessful student that since he did not pass the College Board, he is not college material, and therefore the school is not responsible for his failure. Since the questions are multiple choice, with only one answer permitted, the test may penalize the bright, thoughtful student who can see more than one solution to the problem raised. But unless he "guesses" the right answer, the one that the computer will mark as correct, he is penalized even though he may be logically right. Alternative answers are not accepted, as they are not, also, in the I.Q. tests.

Yale University's Professor Elting Morison told the Commission that his three years of experience in trying to develop a new history curriculum had convinced him that tests have an extraordinary effect on what is taught and how it is interpreted. He would prefer that tests be used to extend the learning process rather than to measure its results.

Learning is not understood theoretically, empirically, or intuitively. Trying to test the results of an ill-understood process might do violence to the process itself.

The Commission further held that students should receive an opportunity to show their best skills and most profound knowledge. Many have an enormous range of special skills, developed to a remarkable degree either as the result of a hobby or because of special talents. Present testing programs tend to mask these, leaving the students unable to show what they do best and failing to give the colleges a full view of their individual capabilities.

Some way should be found to provide potential students an opportunity, through selection from a wide variety of special and far-ranging subject matter, to exhibit their special capabilities. One criticism of the Board's current testing progam is that the tests leave too much of the student's individuality out of effective consideration.

Furthermore, the Commission stresses that the Board's current tests are pertinent only to certain scholastic variables that are significant in schoolwork at all levels. Significantly, it reports:

"While in reality no one can solve anyone's problems of choice, the College Board can give the student, faced with the difficult decisions surrounding the transition out of high school, support equal to that which colleges receive. In short, the Commission thinks that a symmetry or balance should obtain between the services that the Board offers to potential entrants and those that it offers to colleges."

Scores on the SATs reflect at least four factors of ability: knowledge of vocabulary and ability to understand language, ability to deal with quantitative and spatial concepts, ability to reason with concepts either in verbal or quantitative terms, and speed in test taking.

The Commission proposed that the speed factor of all the Board's tests be reduced and that the quantitative emphasis in the SAT be lowered, in favor of measuring developed abilities now done through other tests, such as the Mathematics Achievement Test. Various learning capacities apart from the traditional and more developed abilities could also be measured by sections of the Scholastic Aptitude Test.

It is a challenge to the CEEB to develop such tests and then add them to the SAT. In this way, they might better reveal the educational potential of students who have not had the advantage of a good conventional education.

Present college entrance tests, in common with the I.Q. and achievement tests, are oriented exclusively toward measuring what a student knows or how apt he is at certain skills or how to adapt knowledge relevant to schoolwork. Neither the construction nor the administration of the tests are designed to test the student on anything other than what he has learned in the classroom or at home, and only how this knowledge compares with that of his classmates.

Several suggestions to improve this situation are offered by the Commission. Examiners could discuss with the students possible reasons for choosing alternative answers and could take into account how a student with a different frame of reference might approach the question. Self-administered and self-scoring tests might also be introduced with good advantage to the student. Of course, all this would take extra man power, more examiners, and would cost considerably more than the present mode of testing. But it would be worth the extra funds, since the tests could then become more meaningful to the admissions director and even, of greater importance, to the student himself.

Colleges are urged to replace the SAT's fixed, predetermined one-answer questions with a more flexible assortment of tests. A section could be introduced to measure scholastic learning potential as it now does in assessing the abilities that have already been developed. Again, as in the I.Q. tests, the SATs determine what one has already learned, not the individual's capacity to learn. To make the SAT more representative of the total population, it is necessary to revise our current concept of verbal aptitude as being the major index of intelligence.

As a subgroup of the American population, blacks make lower scores on the SATs than do white students. It has been estimated that not more than 15 per cent and perhaps as few as 10 per cent of black high school seniors score 400 or more on the verbal section, while less than 2 per cent are likely to score 500 or more. Based on these figures alone, few, if any, black students would be admitted to the Ivy League four-year, private, liberal-arts colleges that maintain a cut-off point in the high 600s. Only at the open-admission colleges would they have an equal opportunity of acceptance.

Writing in the *College Board Review,* Drs. Julius A. Davis and George Temp of the ETS stress that many black students bring with them other handicaps, such as inferior preparation, deficiencies in study skills, more frequent origin from broken homes, more apprehensions about what is, culturally, still a new and unknown experience of different values for them.

Calling for a "new look" at how colleges establish admissions quotas, the authors say:

"Admissions practices cannot much longer be determined solely by what technicians have made possible in test construction and prediction procedures. . . . We need to move away from the notion that a limited and stereotyped measure of quality of input alone determines quality of the system and the product."

Instead, Drs. Davis and Temp suggest, we must consider the concept that quality higher education depends on how creatively, efficiently, and effectively the college provides for human growth and development of all individuals who seek a chance to get ahead.

As a result, a widespread practice has emerged on admission committees to give minority applicants special advantages because of their backgrounds. If colleges were to admit a greater proportion of minority students, as they have agreed to do, it will be necessary to have two admissions standards—one for whites and the other for blacks or other minority students.

Whether this is legal will probably be decided by the United States Supreme Court. The Court side-stepped the suit brought by a white candidate who was rejected from the University of Washington Law School, while blacks, with inferior test records, were accepted. Since the student had already entered and was about to graduate from the law school, which he subsequently did, the Court held the case to be moot. The next one brought before the Court may not be.

One college official told me: "Of course, we have two sets of standards. We consider other things besides grades and test scores, such as motivation, for minority students. We're going to admit students on different standards, but they will graduate on the same basis as all other students."

With intensive remedial help, poorly prepared minority students frequently achieve records comparable to their white classmates. Test scores alone, whether from the I.Q. or other tests, are of little value in determining which student is going to succeed in school or college.

At the same time, colleges recognize that many of the minority students that they admit will fail if they do not get special help. Their educational backgrounds have been severely crippled, and, if they are to compete with the more privileged students, they will need considerable remedial instruction to offset their intellectual handicaps.

This view is best expressed by Walter Leonard, in charge of the Harvard Affirmative Action program, designed to recruit minority students and faculty members. Said Dr. Leonard, as quoted in the New York *Times:*

"When you begin to admit minority students, you begin to look at more than just the mechanical scores. A minority student, who, in many instances, has come through a very crippling educational background, one almost designed for failure, but who nonetheless has come through and has reached the point where he's knocking on the grad-school door—well, just the fact of his survival that far becomes a sign of his toughness and is predictive of his ability to survive as a student."

An interesting phenomenon has developed in connection with College Board scores. Over the last ten years the mean scores on the SAT have steadily declined. During the 1962–63 school year, the average score on the verbal was 478 and on the math section it was 502. By 1972–73, the score had dropped to a mean of 445 on the verbal and 481 on the math—a loss of 33 points for verbal and 21 points for math. What is the explanation, if there is one?

"The question of what is causing the drop is something none of us can answer," admits Dr. William Angoff, ETS College Board programs executive director.

Critics suggest that the elementary and secondary schools are not preparing students as well in the basic skills as they did in former years. Or that the tests actually do not measure the intelligence of students, since many schools have rebelled and refuse to structure their curriculum around the questions found in the SATs. Teachers are more willing now, in many instances, to experiment with the "new math" or with advanced methods of teaching English and the language arts. Obviously, these new devices will not accurately reflect a student's ability when he takes an SAT containing material with which he is unfamiliar.

Perhaps it is time that the College Entrance Examination Board adopted the sane suggestions of its own Commission on Tests and drastically revised the tests it now offers to millions of students. It is difficult to understand how these tests can continue to dominate our college and university admissions policies when we find so many flaws in them. The scores have dropped during the past ten years because they do not accurately measure the student's ability. Unless they are drastically and realistically overhauled, the scores will probably continue their descent.

Tests are being used to determine whether a potential employee should be hired or promoted. The courts have ruled that many of these tests are illegal as they do not measure the knowledge and information that the individual needs to know in his job performance. The licensing tests given throughout the country to persons entering vocational or technical fields and occupations are under sharp attack. The criticism comes from the Educational Testing Service itself.

The attack is based on the findings of a five-year study of occupational licensing, sponsored by the ETS. Officials conducting the study interviewed licensing officials, vocational educators, union leaders, and minority-group representatives. The report called licensing a haphazard, unco-ordinated, and chaotic process.

Jumbled testing standards exist. A primary weakness in occupational licensing is the variation in training and experience requirements among state and local governments, together with different sets of test standards. Examinations used by most licensing boards are inadequate and fail to meet modern standards for testing and proper evaluation.

Criticized also is the general secrecy surrounding the licensing examinations which leaves the candidates with little idea of how to prepare for the examinations and provides them with almost no feedback information on their weaknesses if they fail. As a result, the failure rate is high. The candidates were tested in such varied fields as plumbing, electronics, engineering, and automotive work.

The report noted the special licensing problems of persons who are not proficient in English. Men otherwise qualified could not obtain a license because they could not pass the English examinations. Most boards did little to help the candidates overcome this deficiency.

According to the ETS study, the whole testing and licensing field is embedded in a morass of federal, state, and local legislation suffused with tradition and jealously guarded rights. At the state level, licensing by cities should be halted as a first step toward easing barriers to intrastate mobility. Licensing reciprocity between states should also be adopted. Licensing requirements which have no direct bearing on an individual's competency should be eliminated. Perhaps the federal government should take a hand in regulating the tests in an attempt to bring order out of the chaotic conditions that now exist.

Not only in the field of occupational examinations, but in the professions as well, testing has become monopolistic and often acts to bar qualified students. The Medical Aptitude Test, taken by all candidates who seek admission to medical schools, is a case in point. A student may be exceptionally bright, have an A average in college, and be an all-round student, but if he gets a low score on the Medical Aptitude Test, he will usually be denied admission to almost any medical school, let alone the prestigious ones.

No study has yet shown that a medical student who receives a high Medical Aptitude score will, when he enters practice, be a more competent physician than the person who scored lower on the test. No correlation exists between competence on the job, whether in medicine, law, teaching, or auto mechanics, and the scores on I.Q. or achievement tests.

How, then, shall we determine whether a student will become creative, be able to maintain high academic standing, and be a suitable candidate for college or professional school if we disregard the results of the SAT, the I.Q., the MAT, or other tests? An answer is suggested by Professor Michael A. Wallach of Duke University. In his opinion, following extensive studies, talent and creativity can be discovered, not through tests, but through the actual accomplishments of the students prior to their entering college.

He cites these examples that could be useful in determining the abilities of the potentially talented student, regardless of his test scores:

In the field of writing, such achievements have been noted as the student having done creative work in high school, winning a literary prize for creative writing, editing or writing for a recognized journal or periodical.

Science-related accomplishments might consist of winning an award in a state or regional science contest, writing a research paper on pollution or ecology, or continuing unique or long-range scientific experiments at home or in the science lab at school.

Artistic endeavors could be measured by the student's receiving an award in a museum-sponsored competition for paintings or sculpture.

Musical talent might be detected by studying and preparing a musical composition, professional performance at school or in local orchestras, and by concert work.

In the field of political leadership, future success might be deduced from the student's attainments in school, such as the election to the presidency of the student senate, winning an award in a state-wide debating contest, or sponsoring political-action clubs.

Can these future achievements as well as present accomplishments be discovered through high I.Q., SAT., or Graduate Record Examination scores? Not at all.

As Dr. Wallach so aptly stresses, little or no relationship exists between the display of one or another talented accomplishment and a student's location on the academic skills that can be measured. The highest academic scores do not necessarily predict success in after school world activities. Reliance on the I.Q. tests, or other standardized instruments of measurement, can actually prove harmful since the scores rule out many potentially talented students who could, if given the opportunity, achieve far above those of their fellow students who were accepted because of numerically higher scores.

At present, colleges consider the SAT scores to be far more important, in selecting students, than the potential talents that they may possess, as indicated through their school experience. In selecting candidates for law school, for example, candidates with histories of high competence at political leadership activities and debating may make far better lawyers than students with the highest academic record. This is true in the other professions, whether they are science, medicine, engineering, education, music, or art.

The tests that now are used to eliminate students from college, graduate or professional schools should be completely revised or abolished. They are unable to predict the achievements or attainments that the graduates will accomplish after they leave the classroom and enter the "real" world. Employers are not likely to ask:

"What is your I.Q. score?"

"How well did you do on your SAT?"

"What is your scholastic rank in class?"

Standardized tests for jobs and professional position are also generally unreliable. The Miami *Herald* featured a story with the headline:

WRONG REPLY SOMETIMES RIGHT ON TEST

The article reported that the Miami Civil Service director found four major errors that had existed on a police academy entrance examination that the city had used for ten years. The errors appeared in spelling, vocabulary, and the "thought problems" section of the exam, and involved a possible 12 points out of a total score of 424 in the test.

These 12 points might have prevented many applicants from passing the examination, and these persons were thus denied entrance as students to the Academy.

Nearly nine hundred persons took the police academy test, which has since been revised to eliminate the errors. More than fifty of those who took the exam failed by 12 points or less. It is not difficult to recognize what effect the four mishandled questions, totaling 12 points, had on the candidates who failed. Nor is it hard to determine the ineptitude of I.Q. or standardized tests of any kind, whether used for police academy applicants, college candidates, or civil service job seekers.

At present, tests for job applicants are being legally challenged. Many law suits are pending against major corporations and business concerns who are being challenged for using discriminatory and often unfair tests. The Courts have generally held that the tests, when given to job applicants, must relate to job performance. Even if there is no intent to discriminate, Chief Justice Burger has ruled that if it is found that the consequence of a psychological test is discriminatory, then it is illegal.

Writing in the June, 1974, issue of *Psychology Today,* Peter Koenig estimates that from 15 to 20 per cent of the 60,000 complaints that the Equal Employment Opportunity Commission received in 1974 were related to testing.

The validity of I.Q. tests, reports Paul Weckstein, writing in the Harvard sponsored *Center for Law and Education Bulletin,* is questionable unless the tests are given together with other measures that are designed to test actual adaptive ability. The self-fulfilling nature of classification procedures, notes Professor Weckstein, their effects upon teacher expectations and students' self-image, other forms of bias in the performance evaluation, and the inferior quality of lower-track education can be used to explain correlations between test results and later student performance, thus challenging the assumption that the tests are valid.

The use of I.Q., achievement, aptitude, employment, and all other types of tests has now come under strict scrutiny from our courts, if not as yet from the educational profession. Perhaps the I.Q. stranglehold will yet be broken with the aid of the judiciary.

Psychologists and others engaged in standardized testing have had tradition and prestige on their side in support of their testing program. But there is now a challenge to the entire testing practice. Interested parents and educators recognize that a tremendous injustice is often done to test takers, whether they are children in school, adolescents preparing for college, adults in factory shops, or applicants for civil service jobs.

A nineteen-year-old Brooklyn student who failed his art classes both in high school and college recently won the highest award in a cartoon contest. He defeated some of the nation's leading professional cartoonists. The New York *Times* reported that Steve Brodner, who had just completed his sophomore year at The Cooper Union for the Advancement of Science and Art, won the $1,500 award for a cartoon depicting the world overpopulating itself to the point, where, over the course of six consecutive globes shown in the drawing, representing six generations, the world evolved into a skull. Not a single word was used; the cartoon spoke for itself.

Conducted by the Population Institute, the contest sought the best cartoon published between 1972 and 1974, dealing with the population problem.

None of his teachers thought that young Steve had any artistic ability. A high school teacher called his work "glorified doodles." His college teacher gave him a failing grade in drawing.

Commenting on his prize-winning achievement, Steve recalled:

"The teacher would come over and have a fit. We had what you might call an artistic conflict, and she failed me."

Standardized tests of all varieties, just as is the case with I.Q. tests, are meaningless unless they can be used to predict, with some measure of accuracy, the capability of the individual. As of now, they have failed to do this.

What, then, is the purpose for their continued use?

13

The I.Q. and the self-fulfilling prophecy

Liza Doolittle says in George Bernard Shaw's play, *Pygmalion:*

"You see, really and truly, apart from the things anyone can pick up (the dressing and the proper way of speaking, and so on), the difference between a lady and a flower girl is not how she behaves, but how she's treated. I shall always be a flower girl to Professor Higgins, because he always treats me as a flower girl, always will, but I know I can be a lady to you, because you always treat me as a lady, and always will."

Self-fulfilling prophecies operate in the classroom, and affect the

I.Q. in the process, just as Professor Higgins affected Liza. To some teachers a black child is inferior and always will be; a Chicano is unable to learn and therefore is to be placed in the "slow" group. The child from a poverty neighborhood, smelling of stale-food odors, unkempt, unwashed, and unlettered, is hardly educable. The well-scrubbed, well-dressed, and obedient children, in the opinion of many teachers, are the ones who will succeed and benefit from their teaching efforts.

Often, a teacher acts this way because of something else besides the child's appearance and obvious "poor" home background. She has the child's progress and accumulative folder before her, has read it, and noted that the I.Q. score is low. Although she does not know the reasons for this low score, she unconsciously, almost automatically, rates him as a slow learner and a poor achiever.

He is rejected by his teacher and responds accordingly; meanwhile the teacher turns her attention to the brighter, more responsive child. The feelings that a teacher has toward a child significantly relate to academic achievement.

Perceptive and sensitive children recognize this distinction, and teachers usually get what they expect. If the teacher believes that a child is too "dumb" to learn, or that the child is unwilling to pay attention or causes trouble in class and will doubtlessly fail, the chances are that the child will fail.

Psychologists Martin L. Maehr of the University of Illinois and Pamela C. Rubevits of the Comprehensive Child Development Center (Providence, R.I.) measured teacher attitudes toward both bright and average black and white students. The "teachers" were white undergraduates who were taking part in a teacher-for-a-day project to help them decide whether this was the field in which their interests would ultimately lie. This is common practice in many schools and colleges where students are permitted to take the role of teacher for varying periods of time.

In this instance, the student-teachers were assigned to 264 seventh- and eighth-grade children in a small Midwestern city. The "teachers" did not know that they were being observed to discover if latent prejudices existed.

Each of the sixty-six acting teachers was assigned to teach four children for an hour. Two were black and the other two were white. The teachers were told that one of each race was gifted and one was average in both I.Q. scores and in scholastic achievement. Actually, the children were selected at random, and assignments were made without regard to their I.Q. scores or their measured intelligence.

A member of the research team, working on the experiment, sat in the classroom to find out if the student-teacher practiced favoritism. At the end of the class session, the observer queried the teacher about the student's performance in relation to his purported ability and mental alertness.

White students generally received more attention, praise and encouragement in the classroom; blacks were virtually ignored. The supposedly gifted white pupils were rewarded by the teachers, with frequent praise, while the presumably gifted blacks were criticized or chided for minor infractions. Since neither the black nor white children were actually gifted or slow, they were the victims of arbitrary and prejudicial treatment.

The I.Q. test scores, real or imaginary, give the teacher a negative mental image of the child if the score is said to be low, or a positive one if it is believed to be high. The teacher, it has been found, often projects this attitude in the classroom and it reflects in her treatment of the child. We know that the teacher's values, attitudes, beliefs, and expectations have a tremendous impact on the performance of the schoolchildren. Her expectation of the pupil's performance, whether good or bad, may serve as an educational self-fulfilling prophecy. To many teachers, a low I.Q. child will always be a "flower girl." Apparently the teacher gets a more responsive student if she expects greater academic results from him and a negative reaction if she treats the student with a patronizing attitude because she feels that he is intellectually inferior.

In their study on "Self-Fulfilling Prophecies in the Classroom," later expanded into their book, *Pygmalion in the Classroom,* Professor Robert Rosenthal of Harvard University and Lenore Jacobson of the South San Francisco Unified School District stressed that the self-fulfilling prophecy has been observed to operate in the world of work and recreation as well as in education. Here are examples cited by the authors that suggest strongly the influence of expectation upon results:

The Hollerith tabulating machine had just been installed at the United States Census Bureau. It required the clerks to learn a new skill which the inventor, Hollerith, regarded as very demanding. He expected that a trained worker could punch approximately 550 cards per day. After two weeks of apprenticeship the workers began to produce this amount. To go beyond this quota meant, in many cases, physical or emotional exhaustion upon the part of the workers.

Sometime later a new group of two hundred clerks came to augment the Hollerith machine work force. They had had no prior training and did not know that the completion of 550 cards per day was the expected and acceptable quota. Soon the new workers turned out some 2,000 cards daily, and without any ill effects. They just didn't know that they were expected to limit their output at 550, and that if they went beyond this number, they would become physically or emotionally exhausted.

Another example from industry, as cited by Rosenthal and Jacobson:

A number of women applicants for employment underwent an evaluation procedure. Each was administered tests of intelligence and of finger dexterity. The supervisors received the names of the women who had presumably scored either high or low on the tests, although these figures were assigned to the women at random. Thus, a person who was listed with the supervisor as having a high I.Q., might in reality have made a low score on the test, and the one with a "low" label next to her name might in truth be either low or high.

Upon an evaluation at a later date, the records kept by the foremen on the performance of their workers were analyzed. It was found that the foremen evaluated more favorably those workers who they believed to be superior on the bases of their alleged dexterity and I.Q. scores. Even more startling and surprising was the fact that those workers from whom the supervisors had been told to expect superior performance responded with superior work. There was no reason, logically, why a worker should do better just because her supervisor had listed her as "superior," since the individual herself did not know that she had been thus labeled.

Following these unexplained and fragmentary clues, Rosenthal and Jacobson undertook what has since become known as the famous Pygmalion experiment. They designed a project to test the hypothesis that, within a given classroom, those children from whom the teacher expected greater growth in intellectual competence would show greater growth. If it could happen in the factory or the business office, why not in the classroom?

The experiment was conducted in an elementary school, containing six grades, with three classrooms for each of the grades, each with an above average, average, and below average scholastic-achievement level. The teachers were told that the children would be administered the Harvard Test of Inflected Acquisition, a test that presumably could predict academic "blooming" as well as intellectual growth.

This, in fact, was misleading. The test was a standardized relatively nonverbal test of intelligence: Flanagan's Tests of General Ability. One out of five of the children in each of the eighteen classrooms was arbitrarily designated by the researchists as academic "spurters."

Following the so-called "Harvard" test, the names of the "spurters" were given to their teachers as those who, during the academic year, would show unusual intellectual gains, predicated on the basis of the test for "intellectual blooming." The teachers were instructed not to mention the test findings, nor the scores that they had been assigned, to the parents or to the pupils themselves.

As a matter of fact, the children designated as "spurters" or "bloomers," who were destined to outperform their fellow students during the course of the year, were selected at random. The only difference that existed was that in the minds of the teachers who thought that they had a group of children who would do exceptionally well in their studies during the school year and could be expected to outperform the other members of the class.

Four months after the teachers had received the names of the "special" children, the pupils took the same nonverbal Flanagan's I.Q. test. At the end of the school year, the test was once more administered to all of the pupils. Thus, the children were tested before they entered school, halfway through the academic year, and finally at the end of the school year.

The self-fulfilling prophecy worked! At the end of the year, those children in the experimental group dubbed as "bloomers" or "spurters" increased their I.Q. scores, as well as their mental ages, to a much greater extent than the control group or "nonbloomers." Yet, the so-called bloomers, or those whom the teachers had expected to respond favorably, were in no way different from the other children in the class and had received the same instruction.

Teachers were then asked to rate the pupils on such variables as the extent to which they would be successful in the future, and the degree to which they could be described as interesting, curious, happy, appealing, adjusted, affectionate, hostile, and motivated by a need for social approval.

Children who were thought by their teachers to be especially selected were described as being significantly more interesting, curious, and happy, and rated as having a better chance for future success. It appeared obvious that the "special" children were treated more affectionately and with greater understanding than the others.

To the teachers, children from whom more intellectual growth was expected did indeed become more intellectually mature. On the other hand, those children in the control group whose I.Q.'s were similar, or in some cases superior, came to be regarded as less well-adjusted and less bright than the "selected ones."

When teachers expected a child to gain intellectually and grow mentally, somehow that child lived up to their expectations. In one of the three classrooms in the first grade, for example, the experimental children gained an average of 41 I.Q. points, compared with 16 for the controls, a difference of 25 points in the course of the nine-month school year.

The most astounding effect of the teachers' expectations occurred in a second grade where the experimental children gained 22 I.Q. points compared with 4 for those in the control group. Less than half of the control group children gained 10 or more total I.Q. points, while 80 per cent of the "bloomers" gained more than 10 points. One out of five of the "bloomers" gained 30 or more I.Q. points, compared with one out of twenty in the control group.

Evidently the expectations of the teachers greatly affected the reasoning power of the children, at least as measured by the I.Q. tests. Those who were expected to blossom out and become mentally more alert gained considerably more in this area than did their classmates without such high expectations.

Why did the children do better when their teachers expected them to? The children, or their parents, did not know that they were special in any way, or would become spurters. But the teachers knew! The authors suggest these reasons for the gains made by the children, who, logically, had no right whatsoever to be any different from their classmates:

Consciously or unconsciously, the teachers showed their interest in the "bloomers" by what they said and how they said it; by facial expressions, postures, and perhaps by touch; they may have communicated to the experimental children that they expected improved intellectual performance. Such communication, together with possible changes in teaching techniques, may have helped the children learn by enlarging their own self-concept, their expectations of themselves, and their self-motivation as well as their cognitive skills.

What cannot be overlooked is that when teachers expected certain children to improve in their classroom responses and their intellectual growth, their I.Q. scores rose correspondingly. The question to be asked at this point is whether the intellectual development will continue beyond the grades in which the children experienced the self-fulfilling prophecy? The year that followed, when studies were made, showed that these special children continued to progress. For example, their reading achievement was significantly greater than might ordinarily be expected.

Other studies have found similar results. Professor Calvin W. Taylor of the University of Utah, a specialist in creative education, has found that a child usually lives up to what is expected of him.

He comments: "Students try to live up to the concept that teachers have of them. The higher the concept the teacher honestly has of students' potentials, the greater their development is likely to be. In contrast, the lower the concept, the lesser the development."

We find this self-fulfilling prophecy starts early in the life of a child. Take the case of sixty preschoolers from a summer Head Start Program. The children were taught by their teachers to name a series of symbols. Picked at random, half the children were expected to have good symbol learning and the other half poor learning ability.

The teachers were informed who the "bright" and who the "slow" children were in the group. Again, as in the previous instances, although picked at random, 77 per cent of the children alleged to have better intellectual perspectives learned five or more symbols, but only 13 per cent of the children who were arbitrarily designated as "poor" learned five or more.

Could it also be here, as in the Rosenthal-Jacobson Pygmalion study, that teachers who had been given favorable expectations about their pupils tried to teach them more? The difference in learning power was dramatic.

Eight or more symbols were taught by 87 per cent of the teachers who had been led to expect better performance from their pupils, but only 13 per cent of the teachers who expected poor performance tried to teach that many symbols. Again, we find that the children who were expected by their teachers to be superior showed superior performance. Unfortunately, all of the presumptions were based, falsely, on the premise that these children were categorized by previously administered I.Q. tests.

The I.Q. score seems to be in the mind of the beholder. No actual basis of fact existed for the differences except in the teacher's mind.

Not only teachers, but parents as well, can influence the child's physical and mental growth and development, as Professor Don E. Manachek of Michigan State University writes in the Spring 1974 issue of *Today's Education:*

"Once we put labels, such as stubborn or lazy, on a child, we increase the difficulty of ever getting to the why of what he's doing. Those sharp little words have a way of digging grooves in our perceptions, so that it becomes increasingly difficult to see the possibility of other causes or motivations for a youngster's behavior. . . . Once we have a conception of a youngster as being clumsy or a poor reader, or whatever, then it is difficult to change."

Let us explore the Pygmalion effects for educational policies on I.Q. and standardized testing generally. Whether we refer to intelligence or aptitude tests or tests of adademic achievement, we are giving teachers a "handle" with which to project the child's future performance on the basis of past tests. The I.Q. tests are considered as the "raw resources" with which the school must work; achievement scores are interpreted as measuring what the school has accomplished.

If a child's raw resources, as shown by his I.Q. test, are minimal, Professor Jane Mercer observes, then his anticipated achievement is expected to be minimal. The same type of reasoning is also used in estimating the anticipated achievement of groups of children. The teacher often looks at the I.Q. score and forms an immediate opinion as to the capabilities and potential of that child, whether right or wrong.

This reasoning is illustrated in the position taken by Joseph Dionne, vice-president of the California Testing Bureau. He explains that the state board of education is charged with the responsibility of providing students with appropriate knowledge, skills, and attitudes. It does so by allocating resources and providing leadership to develop programs designed to accomplish these ends. It cannot provide for the growth of each of the students without adequate knowledge of what he already knows and at what rate he is apt to learn. Standardized tests can help schools know what to expect from their students. If a district has above-average I.Q. students, that district should have above-average performance on the achievement tests, so the argument runs.

A report is prepared for each child which establishes his anticipated achievement. This report is then computerized and distributed to parents and teachers. If, at the end of the school year, the child's achievement score approximates his anticipated achievement, the teacher feels that she has done her best and the parents are so advised.

This computerized, self-fulfilling prophecy provides almost instantaneous feedback to teachers and parents. However, if the child comes from a poverty-level or minority background, he may not do as well on his I.Q. test. His lower performance, nonetheless, is interpreted to mean that he lacks intelligence and has less aptitude for learning than children with the higher I.Q. scores.

Accordingly, if the student does not do well on the school program, for whatever reason, the school can, by way of putting the blame elsewhere, point to the low I.Q. score and explain to the parents:

"We did the best we could with the material with which we have to work. Your son, you can see, just does not have the ability to learn as well as our other students."

That is the easy way out, of course. The I.Q. test scores become the scapegoat for anything that may go wrong in the school system or the classroom.

The present evidence, in the opinion of Dr. Mercer, does not justify the educational practice of using intelligence test scores as "input" variables to establish a child's "raw resources." From these resources, the schools are able to create a self-fulfilling prophecy by predicting the anticipated achievement score for individual children. Since the I.Q. tests and the achievement tests measure essentially the same intellectual qualities, they are highly correlated. Both are heavily influenced by the sociocultural background of the child.

A fundamental confusion in the testing procedure, particularly as it pertains to the I.Q., is the error of mistaking prognosis for diagnosis. Prognosis estimates the probable future success of the child and attempts to predict the outcome, to see how it correlates with the I.Q. score. However, diagnosis investigates the probable cause or nature of a given condition that may exist within the child's makeup and seeks remedies for its correction if that may be found necessary.

Binet's original test, as we know, was designed specifically for prognosis—a prediction that might help determine which children would succeed in the regular school program without special help. However, the I.Q. test, going beyond Binet, is now frequently used as a method to diagnose the child's ability. Too many educators, psychologists, and clinical researchists refer to the I.Q. score as a measure of the child's "raw resources," an entirely wrong assumption.

Nor can we overlook the fact that the criterion used to establish the validity of an intelligence test is the same as that used to establish the validity of an achievement test. Both are now used to predict a child's academic performance, his ability to function in the classroom, and to suggest to the teachers the outer limits that they can expect from a child with a low I.Q. or an equally poor achievement score.

If a child scores 75 on an I.Q. test, the school can usually predict that he needs special help beyond that offered in the regular classroom. The same prognosis can also be made from an academic-achievement test. These tests tell us the scores but they do not tell us why the child scored low or how much extra assistance he may need to maintain his standing in the classroom, on the same basis as other students who have high I.Q. scores.

The net effect, warns Dr. Mercer, has been to shift responsibility for the educational failure of underprivileged or minority children from the schools to the individuals themselves and their families. If the school fails to educate children and can show that these children have a low I.Q. test score, then the school has been able to absolve itself of responsibility for its academic deficiencies. It can interpret the low test scores as a sign of low potential and proclaim that the child is unable to succeed because he does not have the capacity to learn.

Here the self-fulfilling prophecy comes into full play. The teachers, looking at the I.Q. scores, conclude that the child just "doesn't have it" and do not expect him to succeed, whether he tries or not. The child has been computerized and is marked as lacking in academic or mental ability.

Many studies have shown that academic achievement is highly correlated with the student's economic background. Few, however, have attempted to explain exactly how the school helps to reinforce the class structure of society or how the I.Q. can be raised.

Professor Ray C. Rist of Washington University has researched the self-fulfilling prophecy in ghetto education. He has explored the process whereby expectations and social interactions give rise to the social organization of the class. And he found that expectations of the child's abilities, as early as the kindergarten years, may influence the youngster for many years of his school life.

In his study, Dr. Rist found that teachers possess a roughly constructed "ideal type," a gathering of all the characteristics which are necessary for a student to achieve success both in and out of school. Upon first meeting her students at the beginning of the school year, the teacher involved in the Rist project made subjective evaluations of the traits she deemed to be desirable and acceptable.

On the basis of her evaluation, the class was divided into two groups—those who were expected to succeed, the fast learners, and those expected to fail, the slow learners. Different treatment was accorded the two groups in the same classroom. The groups designated as fast learners, with high I.Q.'s, received the majority of the teacher's time, reward, and attention.

Those designated as slow learners were taught infrequently, subjected to more frequent control-oriented behavior, and received little, if any, help from the teacher. The interaction between the teacher and the groups in her class became rigid, taking on castelike characteristics during the school year. The gap in the amount of education the two groups received widened during the year.

A similar process took place in later years. Teachers of the same students in upper grades used information related to past performance as the basis for class grouping.

The Rist report is based on a study that spanned two and one half years with a single group of children. He found within the class the beginning of a caste system, based on socioeconomic conditions. The schools were not able effectively to close the achievement gap that resulted from separating the children on the basis of societal factors rather than intelligence.

It is worth while at this point to quote from the famous Coleman Report (James S. Coleman in *Equality of Educational Opportunity*):

"One implication stands out above all: That schools bring little influence to bear on a child's achievement that is independent of his background and general social context; and that this very lack of independence effect means that the inequalities imposed on children by their home, neighborhood, and poor environment are carried along to become the inequalities with which they confront adult life at the end of school.

"For equality of educational opportunity through the school must imply a strong effect of schools that is independent of the child's immediate social environment, and that strong independent effect is not present in American schools."

Certainly the inequalities of the home and neighborhood, as cited by Coleman, were found by Dr. Rist. Data for his study were collected by means of twice-weekly half-hour observations of a single group of children in an urban school, who began kindergarten at the age permitted by school law in the community. Observations were conducted throughout the kindergarten year and again in the first grade and the first half of their second grade.

Prior to the beginning of the school year, the teacher possessed different sets of information regarding the children she would have in her class. The teacher was supplied with the child's name, his age, parents' names, home address, phone number, and whether he had had any preschool experience.

Two days before school opened, the social worker attached to the school provided the teacher with a list of all children who lived in homes that received public welfare funds.

A third source of information was gained as a result of the initial interview with the mother and child during the registration period. A major concern was the gathering of medical information about the child, as well as finding out if there was any specific parental concern related to the youngster. Twenty-eight items were disclosed, such as thumb-sucking, bed-wetting, loss of bowel control, lying, stealing, fighting, and laziness.

Finally, the teacher gathered information concerning her own experience, if any, with older brothers or sisters of the children who might have been in one of her classes in the past. The teachers' lounge became the location in which teachers in the building would discuss the performance of individual children, as well as make comments concerning the parents and their interest in the school and their children.

Admonitions were given to teachers, by their friendly colleagues, to "watch out" for a child believed to be a "troublemaker."

In this way a variety of information concerning students in the school was shared, such as academic performance, behavior in class, or the relation of the home to the school. However, not one of the sources of information was directly related to the academic potential of the incoming kindergarten child. Instead, they revealed such facts as financial status of families, medical care, presence of a telephone in the home, and the structure of the family in which the child lived.

On the eighth day of school the kindergarten teacher made her permanent seating assignments. During this short time she had observed the children within the classroom setting, their behavior, dress, mannerisms, physical appearance, and performance.

It was evident that the teacher had already formed opinions concerning the capabilities and potentialities of the children. Within a few days, only a certain group of children were called upon to lead the class in the Pledge of Allegiance, read the weather calendar each day, come to the front of the class for "show and tell" periods, pass out materials, be in charge of playground equipment, or lead the class to the library or on a school tour.

Three tables were set up by the teacher. The first criterion appeared to be physical appearance of the child. Children at table 1 were dressed in clean clothes, while most of the children at table 2 and table 3 were poorly dressed. Their clothes were old and dirty. On cold days table 1 children dressed warmly while the children at the other two tables wore thin summer clothes even in winter. Some of the children at tables 2 and 3 came to school with an odor of urine on them.

A second major criterion that separated the children was their behavior among themselves and with the teacher. Children who developed as leaders within the class and spoke more often to the teacher were placed at table 1.

Use of language within the classroom appeared to be the third major differentiation among the children. Those placed at the first table displayed a greater use of standard American English within the classroom, while those at the other two tables responded in slang or ghetto dialect.

The final apparent criterion by which the children at the first or "elite" table differed from the others consisted of a series of social factors known to the teacher prior to her seating the children. At table 1, none of the families were on welfare, no family income fell below $3,000 a year, fathers were employed, more parents had attended high school, and more of the families had both parents living in the home.

Evidently, the teacher had developed her own expectations about the potential performance of each child and then grouped the children according to her perceived similarities in expected performance. The children were grouped solely on the subjective "intuition" of the teacher. They had not, as yet, had I.Q. tests nor any of the reading "readiness exams," unreliable as they are.

The teacher said that children at the first table consisted of her fast learners, while those at the other two tables "had no idea of what was going on in the classroom."

Says Dr. Rist: "What becomes crucial in this discussion is to ascertain the basis upon which the teacher developed her criteria of fast learner, since there had been no formal testing of the children as to their academic ability or capacity for cognitive development."

The assessment of what the children could accomplish was made after only eight days in kindergarten! Those children who most nearly met the teacher's ideal type of the successful child were chosen for seats at table 1. Children who had the least "goodness to fit" were placed at the third table.

What served as the criteria? The attributes most desired by educated members of the middle class—the ability to become a leader, a neat appearance, coming from an educated family, a mother or father who was employed, and a family that lived together.

Here once more is the self-fulfilling prophecy of success or failure. After eight days, the teacher organized the classroom according to her expectation of success or failure. That became the basis for differential treatment for the remainder of the school year. From the day that the children were assigned permanent seats, the activities hinged on two premises: those expected to learn and those destined to fail.

Here are examples of how failure or success can be influenced, directly or indirectly, by the teacher: although the blackboard was long enough to extend parallel to all three tables, the teacher wrote the assignments, such as the arithmetic problems, letters of the alphabet, or various illustrations, on the board in front of the students at table 1. It is an unintentionally cruel and sad instance of how, inadvertently or not, a teacher can hurt a child's ability to learn.

Take this example: Lilly stands up out of her seat. The teacher asks Lilly what she wants. Lilly makes no verbal response to the question. The teacher then says rather firmly to Lilly, "Sit down!" Lilly does. However, Lilly sits down sideways in her chair, so she is still facing the teacher.

The teacher instructs Lilly to put her feet under the table. This Lilly does. Now she is facing the front but in this position she cannot see the teacher or the blackboard clearly. The teacher is demonstrating to the students how to print the letter "O" and other letters of the alphabet. All of this is missed by the child. She is afraid to sit sideways as she doesn't want another reprimand.

By the end of the school year the self-fulfilling prophecy had become apparent. Lack of communication within the classroom with the teacher, lack of involvement in class activities, and infrequent instruction characterized the situation of the children at tables 2 and 3. Throughout the year, the "elite" children at table 1 were favored.

After the school year had closed, Dr. Rist asked the teacher to comment on the children in her class. Of those at the first table, she noted:

"I guess the best way to describe it is that very few children in my class are exceptional. I guess you could notice this just from the way the children were seated this year. Those at table 1 gave consistently the most responses throughout the year, and they all seemed most interested and aware of what was going on in the classroom."

Here are the teacher's comments concerning the other children: "It seems to me that some of the children at table 2 and most of the children at table 3, at times, seem to have no idea of what is going on in the classroom and are off in another world all by themselves. It just appears that some can do it and some cannot. I don't think that it is the teaching that affects these children but they are just basically low achievers."

Not only did the teacher indicate her low esteem of the "inferior" children, but their classmates did, too. Children at table 1 learned, through their teacher, how to behave toward other children who came from low income and poorly educated homes. The teacher, who came from a well-educated, middle-income family, and the children from table 1, who came from a similar background, responded to the children from squalid or poverty homes in a manner strikingly the way their teacher did. Ridicule, scorn, and sarcasm were often used by both the teacher and children at the first table, in their relationship to the other youngsters.

When school reopened after the summer vacation, eighteen of the kindergarten children were assigned to a first-grade teacher. Of these, seven were from the previous year's table 1, six from table 2, and five from table 3.

The first-grade teacher also divided the children into three groups. The children whom she placed at table A had all been in the table 1 group in kindergarten. Not a single child who had been at tables 2 or 3 in kindergarten was placed at table A in the first grade. Instead they were placed at tables B and C.

The seating arrangement that began in kindergarten, as a result of the teacher's definition of which children possessed or lacked the ability to succeed in school, continued. No upward mobility occurred. Of those kindergarten children listed by their earlier teacher as "failures," not one was assigned to the table of the "fast learners" when they entered first grade.

Because the kindergarten teacher had devoted more time to the children at table 1 than to the others, they had completed more material at the end of the school year and were, in fact, the only students in the entire group who had been prepared to undertake first-grade reading material. Now the rope began to bind the children in an academic noose from which escape at this stage, or at almost any stage of their school lives, was virtually impossible.

We now move to the second grade. Of the original thirty students in kindergarten and eighteen in the first grade, ten were assigned to the second-grade class. Again, the children were divided into three groups: the first she called "Tigers," the second was labeled the "Cardinals," and the third was designated as "Clowns." Whether this was done intentionally, to hurt the slow learners is hard to say, but children are sensitive and to be called clowns does not help their self-image any.

The seating arrangement was established on the third day of school! No student from the first grade who had not sat at table A was moved up to the "Tigers." Those who had been at tables B and C were placed in the average or "Cardinal" group. Finally, the "Clowns" consisted of six second-grade repeaters, plus three new students. Of the ten original kindergarten students who came from the first grade, six were "Tigers" and four "Cardinals." The distribution of socioeconomic facts that set off the children in kindergarten continued onward, unchanged and unchecked.

Past performance based on the teachers' expectations of how the child *might* perform governed the seating arrangement. And this arrangement determined the kind of schooling the child would receive during that year and years to come.

The second-grade teacher examined the accumulative record sheets from kindergarten and first grade, examined the I.Q. scores, the reading or arithmetic scores, looked into the parental occupations, and read the evaluation from both the kindergarten and first-grade teachers.

To a major degree, the reading scores made at the end of the first grade served as the basis for the new grouping. The "Tigers" were designated as the highest reading group, the "Cardinals" were average or in the middle, and the "Clowns" were assigned a first-grade reading book, although many were second-grade repeaters and could read beyond first grade.

Again we find the caste system with its self-fulfilling prophecy, dictated by I.Q. and reading scores. The three groups had different reading books. It was the school policy that no child could get a new book until the previous one had been completed. There was no way for the child to advance, even if he was competent and had become a "late bloomer," as he was required to continue at the pace set by the rest of his reading group. Incredible as it sounds, the teacher did not allow individual reading so that a child might finish a book on his own and move ahead. This he was not permitted to do.

No matter how well a child in the lower reading group might now read, he was destined to remain in the same group, reading the same books as his fellow students in this particular section. A slow learner had no option but to continue to be a slow learner, regardless of his performance or potential, because his teachers had signaled him out as such. And a slow learner he remained, not getting the help that the more advanced children were receiving.

Reflect back: the kindergarten children were assigned to their groups after eight days in school. Those placed in the fast group were always encouraged to advance, and they were taught how to read. The others were neglected, not only in learning basic skill subjects, but in every other way. Now we note that the child's progress through the early grades of school appeared to be preordained from the eighth day.

In the second grade, placement was made after the third day. Here the "Tigers," or highest group, received the most attention; the "Cardinals," or average group, a moderate amount; while the "Clowns," or the low children on the academic totem pole, were virtually neglected. Their teacher did not expect them to succeed, and they lived up to her expectations.

These children are similar, in many respects, to others elsewhere who are being deprived of their rightful educational opportunities in schools throughout the country. On the basis of superficial, unscientific, and utterly irrelevant criteria, teachers assign children to groups that are designed to fail. Neither the children nor their parents realize what is taking place.

As Dr. Rist contends:

"Through ridicule, belittlement, physical punishment, and merely ignoring them, the teacher was continually giving clues to those in the high reading group as to how one with high status and a high probability of future success treats those of low status and a low probability of future success."

It is bad enough to be labeled as a slow learner when the facts do not warrant this label, but it is even worse to be treated as one undeservedly. Tell a child that he is bright, and he will do his best to prove to you that you are right. Tell him that he is dumb, a clown, a pumpkin head, and he will not disappoint you.

This story may be apocryphal, but it is all too likely to take place in our schools today. In a school that used the tracking system extensively, an IBM computer was incorrectly programmed. It sent the "slow" students into the "Tigers" or "Bluebirds" top group, and the bright ones to the "dull" section, or the "Clowns." A year later, when the error was brought to light, the slow pupils were behaving as though they were bright, and the bright ones had become dull and listless.

The "Clowns" had turned into "Tigers," thanks to a misplaced comma in a computer. And the "Tigers" meekly assumed the role of the "Clowns." How often do our teachers misplace students so that their potential is wasted! When I.Q. scores are used to separate children, and teacher evaluations place them in castelike tracks, might it not also be possible that the teacher, similar to the computer, can make the wrong decision through a misplaced comma or prejudicial judgment? Decisions are too often made on the basis of middle-class standards that are expected of the students, not learning ability.

Actually, there is little new in the Pygmalion concept. It is usually called by a different name—self-confidence. The image that a child gets of himself in school or at home is the combined results of the I.Q. tests, the teacher reaction to his educational needs, and his parents' acceptance of him as an individual in his own right.

The effects of teacher expectation, the psychology of the teacher's behavior, her reaction to her students, and the inevitable subjectivity that surrounds our teaching profession today are all part of the I.Q. bind in which the schools have placed our children.

14

You don't need a high
I.Q. to be creative

People with high I.Q. scores are not necessarily those who become political leaders, artists, writers, poets, scientists, musicians, or successful businessmen and businesswomen. History is replete with the names of men and women who were low academic achievers and late starters, but became creative in later life.

Examples: Winston Churchill failed English in his early years in school but later won the Nobel Prize for Literature. Albert Einstein had trouble with high school mathematics, only to develop the revolutionary, world-shaking theory of relativity. Louis Pasteur wasn't known as a scholar but through work with "pasteurization" he saved millions of lives. Thomas Edison, one of the greatest inventors this country has ever produced, was called a dunce by his teachers and left school as a failure and dropout.

These, and hundreds of others like them, were underachievers, who did not "blossom" early in youth and would not have been admitted to the better schools and colleges of their day if admission standards had been based on the I.Q. test scores alone, as they are now in many instances.

Studies by Torrance, Guilford, Taylor, Getzels, Jackson, and other prominent psychologists have shown that the creative child is not necessarily academically gifted, as measured by the conventional I.Q. scale. The Stanford-Binet, WISC, Otis-Lennon, Lorge-Thorndike, Peabody, or any of the numerous tests commonly used to measure a child's I.Q. do not measure creativity, imagination, curiosity, or potential leadership.

As presently conducted and utilized, the I.Q. tests screen out a large proportion of creative children. This is a waste of an important national resource at a time when we need as many creative leaders as we can possibly train.

The search for tests to assess creative thinking has been carried out for more than a decade by Dr. E. Paul Torrance, formerly of the University of Minnesota, now in the psychology department at the University of Georgia, as well as by a growing number of other educators who agree that you don't have to possess a high I.Q. to be creative.

Considered to be one of the nation's foremost authorities in the field of creative education, Dr. Torrance has experimented with a variety of approaches, ages, and socioeconomic groups in trying to produce tests which can, to some degree, measure creativity.

Foremost among the tests in the area of creativity, and the one generally accepted as valid, is the Torrance Tests of Creative Thinking. It consists of a battery of tests that sample many types of creative thinking, action, and ability. The tests consist of a series of verbal and figural tasks that require thinking analogous to that involved in recognized creative activities.

For example, the Verbal Tests require such pupil responses as asking questions about pictures, suggesting how an object can be improved, and imagining outcomes of improbable and bizarre situations. In the Figural Tests the pupils are asked to complete open drawings, construct new pictures, and elaborate on common shapes.

These tests are designed, basically, to help teachers and parents become aware of potentialities in children that might otherwise go unnoticed. High creative potential of children may be discovered in these tests which also provide ways to identify and assess individual differences as a step toward individualized teaching. They may serve, as well, as clues for remedial and therapeutic programs.

In Torrance's test on "Thinking Creatively with Words," children respond to such questions as "ask and guess" about a picture, guess at the consequences of various statements, the unusual uses of cardboard boxes, or unusual questions which might begin with the words "just suppose." In the test on "Thinking Creatively with Pictures," children concentrate on picture construction, picture completion, or on how many objects can be made from a group of circles.

The above is a sample of the way "creativity" is tested. There are many variations, but they all have the same objective, that of trying to find if the child, or adult, has any unusual qualities that are not brought out into the open through superficial testing procedures.

Can creativity be taught? Or even more important, can it be detected and encouraged in the classroom? Many psychologists now agree, although they have their critics, that there are two types of talent: academic and creative. Since it has become obvious, over the years, that the Binet and other similar I.Q. tests do not measure creativity, one cannot say that a child does not have creative talent because he has a low I.Q. Many of the special programs for gifted children, almost always based on high I.Q. scores, may prove harmful to the creative child who does not conform to the standards expected of him by his teacher or parents.

Whether creativity can be assessed to some degree of accuracy through the newly designed tests is subject to a bitter controversy, not quite as sharp as that which has divided the academic world on the reliability of the I.Q. tests, but, nonetheless, of growing concern to educators who believe that there is more than one aspect to intelligence. Indeed, Professor Guilford has isolated 120 separate components of the child's intelligence, which, in his opinion, are significant in the measurement of any child to determine existing or potential ability.

Claiming that creativity cannot be measured, let alone taught in the classroom by conventional methods, Dr. Robert L. Ebel, former president of the American Educational Research Association, maintains that those who try to teach people to be creative in a general way, or who test children for creativity, are doing little but chasing a will-o-the-wisp. Creative achievement, in his opinion, depends on special abilities and a special personal inner drive to create original design, write poetry, or fashion clay or cloth into unusual objects.

Answering these and other criticisms leveled at those who would separate the I.Q. score from the creativity score, Dr. Torrance asserts that the skills of creative thinking can be taught and are applicable to classroom situations. Of course, teachers are a key here, too, as they are in any teaching situation.

Dr. Torrance has found that a correlation exists between the early detection of creativity and the later performance of those who gave evidence of having creative talent. Dr. Torrance gave a series of creativity tests to high school students, while he was in Minnesota, and he found that performance on the tests related significantly to their creative achievements as adults, twelve years later.

Children designated as creative in the Torrance tests later obtained original and exceptional achievements in art, writing, and scientific projects. The students were asked to list three peak achievements that, to them, epitomized the highlights of their career up to the present time. A significant difference was found between those who had, earlier in high school, been labeled as creative children, and those found to be noncreative.

A student who, while in high school, was ranked as highly creative, twelve years later ranked his "peak achievements" as first, "research in enzymology of human lactate dehydrogenase and development of an electrophoretic assay system for quantification from serum." His second "peak" achievement was listed as the "planning and construction of my cabin in northern Minnesota," while his third was in the area of his hobby, oil painting.

Another student in the high creative group stopped working for a stock brokerage firm, not because the work was bad, but "very silly" and dead-ending. She is now in Spain, has written three novels, compiled a volume of poetry, and has written and performed songs for the guitar, which she plays professionally.

A rather common note in the accounts of the high creative group is the desire to escape, at least temporarily, from society's "rat race," and then to return and contribute in some unique way to society.

On the other hand, those who were labeled as "low creatives" while in high school, reported as their peak achievements "copout" or "dropout" experiences, unaccompanied by any form of constructive action, either in their own personal lives, or as a contribution to society. For example, one of the men in this group listed as his three best achievements, those of which he could boast the most and of which he was proudest: dodging the draft, dropping out of college, and taking LSD.

From the results of this experiment, Dr. Torrance concludes that young adults identified as highly creative while in their early years in high school more frequently than their less creative classmates, as measured by the creativity tests, attained their peak creative achievements in writing, medical and surgical discovery, research, musical composition, style of teaching, and human relations.

On the elementary school level, too, creativity can be unearthed and taught by alert, sympathetic, and understanding teachers. Reporting on a study he made with two first-grade classes, Dr. Torrance found that the creative growth and creative functioning of the children in an experimental program substantially exceeded that of the control group who were not subject to any deliberate teaching effort to develop their creative ability. Children who are involved in creative learning and more unusual teaching are motivated to read more books, ask more questions, conduct more challenging experiments, and develop their creative endeavors outside the classroom in ways that are foreign to the routine-minded child who does not see beyond his class reader.

Today, I am pleased to note, more classrooms are using educational products to stimulate children's creativity and imagination. These include a great variety of books, films, recordings, games, and other materials designed to facilitate creative learning and teaching. An attempt to develop creative thinking has become an integral part of almost all methods of implementing the curriculum in forward-looking schools.

How much do we know about the role of the I.Q. and creativity in education? Some critics maintain that the experimental and evaluative studies, made by Dr. Torrance and his colleagues, are unreliable because they are based upon "so-called" creativity tests for which there is no evidence of validity, and that the link between test performance and real-life achievement does not exist and cannot be measured.

This is a controversy that may take years to resolve with finality, but enough evidence exists to indicate that creativity can, to some extent at any rate, be detected, nourished, and made to bloom. It depends, of course, on how one defines creativity. A person may be creative in many ways. He can be a pediatrician, for example, as was William Carlos Williams, who was also a Pulitzer Prize-winning poet. Leonardo da Vinci was a talented engineer and a memorable great painter. Albert Schweitzer was a world-famous physician and a superb interpreter of Bach in his organ playing. There was no way that an I.Q. test could have measured the talents of these men.

Moreover, although it is recognized that socioeconomic and racial differences are inherent in the standardized I.Q. tests, this is not true for tests designed to measure creativity. Various studies have shown that when creativity tests were given to groups of black and white children, the black children excelled the white ones on certain tasks in the test and the white children excelled the blacks on others. A similar situation took place when socioeconomic status differences were studied.

A major reason may be that the items found in creativity tests are not multiple choice, with only one answer marked "correct." A child may respond to most of the items on the test in terms of his own life experience. This, of course, is not possible on the I.Q. tests.

Creative abilities are not inheritable. You don't have to be the son of a scientist to become a scientist, or the daughter of a painter to follow in your father's footsteps. There is no 80–20 ratio for creative heredity, as Dr. Jensen says there is for the I.Q. scores. Educators and parents can modify the creative abilities of their children. Educational programs that build competencies in creative thinking can prove successful in developing the latent talents of their pupils.

Psychologist Susan Houston, a colleague of Dr. Torrance, has identified a number of reasons why disadvantaged black children customarily get lower scores than advantaged white children on scholastic achievement and I.Q. tests, so heavily loaded with verbal items. She maintains that, ironically enough, their creative talents actually interfere with their success on the I.Q. tests.

In her studies of poor children in the South, who lacked material playthings, the psychologist found that these children engaged in constant play language and verbal contests among themselves, of a primitive nature, perhaps, but requiring ingenuity and the thought process. For example, they made up games and situations with high creativity value, although they did not realize that they were doing this. They also fabricated, elaborated upon, and spun out highly imaginative stories, all part of the creativity process, but a natural outlet for children who had to rely upon their own limited home or street resources for their "fun and games."

They interacted more with one another and developed skills in group interaction which far excelled those of other children of the same age.

From George Witt's long-range experiment, cited in the 1971 *Journal of Research and Development in Education,* we know that it is possible to develop high levels of both academic achievement and creative talents among disadvantaged children who are identified early in their school or even preschool lives as having creative potential. The children were given an opportunity to build upon their exceptional creative abilities. Second- and third-grade children, selected on the basis of creative talents, have distinguished themselves in one or more of the creative arts, sciences, and literature.

Five-year-olds were able to attain unusual heights in original thinking. They showed enormous growth in both verbal and nonverbal areas, excelling the control groups with which they were matched on every measure of originality devised for them. In some instances children at the end of their first grade, having been "taught" creativity, received higher scores on creative talents, originality, and imagination than did fifth-grade children.

A group of six-year-olds had entered upon special training in creative abilities at the age of three, prior to kindergarten. Now, in the first grade, they had progressed to an amazing extent. A visit to their classroom showed that they worked quietly as individuals and in small groups, learning, inquiring, and experimenting. Their teacher was delighted. The six-year-olds were self-disciplined. There was no bickering, fighting, or pushing, the kinds of behavior normally found in first-grade classes.

A creativity test given to them at this time showed that these children produced far more original ideas on both the verbal and figural measures of creative thinking than did a control group of first-graders, as well as a number of other first-grade classes tested during the year.

An alert teacher, aware of the importance of bringing out the creative talents within her children, can prove extremely helpful to those who score low on the I.Q. tests, yet are basically intelligent and possess untapped abilities.

Jimmy was always looked upon as a dreamer. As a fourth-grader he lagged behind his classmates in reading and arithmetic. And no wonder: from kindergarten on, when his I.Q. was listed as 85 he found himself neglected by his teachers, always relegated to the back row. But then came a creativity test, offered on an experimental basis. The psychologist was amazed at Jimmy's responses. Although looked upon as the "dummy" of the class when it came to reading or writing, he came out near the top of his class on virtually every aspect of the test on creativity. He had the finest imagination; he could outguess his classmates on the "guess what" section of the test. He listed scores of unusual replies to many of the routine questions.

Above all, the test opened the eyes of Jimmy's teacher. Suddenly she realized that the lad could draw, that he was adept with his paintbrush. Primitive, to be sure, but so was Grandma Moses. The teacher encouraged him to draw. Now a sparkle came to Jimmy's eyes, the eyes that had for many years in school been dull and listless. His posters were displayed on the bulletin board, with his name in the right-hand corner, large enough for all to read. For the first time, probably since he entered school four years ago, he received a word of praise from his teacher, compliments from his classmates, rather than scorn.

Then Jimmy showed other creative talents. He became the class storyteller, using his brilliant imagination to compensate for his grammatical lapses.

"Tell us a story, Jimmy," his classmates begged, during the "free" period. And Jimmy obliged. His fantasy and vision roamed, and the tales he spun so naturally captivated the excited children.

"Jimmy is a new boy now," his teacher told me, a smile engulfing her face. "Forget his I.Q. I'm going to throw that score out. I've asked the guidance counselor for a retest."

The new score was a respectable 118. Not a genius, but then, not a clown. Given an opportunity to express his creative abilities, he blossomed forth as a happy, earnest, well-behaved child. If it had not been for the test on creativity, and if his storytelling abilities and artistic talents had not been discovered, Jimmy would have remained the clown of the class until his peak achievement would have been to "drop out."

"His classwork has improved, too," his teacher marveled. "He is not the class dunce any longer. He is one of the group, fully accepted, as well as respected and admired."

Just what constitutes a suitable environment to encourage creativity has led to much controversy. However, it's obvious that the classroom was just what Jimmy needed, plus, of course, the encouragement that his teacher gave him. It is altogether possible that creative talent will perish under the prolonged stress of unfavorable circumstances and constant neglect, as indeed it surely would have with Jimmy.

Is there any way that parents and teachers can recognize the child who is creative, so as to encourage him to achieve greater heights? The I.Q. score will not give the necessary clue, or any clue at all. What, then, will? Dr. Torrance suggests that parents or teachers should seek these traits, characteristics, or attributes in the child:

Ability to express his feelings and emotions, enjoyment of and ability in visual art, expressive speech, unique solutions in problem-solving, fluency and flexibility in nonverbal media, expressiveness of gestures, body language, humor, richness of imagination in informal language, emotional responsiveness, enjoyment of and ability in music, rhythm, dance, or dramatics.

Academic grades and I.Q. scores cannot predict creative potential in the child, nor is sheer accumulation of knowledge any indication. Many persons well versed in the academic field, fountainheads of encyclopedic knowledge, show little creative talent.

Creative children have strong drives toward music, art, writing, invention, or dozens of other traits not uncovered by the traditional I.Q. test.

An attempt to differentiate between the highly creative and the high I.Q. adolescent has beeen made by Professors Getzels and Jackson of Chicago, in a U. S. Office of Education sponsored study. They examined the achievement, fantasy production, school performances, and teacher preferences of two types of students—those exceptionally high in creativity but not in I.Q. scores, and those high in I.Q. scores but not in creativity.

All of the students enrolled in a Midwestern private high school were given I.Q. tests, using the Stanford-Binet, the WISC, or the Henmon-Nelson. They were also tested on these five creativity items: word association, uses of things, hidden shapes, fables, and makeup problems.

Interestingly enough, the intellectually high I.Q. group, rather than the high creative group, was preferred by the teachers, when asked whom they would like to have as students in their classrooms. It is not difficult to understand why. Those in the creative group made greater use of stimulus, free themes, unexpected endings, humor, incongruities, and playfulness—qualities which disturbed at times the routine and classroom procedures of the teacher.

Here is an example of the different approach used by the high I.Q. and the high creative children, cited by Getzels and Jackson:

The students were asked to tell a story about a picture, without a caption. All they saw in the picture was a man, evidently flying in an airplane, sitting on a reclining seat, possibly returning from a business trip or conference.

A high I.Q. student wrote: "Mr. Smith is on his way home from a successful business trip. He is very happy and he is thinking about his wonderful family and how glad he will be to see them again. He can picture it, about an hour from now, his plane landing at the airport and Mrs. Smith and their three children all there welcoming him home again."

A child in the high creative but not necessarily high I.Q. group wrote:

"This man is flying back from Rome where he has just won a divorce from his wife. He couldn't stand to live with her any more, he told the judge, because she wore so much cold cream on her face at night that her head would skid across the pillow and hit him in the head. He is now contemplating a new skidproof face cream."

Another picture showed a man evidently working late at night, or very early in the morning, at his office.

Wrote a high I.Q. student:

"There's ambitious Bob, down at the office at six-thirty in the morning. Every morning it's the same. He's trying to show his boss how energetic he is. Now, thinks Bob, maybe the boss will give me a raise for all my extra work. The trouble is that Bob has been doing this for the last three years, and the boss still hasn't given him a raise. He'll come in at nine o'clock, not even noticing that Bob has been there so long, and poor Bob won't get his raise."

This is what a student with a high creative score wrote:

"This man has just broken into the office of a new cereal company. He is a private eye employed by a competitor firm to find out the formula that makes the cereal bend, sag, and sway. After a thorough search of the office he comes upon what he thinks is the correct formula. He is now copying it. It turns out that it is the wrong formula and the competitor's factory blows up. Poetic justice!"

These themes were written in group sessions, with a maximum writing time of four minutes per story. Note that the high creative students bring out such unique expressions as "skidproof face cream" or "cereal that will bend, sag, and sway." Getzels and Jackson observe that the ability to restructure stereotyped objects with ease and rapidity, almost naturally, appears to be the characteristic mark of the highly creative child as opposed to the one with a high I.Q. score.

The essence of creativity, it would appear, lies in the ability to produce new forms, to join elements and situations that are usually thought of as being independent or dissimilar. The creative child, going beyond the art of seeing the bizarre in what may appear to most of us as routine, can inject new meanings into everyday situations, giving them social value.

Moreover, the attitudes and goals of the two groups of children are different. The high I.Q. children ranked the qualities in which they would like to be considered outstanding in this order: character, emotional stability, goal directednesss, creativity, wide range of interests, high marks, high I.Q. score, and a sense of humor.

Creative children listed the traits that they thought to be of greatest importance to them this way: emotional stability, sense of humor, character, wide range of interests, goal directedness, creativity, high marks, and a high I.Q. score.

Children in the creative group gave "sense of humor" an extremely high ranking, but thought a high I.Q. score to be the least important trait of all, as far as they were concerned.

Evidently the high I.Q. adolescent wants and admires the qualities he believes make for adult success and appear to be similar to those that his teachers prefer. Little wonder, then, that the teachers would rather have a roomful of children who have high I.Q. scores but may be short on the creative side.

On the other hand, the creative child favors personal qualities which have no relationship to those that make for adult success. In some ways, too, they are the reverse of what the teachers favor. The creative student appears to be more rebellious and more independent in his thinking and actions than the high I.Q. child as far as adult standards of success are concerned. In most respects, the student with a high I.Q. score is complacent, realistic, and wants to succeed in an adult world once he leaves the classroom.

But the creative child wants to free himself from the usual, to diverge from customary behavior, enjoy the risk and uncertainty of the unknown. He would follow the advice of Robert Frost who chose the least traveled road, "and that made all the difference."

For whatever reason, the high I.Q. students possess ability but need to focus on the usual, to be channeled and controlled in the direction of right answers and socially accepted solutions. They shy away from the risk and uncertainty of the unknown. Rather they seek safety and security. They tend to converge upon stereotyped meanings, to perceive personal success by conventional standards, to move toward the model provided by their teachers, to seek careers that conform to what is expected of them and that will guarantee success and social acceptance.

On the other hand, the high creative students diverge from stereotypes. They seek careers that do not usually conform to what society, their teachers, their classmates, or even their parents expect of them. They are the ones who follow their own beliefs and ideals, who express themselves freely and are known as nonconformists, much to the dismay, or sometimes delight, of their family, friends, or teachers. In every respect, they are the divergent thinkers, unaware of the reactions that they may cause in following their own paths.

"Johnny may be bright—he is always coming up with unexpected ideas—but he sure is a pest," says Mrs. Jones, the prim third-grade teacher. "I wish he were more like Thomas, who is neat, pays attention to what I say, and never forgets to do his homework. Too much daydreaming is Johnny's problem, if you ask me. I wish he could be transferred to another class."

Obviously, the creative child needs an imaginative, sympathetic, nonconforming, creative teacher. In describing one of the three creative teachers he had known during his school years, author John Steinbeck wrote:

"She aroused us to shouting, bookwaving discussions. She had the noisiest class in school, and she didn't even seem to know it. We could never stick to the subject, geometry, or the chanted recitation of the memorized phylo. Our speculation ranged the world." A good creative teacher!

Writing in the Harvard-sponsored *Inequality in Education,* Dr. Shephard Ginandes reports that many of the students he meets are tracking victims. Some are tracked lower than they should be, while others are tracked with the intellectual elite, above their ability. When a student is placed in a group below his mental or intellectual level, he becomes bored and stifled. His desire to learn frequently withers, wanes, and ultimately dies. To him, school becomes a perpetual torture.

When students are unfairly tracked into an advanced program, they, too, are often beset with excessive pressure from their teachers. Scorn and criticism may be leveled at them, such as: "Surely you can do better than that. You are in the advanced, bright group, you know."

Thus we find that in the slow tracks, mediocrity and boredom frequently exist. In the fast, accelerated groups, anxiety and loss of self-image can take place.

For the creative child, with or without a high I.Q., the atmosphere in a tracking program limits his exposure to a variety of experiences, and he is punished, emotionally if not physically, because he is "different." He soon realizes that orderliness, systematic thinking, promptness, neatness, and general conformity to middle-class values are the qualities desired, often demanded, by his teachers and their supervisors. But he also recognizes, try as he may, that he will never be able to perform, and still be true to himself, within those structured limitations.

Teachers, too, suffer from the rigid standards of behavior and curriculum requirement imposed upon them by their principals and administrators. A highly creative high school art teacher was dismissed from a post she had held for some years because she did not conform to unyielding regulations. The main complaints against her were that she permitted too much student movement in her class, her classroom was untidy, the blackboards were not washed clean at the end of the day, and she permitted the class to deviate from the requirements set by the school board.

In every respect she was a creative teacher, but she was charged with disobeying school rules generally and was seen, by those in authority, as an "odd ball," unlike the conventional and obedient attitude expected of teachers. Like so many of her students, who were responsive and appreciative of her unorthodox methods, she felt that rigidity and conformity to arbitrary, sometimes unnecessary, rules were less important than evoking the utmost creative talent in her students.

A teacher of English was not given tenure, at the end of her third year of teaching, because an administrator, entering her high school classroom, found her students dancing and cavorting around the room to poetry of e.e. cummings, played on a victrola. Her explanation that poetry is music and that the students were discovering its rhythm and its beauty through this original method was not accepted.

"We don't teach poetry that way here," the supervisor told her, with finality.

The attitude of many school boards is that all students should be exposed to the more routinized, traditional, conventional teachers. Creative children, accordingly, will be confined in class situations where the teachers are bound by their own rules to stress the routine side of education and to be unaware of the needs, desires, goals, ambitions, or emotional makeup of these children.

A skilled teacher learns to structure the classroom setting in a way to elicit talent, as well as creative and original thinking in her students, if her school board or supervisors so permit. She can become active in structuring a variety of situations, in posing "thought" not "textbook" questions, in observing the reaction of the students, and in stimulating and challenging the talents that many creative children possess. In this way, teachers may discover that nearly all students have some degree of creativity or some undiscovered talent, ready to be brought to the surface by a sympathetic and understanding teacher.

To help develop students' abilities in creative thinking, for example, a teacher had her class project the economic and social situation it will face twenty-five years hence, by asking the students to imagine that they were all delegates to the United Nations or members of the Cabinet of the President of the United States.

Another teacher asked her twelfth-grade class to compile a book of twentieth-century American poetry. This involved intensive reading and research, plus an introduction written by each student who gave reasons why he selected the particular poems. The teacher thus used literature, grammar, punctuation skills, and composition writing as a clever and challenging project in an English class. Moreover, the students enjoyed their assignment and used their creative abilities to the fullest.

A first-grade teacher took her class to a bakery where they watched the making of bread as it was prepared for baking. They saw the ovens, the dough being kneaded, and the finished product. The teacher followed up this visit for the day in the classroom by teaching them, when they returned to school the next day, about the various grains which are used in bread in many countries around the world. As they learned about these faraway countries, she told them something about each land's history and geography, using slides, movies, and pictures. She brought in materials for breadmaking and the first-graders mixed them, then baked them in the oven of the stove in the teachers' room. The parents' reaction to this project was that their children showed a new and tremendous interest in "how things are made." If any creativity lay within the child, he was stimulated, with the help of this kind of teaching, to develop it.

At a school in Utah, as reported by Professor Taylor, teachers used the teaching-for-talents approach within the regular curriculum. Talent totem poles were designed to illustrate this multiple-talent pattern. Cartoon drawings representing individual pupils were ranked on each of the six talents that were to be developed. The teacher placed the names of her twenty-eight second-graders on each of the totem poles, after working with every pupil to discover which talents he possessed and in which he excelled. She found that every pupil was well above the class average in at least one creative talent, and that the child was delighted to see his name high up on the totem pole.

High I.Q.'s and creativity did not, in any way, correlate at this school. The seven children who scored highest on academic talents were less promising as a group than any of the three academically lower groups on such talents as creating, planning, communicating, forecasting, and decision-making.

Academically talented children were found to have high ratings on talents that are necessary to get good grades in school, such as receiving, storing, and retrieving information—in other words, memorization and recall. Since they can reproduce information that they have memorized, they also do well on I.Q. and standardized achievements tests.

The creative thinkers, unlike the high I.Q. "memorizers," are able to develop original ideas and methods. They may take a unique way to solve problems, but they usually find the appropriate means to do so. Dr. Taylor, who conducted the Utah experiment, makes the following observations:

Students who are talented in planning have the ability to organize their time, work, play, and associate effectively with other people. Those talented in communicating are able to express themselves fluently and effectively. They are also able to understand others in their various methods of communication.

Children talented in forecasting have the ability to predict outcomes of problems or situations. They can forsee difficulties or conditions that will require future adjustments and new solutions. The creative teacher uses these talents in both the classroom and in her program planning.

Talented, decision-making students have the ability to view many alternatives, to gather relevant information from many sources, to come to a logical decision, and to explain, justify and, if necessary, defend it.

Despite the knowledge that we have gained from the studies made by Taylor and other psychologists dealing with creativity, few students benefit from new research-based opportunities to develop their intellectual talents, other than academic, in the regular classroom. As a consequence, many apparently successful students may actually be handicapped for the rest of their lives, never having recognized or fostered their creative talents. Teaching primarily for scores on the I.Q. or standardized achievement tests can often result in depriving students of much of their potential creative abilities. Moreover, if this pattern persists, as it so often does, during the school years of the child, many of his talents and abilities may never be discovered or cultivated and may be permanently buried.

Along with existing tests of neglected talents, developed in recent years, appropriate new tailor-made measuring devices have been constructed and used at several schools. For example, the Student Activities Questionnaire is a multiple-choice, classroom-climate test developed for fifth- and sixth-grade children. It presumes to yield these eight measures of academic and creative information concerning each child: Individualized instruction, enjoyment of school, classroom participation, career development, self-concept, independent development, democratic classroom control, and multiple-talent experiences. Other pertinent items that can be measured, such as human relationships and values, can readily be added when deemed important.

The program works. Fifth- and sixth-graders at the Utah school were compared on the Student Activities Questionnaire and other measures with children of similar grades from another school, serving as a control group. The experimental school outscored the controls in every one of the fifty-eight comparisons that were made.

Carrying the experiment further, it was found that the children who had been involved in the special creative program adapted themselves better to junior high school and functioned much better than a comparable group of classmates who had attended a structured, traditional elementary school.

The multiple-talent teaching approach conceives of students as thinkers, not merely learners. Teachers who employ this method allow youngsters to think, plan, and produce. In this way, programs are designed for the child, not for a teaching program.

In a New Hampshire vocational technical college, where one third of the students usually drop out at the end of the first year, all of the first-year students who were placed in the multiple-talent program returned the following year. They had more fully developed those talents which, it was fully expected, would help them advance in their careers and professions after they had completed their schooling.

At present, the emphasis is almost entirely on the academic side of the child's development, based on the I.Q. score. Creativity is all too often neglected. But it is just as important as high grades or a high I.Q. Creativity can be cultivated, depending on the teacher, the curriculum, the school philosophy, or the proper motivation of the child. A creative child, working with a creative teacher, will not be bound by rigid, inflexible academic rules or regulations.

There is no limit as to what can be accomplished if the parent or teacher understands the child's needs and then permits him to express himself in his own manner, unorthodox as it may be. Unfortunately, because the emphasis is almost entirely on the verbal or mathematical I.Q. score, thousands of young boys and girls are overlooked each year, their talents undiscovered and uncultivated.

Who knows how many Einsteins, Beethovens, Edisons, Pasteurs, or Shakespeares, how many musicians, artists, scientists, or physicians are lost to the world because we do not recognize that creativity can be developed and nourished in the classroom and home, completely freed from the ever-recurring, threatening shadow of the I.Q. score?

We must recognize that often the creative child is the nonconformist, the unruly child, the one who causes his parents and teachers heartache, pain, and administrative problems.

Rather than having him sent to the principal's office or banished to his room, the rebellious child should be considered as the unhappy child whose peculiar talents and creative abilities are ignored and repressed. The daydreamer in the classroom is bored because the math class, or the lesson on grammar, is dull and meaningless to him. While listening to a boring lecture or discussion, he is perhaps thinking how he can make or invent a new type of airplane or write a really good detective story.

He may be a late starter, a poor academic student, a difficult and unruly child, but we must remember that he marches to the beat of a different drummer.

Human intelligence has been broken down into various components. Out of Dr. Guilford's studies has come a unified theory of human intellect. This concept organizes the known, unique, or primary intellectual abilities into a single system and is called the "structure of intellect."

Some persons do well on certain sections of an I.Q. test and poorly on others. What are the various aspects of intelligence that bring about this diversified pattern?

Cognition and memory are two areas of this variation; in simpler terms, we can call them discovery and retention. We conjecture in different directions in divergent thinking, but, in convergent thinking the information can lead to only one answer, the one that is called the "right" one. Evaluation of material is a process of reaching decisions as to goodness, correctness, suitability, or adequacy based on knowledge, memory, and an individual system of values. Still another way to classify intellectual factors is response to certain material or content which involves figural, symbolic, or semantic meanings.

In one of Dr. Guilford's tests for intellectual creativity, the student is expected to express novel, unusual, clever, or farfetched ideas. An illustration of this type of intellectual probing is offered by Dr. Guilford under the title "The Plot Titles Tests." A short story is presented. The student is then asked to list as many appropriate titles as he can as a title to the story.

For example, one story describes the plight of a missionary who has been captured by cannibals in Africa. He is in the pot and about to be boiled when a princess of the tribe obtains a promise for his release if he will become her mate. He refuses and is boiled to death.

In scoring the tests, the responses are separated into two categories, clever and nonclever. Examples of clever, or creative, responses are considered, among others to be these: "Pot's Plot," "Potluck Dinner," "Stewed Parson," "Goil or Boil," "A Mate Worse than Death," "He left a Dish for a Pot," "Chase in Haste," and "A Hot Price for Freedom."

Noncreative, nonclever responses are seen as these: "African Death," "Defeat of a Princess," "Eaten by Savages," "The Princess," "The African Missionary," "In Darkest Africa," and "Boiled by Savages."

Another test of originality and creativity asks the students to write "punch lines" for cartoons, a task that often challenges the students to present out-of-the-ordinary, nonroutine answers.

Since fifty intellectual factors are already known, there are at least fifty ways of expressing intelligence, few of which can be detected on the traditional I.Q. tests. Dr. Guilford has prepared a theoretical model, or structure, of intellect that predicts as many as 120 distinct abilities, with the possibility that it may go well beyond this number.

How, then, can we say that a child's I.Q. is 110, 130 or 150, based on an intelligence test that measures only two of these more than 120 abilities? A multiple-score approach for the further assessment of intellect, whether academic or creative, appears obvious. Broad categories of intelligence must be considered; concrete, abstract, and social intelligence cannot be overlooked or discarded.

The implications for education, and this includes teachers, parents, and students, are momentous. If education has the stated objective of developing the intellect of students, each intellectual factor provides a particular goal that must be uncovered, developed, and encouraged.

Considering the tremendous variety of abilities that are found in the intellect—at least 120 isolated by Dr. Guilford—educators must ask whether appropriate balances are being made not to neglect one aspect of schooling and overemphasize another. We may need a better balance of training in the divergent-thinking intellectual areas as compared with training in convergent thinking and in critical thinking or evaluation.

Schools are presently biased in favor of convergent thinking, and this is the mainstay of our I.Q. tests. Creativity, as expressed through divergent thinking, is frowned upon and given short shrift in schools today. We attempt to teach our students how to arrive at answers that society or its majority members say are "correct." Outside the arts, and not always there, we have generally discouraged the development of divergent-thinking abilities, perhaps unintentionally, but effectively nonetheless.

Failure to distinguish between convergent and divergent talent in our schools may have serious consequences for the future welfare of our society. Both types of talents are sufficiently important to warrant attention in educational theory and practice. It is unwise to think of divergent fantasy as simply rebellious or unconventional career choice as invariably unrealistic rather than courageous. Actually, a multidimensional approach to the study of creativity will help develop an increased appreciation of the "motivational and cognitive variability of children."

Further evidence that points to the premise that the I.Q. is not an indicator of creativity comes from a research project conducted by Professors Michael A. Wallach and Nathan Kogan. They define creativity in these two ways:

First—The flow of ideas. The teacher and parent should consider how unique and abundant are the kinds of ideas that a child can provide when contemplating various sorts of tasks.

Second—The establishment of an environment for the student in which he feels free to experiment with ideas and inventions at his own pace. He is to know that these are not going to be tested and evaluated by the usual educational standards.

The procedure involved in the experiment with fifth-grade, middle-class children, by Professors Wallach and Kogan, consisted of testing each child separately. The child was asked to suggest possible uses for each of several everyday objects, or to describe possible ways in which each of several pairs of objects, with which they were familiar, were similar to each other.

For example, in one case, the child was asked to suggest all the different ways in which we could use such objects as a newspaper, a cork, a shoe, or hair.

"Rip it up, if angry," was a unique response for the use of a newspaper; "make paper hats" was not considered especially unusual.

In another instance, the child was asked to suggest the similarities that might exist between a potato and a carrot, a cat and a mouse, milk and meat.

A unique response, showing creativity, for the way milk and meat were similar might be the one suggested by a child: "They are both government inspected." The answer, "They come from animals," was not considered unique or unusual.

In yet another test, the child was asked to indicate all the things that each of a number of abstract drawings might represent. For a triangle with three circles around it, "Three mice eating a piece of cheese" was called creative originality, while "Three people sitting around a table" was scored as being a routine answer, without any original talent expressed.

The number of ideas that a child suggested and the originality of those ideas were recorded. In addition, a variety of traditional techniques, or the usual I.Q. test, was used with the same children to assess general intelligence.

A significant finding was that a correlation did not exist between intelligence, as measured by the I.Q. test, and creativity, as shown in the test for originality and uniqueness. A creative child was just as likely to have a low I.Q. as a high one. The researchers found that the chances that a child of high intelligence would also display high creativity were no more than fifty-fifty, or merely a chance relationship without significance. It would appear that, in schoolchildren at any rate, creativity is a different type of cognitive excellence than is general intelligence.

How would Bach, Beethoven, Brahms, Picasso, Van Gogh, Stravinsky, Browning, Keats, or Rodin have fared on an I.Q. test slanted toward mathematics, neglecting art, music, or literature in any form?

Psychologists studied two hundred young artists who were, for the most part, still students at one of the leading art schools in the country. Some of them were already winning prizes in competitive shows, exhibiting in professional galleries, or supporting themselves on the proceeds of their artistic skills.

The study compared the art students with a cross section of the college population as a whole to see how values might differ on these six dimensions or traits: economic, aesthetic, social, political, theoretical, and religious.

While economic values were near the top for the average college student, the art student ranked financial values and the desire to make money near the bottom of the list. On the other hand, the artists had much higher aesthetic values than the other students. Nothing but art seemed to be of real importance and to have a sustaining interest for the young artists.

Second to the aesthetic values held high by the art students came the "theoretical" values. This confirms the results of other studies that found creative persons in various professions to hold both aesthetic and theoretical concepts as being among their most desirable characteristics. This might also suggest why artists generally, with exceptions of course, are likely to be economically poor, in comparison with the rest of the population, and are lonely and disapproved of, or even rejected, by society. They are looked upon as "different," living a Bohemian life in an unheated attic. Does this bother them? Apparently not at all.

From the study emerges a personality profile of the artist as self-sufficient, introspective, and socially withdrawn, by the prevailing standards of American society. These traits are linked to creativity. A personality test, similar to the one given to the artists, was also administered to three hundred eminent scientists. The composite profile of the scientists bore a striking resemblance to that of the artists, suggesting that creativity has common traits.

Various I.Q. tests were given to the artists. They were found to be of average intelligence, at least as indicated by the scores they made on these tests. Thus, although a person can become a noted artist without possessing a high I.Q., these tests would screen out the potential artists from any academic or artistic program that depended solely on the I.Q. scores or, at the least, placed substantial faith in them.

Creativity can be encouraged, nurtured, and measured directly through tests, indirectly through observation. The creativity tests are still imperfect and should only be used as a guide. But they do indicate the latent talents of young as well as mature students. It is rather obvious that the I.Q. tests do not measure, and are not able to predict, the creative child.

New "I.Q." tests should include C.Q. for Creativity Quotient, P.Q. for Potential Quotient, S.Q. for Social Quotient, A.Q. for Academic Quotient, E.Q. for Emotional Quotient, S.Q. for Social-economic Quotient, and D.Q. for Disadvantaged Quotient. In fact, if we must have tests, let's develop a complete alphabetical scale, similar to the alphabet soup that children love to eat, which may, or may not, be nourishing for the child's education if it can help develop more facets of his intellect than the rigid and circumscribing I.Q. score.

Or better still, let's eliminate all of the existing I.Q. tests that have a destructive, rather than constructive, influence on American education.

15

What research has found
out about the I.Q.

As we have seen, enough evidence exists, through a half century of research, to suggest strongly that I.Q. scores have little value in predicting a child's future potential. Children, like adults, respond to the type of stimulation, both in school and at home, that can encourage them to succeed. The parent, the teacher, or even the scout leader can influence the growing child and infuse values and goals into his life that will motivate him toward success and fulfillment.

The I.Q. is not static. It can be manipulated through special environmental changes. Even in the case of mentally retarded children placed in selected training schools, psychologists Benjamin M. Braginsky and Dorothea D. Braginsky found that the retardate's life can frequently be "normal" and that many of these children are adept, rational, and resourceful.

They also learned that the so-called retarded child or adult can, to some extent, control his I.Q. performance. If he so desires, he can register a lower score; if motivated for his benefit to do so, he can raise his I.Q. score. The Braginskys reported their findings in the March 1974 issue of *Psychology Today*.

They administered an I.Q. test to children sequestered in an institution for the retarded. Each person took a short vocabulary test and when the paper was completed it was, ostensibly, crumpled and tossed into a wastebasket, with the remark that this was just a trial. It wasn't! The real test would begin soon, they were told, and were informed that they were being tested because state officials wanted to select a number of them for a program in another institution.

The examiner explained that she was unable to disclose any further details, but she did infer that the change would be rather unpleasant. Some of the inmates tested were told that only those who received high scores would be transferred out of their present institution into a new program. Others were told just the opposite—that those with low scores would be the "fortunate" ones to be chosen. A control group took the test without being given any information. All the children were selected at random.

Ranging in ages from twelve to sixteen, the children had averaged four years at their present institution. Would they want to leave the place where they were relatively secure? The Braginskys found that those who believed high scores would be selected showed a decline in intelligence by more than one and one half mental-age years, compared with the "trial" test that they had taken, while those who expected only low scorers to be chosen raised their I.Q. scores by more than two mental years. About 50 per cent of the group that was motivated to raise the I.Q.'s obtained almost average scores, indicating that they were hardly retarded. However, since this was an experimental project, they remained at the institution.

The control group, not being motivated one way or the other, showed no measurable change from the first to the second test.

When it served their interests, the children manipulated their I.Q.'s to appear either bright or retarded!

Teachers have frequently observed that many of their pupils seem much brighter than their I.Q.'s would indicate. They often appear much brighter in many nonscholastic ways, such as judgment in problem-solving and in interpersonal relationships. The untapped reservoirs of mental ability of all children should be marshaled for educational purposes, stimulated and encouraged by enrichment programs.

These programs continue to challenge the genetic-inheritance theory of the I.Q. scores. Studies dealing with inherited traits have been confined to a large extent to white populations and largely to normal environments. How relevant is the theory of genetic factors as they relate to other populations, and particularly those who come from underprivileged environments?

In the view of Professor James F. Crow, a geneticist at the University of Wisconsin, we are at present deeply concerned with culturally disadvantaged groups and racial minorities. Since races are characterized by different gene frequencies, there is no reason to assume that genes for behavioral traits differ. But this is not to say, Dr. Crow stresses, that the magnitude and direction of genetic racial differences are predictable.

A high heritability of intelligence in the white population would not, even if there were similar evidence in the black population, tell us that the differences between the races are genetic. No matter how high the heritability rate, there is no assurance, the Wisconsin geneticist points out, that a sufficiently great environmental difference does not account for the difference in the two groups.

Society must recognize that there is a considerable genetic variability for all kinds of traits, including intelligence and special talents. But this variability is not the exclusive property of any race or group.

Intelligence is developed through experience, in the opinion of Professor David Elkind of the University of Rochester. He defines intelligence as an extension of biological adaptation which has the ability to develop in response to internal processes as well as environmental changes. The psychometric approach regards intelligence as capable of being measured and holds that such measures can be used to assess the extent to which nature and nurture contribute to intellectual ability.

Self-motivation is a basic indication of intelligence that cannot be measured. The educational practice that would best motivate children in the Piagetian or Montessori sense would be the provision of "instant areas" where children could go on their own for long periods of time. Only when the child can choose an activity and persist at it until he is satiated can we speak of true intrinsically motivated behavior. Dr. Elkind has had impressive results in motivating children to utilize their intelligence to its fullest in his work at the World of Inquiry School in Rochester. Pupils were found to seek higher achievement goals and were more positive in their own self-evaluations than were their matched controls who attended other schools that did not make any special effort to change the traditional teaching practices.

Evidence exists that "late blooming" occurs, that some persons rise dramatically in their relative positions even in late adolescence. When severe deprivation in the home, or in the slum child, is counterbalanced by attractive and meaningful school programs, upward I.Q. changes frequently are found to occur. The more severe the deprivations found in the slums, the greater is its effect on the I.Q. score.

Child-rearing practices of disadvantaged groups, holds Professor Lee J. Cronbach, Stanford University psychologist, are stubborn obstacles to the achievement of quality and educational equality. New instructional techniques are necessary to develop learning ability and better self-concepts. Here, again, education must encompass parents as well as children.

Denouncing the devastating implications of I.Q. tests, and the imprecision of their measurement, Professor William F. Brazziel of Virginia State College warns that a caste status has taken place in our schools. Children will learn effectively if the teacher stresses listening, reading, discussion, peer-group interaction, library resources, or teacher-pupil relations, and ignores completely the I.Q scores that are tagged to each one. Making the same test score is not important educationally.

An Ethnic Success Quotient is proposed by Professor Brazziel. Under this E.S.Q. test, a Richmond-born Episcopalian of English stock, from a family with an income of $12,000, would be declared below average intelligence if his Stanford-Binet score was 120 or under. A score of 100 would place him in the low-normal or retarded class. On the other hand, a Beaufort County, South Carolina, poverty child with an I.Q. of 100 would be placed in the bright group on the basis of the Ethnic Success Quotient concept.

In the long run, the Virginia psychologist maintains, the most potent strategy will prove to be a combination of early stimulation and integrated schools with teachers free of racial and social prejudice. If the child is to succeed, the I.Q. would necessarily have to be eliminated. This would also eliminate the self-fulfilling prophecy of failure, unconsciously and subtly fostered on the child who scores low and is discouraged to achieve since he is relegated to the "failure" section of the school.

Although clinical psychologists have accepted the I.Q. test as an adequate measure of practical or potential intelligence, Dr. David Wechsler, whose WISC tests are so frequently used in our schools today, suggests that general intelligence cannot be equated with intellectual ability, but must be regarded as a manifestation of the personality as a whole. Factors other than intellect enter into our concept of general intelligence.

Research points to education as one of the key factors in the fluctuations of the I.Q. scores. Dr. E. L. Thorndike, for example, concluded that there is an essential relationship between the highest grade completed by an individual and his I.Q. score. The famous Columbia psychologist studied a group of boys who had obtained the highest scores on an intelligence test, contrasted with boys of the same original group who had made the lowest scores. He selected forty boys of a group of seven hundred and contrasted them with forty others. The first forty had made the highest I.Q. scores on a retest, the second forty, the lowest.

The ablest forty, in terms of I.Q. scores, were only four months older than the least able, when each of the eighty left school. However, the ablest forty graduated from high school, in contrast to the other forty who had dropped out at the end of the eighth grade. Although they were just about of equal age when school ended for them, one group had finished high school while the other group only went through eight grades. Obviously, this latter group had to repeat various grades in elementary school.

From his research with these boys, and numerous other studies that he made, Dr. Thorndike concluded that an intelligence test score of an adult cannot be interpreted as evidence of original inherent ability. Rather, the status of an adult on an I.Q. test represents the interaction between his basic ability and the circumstances that enabled him to continue with his education.

President John R. Silber of Boston University, a Fulbright scholar in Germany and a Fellow of King's College, London, points out that it is becoming increasingly difficult to discuss the I.Q. controversy surrounding the work of Professors Jensen, Herrnstein, Bronfenbrenner, Eysenck, and Shockley. Each of these scholars has been in some way harassed by those opposed to what they think is his idea.

When Professor Bronfenbrenner spoke at Boston University in 1972, a mob demanded that he recant his former errors. In the spring of 1974 Professor Eysenck was physically assaulted at a lecture, and at one major university after another Dr. Shockley has been denied a platform.

In arguing for the right of these scholars to present their views, even though they may be contrary to the beliefs of some segments of our society, President Silber notes:

"Suppose we were able to measure a significant difference in I.Q. as between blacks and whites. First of all, we might develop once and for all a *reductio ad absurdum* of the concept of I.Q. as a measure of intelligence independent from environmental influences. If this be a myth, it is clearly one best put to rest, and the sooner the better.

"Second, we would almost certainly observe a substantial range of overlap between blacks and whites, a circumstance which ought to be sufficient to render absurd any pride of intelligence in either race.

"Third, if I.Q. were recognized not only as a reflection of native intelligence but also (as it almost certainly is) a response to environmental influences, then the I.Q. differential between blacks and whites would itself be a measure of the cultural deprivation of blacks and a way of quantifying for Congress and the state legislatures their obligation to take remedial steps in providing equal opportunity for the black community."

No racist implications, wrote Dr. Silber in the August 1974 issue of *Encounter,* need follow from the most rigorous scientific examination of the concept of I.Q.

Professor Robert B. Zajonic of the University of Michigan, and director of the Research Center for Group Dynamics, has found, through his research, that intelligence decreases with family size. He explains that the larger the family, the lower the over-all level of intellectual functioning.

Children, after all, may have a negative effect on the intellectual level of their parents. Writing in the January 1975 issue of *Psychology Today,* he comments:

"Ask kindergarten teachers, who often complain that they must regress to the verbal level of their charges. Parents who interact frequently with large numbers of intellectually immature children may suffer a similar fate."

This means, reports Professor Zajonic, that if you switch from your present intellectual environment to a superior one, your intelligence will increase. And, he adds, if you do this whenever you reach the level of your current surroundings, your intelligence may keep on growing indefinitely.

Rather intriguing! A child's I.Q. may depend on the number of siblings he has, the order in which he was born, and the frequency of births in the family. Since the 1973 Census report shows that the average family size for blacks with children is 2.52, compared to 2.13 for whites, and that while only 2 per cent of white families have six or more children, more than three times as many black families are that large, the difference in I.Q. between blacks and whites (if Jensen et al are correct) may be caused not by lack of native intelligence but because of more children per family.

As far back as 1912, Dr. W. C. Bagley upheld the views of the environmentalists when he stated that, except for a few cases of pathological deficiency, the factor of heredity plays a very small part in human life, as compared with the influence of environment. We know that many other geneticists and clinical psychologists take vigorous issue with this view. They also base their views on research findings.

Probably the genetic view is best expressed by Sir Cyril Burt, who maintains that the child's innate endowment of intelligence sets an upper limit to what he can possibly achieve. No one would expect a Mongolian imbecile, with the most skillful coaching in the world, to attain the scholastic knowledge of an average child. In the same way, he adds, no one should expect a child who is innately dull or whose inborn ability is merely average to win first class honors at Oxford or Cambridge.

Although an I.Q. score derived from tests alone falls far short of being trustworthy, yet, says Dr. Burt, educational authorities cannot afford to risk spending money on children where heavy odds exist against their academic success. He quotes a university teacher as justification for his position:

"That section of the middle class which seeks, by paying fees that it can ill afford, to assist its children to climb, via a 'public school' or an independent grammar school, to a University education and a good honors degree in the humane subjects is animated by a traditional morale which is comparatively rare in children and parents from other classes. Those who nowadays come here on grants, at no cost to themselves or their parents, are, on the whole, most irregular attendants and the least satisfactory students."

However, Dr. Burt modifies his statement on the overriding importance of inherited traits, as he calls for further examination of the influence of genes on I.Q. scores. He comments:

"To my mind the most pressing need at the moment is for more extensive research. Hitherto the most active investigators have been research students with little or no experience of the ways of children, or the conditions of the classroom; they have to rely on the good will of the busy teacher."

An important factor is getting accurate I.Q. scores through psychologically oriented research programs: the motivation of children who are "guinea pigs" in the experiment. Often children will not do their best when tested as part of a research project that has no meaning to them and is utterly boring as well. But if the child knows that the score that he gets on the test will make a difference to him personally, that it may mean getting a scholarship, or being admitted to a better school, he can be expected to put forth greater effort to improve his I.Q. score.

Recall how the children manipulated their I.Q. test scores in the Braginsky study when they thought a higher, or a lower, score would send them away from an institution to which they had become accustomed, to a place that was described to them as being less desirable.

The concept of general intelligence, despite the fact that it has been maligned, discarded, or ignored, still has a rightful place in the science of psychology and in the practical affairs of men, in the opinion of Dr. Quinn McNomar, former president of the American Psychological Association. He observed that many psychologists have long recognized that identification in terms of high I.Q. is too narrow—those gifted in such areas as art and music are necessarily overlooked and remain undiscovered through existing intelligence tests.

Studies of the interrelationships among human abilities indicate that there are two basic types of intelligence. These are described by Professor John L. Horn of the University of Denver as fluid and crystallized. Fluid intelligence is formless and relatively independent of education and experience. On the other hand, crystallized intelligence increases with a person's education and experience. The concepts we possess at any one time may well be a residue of previously acquired intellectual knowledge and ways to use our brain. It is important to recognize that lack of facility or familiarity with special ideas or information does not mean that a child has failed to develop his intellectual abilities, even though the I.Q. tests may make him appear to be mentally slow or culturally inferior.

Just as verbally oriented tests penalize the child who has not had the formal schooling or adequate home atmosphere to develop a large vocabulary, so many tests of mathematical aptitude rely heavily on the use of conventional formulae taught in school, Dr. Horn stresses. A child who has learned only a few of the verbal or mathematical abstract concepts will generally do poorly on I.Q. tests, but that does not mean necessarily that he lacks basic intelligence.

Taking another viewpoint, Professor Jules Henry of Washington University points out that among children from poor families, physical survival must take precedence over every other consideration that may affect the family. Immediate and physical motives are downgraded by educators and psychologists, with the emphasis placed on goal-striving, status-seeking, and planning. By such middle-class standards, the children in the lower socioeconomic levels, or even those considered "average," are seen to have little or no motivation to succeed.

In his study that took place in a low-income housing development in St. Louis, Professor Henry found that extremely poor children lack the structure on which conventional educational patterns can be built, both by feeling and understanding. Their backgrounds do not possess the elements necessary to achieve success in either education or work careers. Their homes were found to be crowded, full of disturbances, and physically and personally disorganized. They do not operate on schedules that pay much attention to school concepts of time, self-discipline, or a sense of obligation.

Even the children most willing and able to learn in a class of thirty to forty-five pupils were under tremendous pressure from their nonachieving and disinterested classmates to stop trying and to join them in their "do nothing" educational attitudes. Actually, this poor motivation of the low achiever is but one more side effect of a whole mountain of pressures and frustrations which have surrounded him and, in a sense, overwhelmed him since birth.

Short of reforming or changing the world in which he lives on a day-to-day basis, how can we stimulate and challenge the slum child to greater school achievement? It will not be enough to improve teaching methods and curricula, Professor Henry firmly believes. The entire fabric of the school system may need a severe and drastic overhauling to meet these challenges. This would most certainly include adult or parent education classes. Somehow, the children need hope in order to achieve, they must see that they have a definite goal, that their future is not altogether bleak and hopeless. And so do the teachers and counselors who work with them.

To forecast the educational or social growth of children who enter school at age five or six, based on I.Q. tests, without considering their normal growth variations, is a travesty on the educational process, warns Professor Estelle Fuchs of Hunter College. Yet we know that in the first few months of a child's school life, a relatively inexperienced teacher may find herself in the untenable position of literally deciding the academic future of her pupils. She is asked to assign children on the basis of an unknown quantity to sections that she will call "superior," "average," or "dull." This may often result in a lifetime of educational distortion for the children so selected.

Moreover, the structure of the school and the attitudes of teachers and administrators affect the development of the children's intellect. The impact of the actual school experiences and the context in which it occurs can well explain the academic failure of many children. Putting aside the I.Q. tests entirely at this point, we are concerned with the plight of children who are misplaced in classroom situations because of the accident of geographic birth, color, race, or ethnic derivation.

Another factor to suggest that environment plays an important role in deciding whether a child is going to be educated as a slow learner or retardate is lack of medical facilities and child-rearing know-how by his parents. Mental slowness may have an organic base associated with premature birth. Lack of proper nourishment and improper health care during the prenatal period often affect a child's later intellectual capacity. This condition does not depend on race or slum living—it can take place in the average, or middle-class, family as well as the poor.

Too many hyperaggressive or environmentally retarded children become dropouts or delinquents. They can be helped through understanding, a sympathetic teacher, and a positive approach to their learning problems. Research has shown that through various techniques, the I.Q. scores of children can be raised by 30 or more points. If we continue to use the I.Q. as an index of intelligence or potential ability, this holds great promise for the future development of children who are now doomed to failure because they have been branded as clowns or pumpkin heads.

The United States is not the only country where the I.Q. plays a vital role in the education of its children. Professor David H. Hargraves offers an incisive study of a secondary modern school in England that points to the evils of tracking—called "streaming" in England—in molding the structure of social relations of children while they are in school.

In Great Britain, as well as in many European school systems, students are rigidly segregated early in their school lives. The notorious "11-plus" practice, in which children at age eleven take an examination to determine whether they are to go to a school leading toward university training, or are to remain in elementary school and later enter a vocational or technical school, has taken its toll in emotional and even physical breakdowns.

A popular explanation for the greater percentage of failure and misbehavior among low I.Q., or noncollege-bound, students is that they come from homes that fail to provide the same ambitions or conforming attitudes as college-bound students get.

But Dr. Hargraves emphasizes that whatever the differences that the students bring to school, they are magnified by what happens to them once they enter. This is caused in large measure in England because the "low stream" children are the victims of mediocrity and failure in their relations with their teachers in both academic performance and classroom behavior.

Teachers of "high stream" children expect higher performance and get it. Those in the lower streams are seen by their teachers as limited in ability, as troublemakers, and are treated accordingly. In a "streamed'" school the teacher categorizes each pupil not only in terms of the inferences he makes of the child's classroom behavior, but also from the child's "stream" level. The teacher expects certain kinds of academic achievement and classroom behavior from members of the different "streams."

Assignment to a lower stream means that a child is immediately immersed in a student subculture that stresses and rewards antagonistic attitudes and behavior toward his teachers, reports Dr. Hargraves. If a boy is assigned to the "A stream," he is drawn toward the values of his teachers, not only by the higher expectations and more positive rewards from the teachers themselves, but from other students as well. The converse is true for lower-stream boys who accord each other high status for doing the opposite of what the teachers demand or expect in the way of good behavior.

Because of class scheduling, little opportunity develops for interaction and friendship across streams. The result is a progressive polarization and hardening of the high- and low-stream subcultures between the first and fourth years of school and a progressively greater negative attitude across stream lines, with predictable consequences. All of this follows from the "streaming," which is based on various standardized and I.Q. tests.

In *Under Which Lyre,* the poet W. H. Auden writes:

Thou shalt not answer questionnaires
     Or quizzes upon World-Affairs,
Nor with compliance
Take any test. Thou shalt not sit
With statisticians nor commit
     A social science.

How many parents, teachers, and children would agree with this famous poet that thou shalt not take any test!

Dr. David Z. Robinson, vice-president of the Carnegie Foundation, argues against I.Q. test taking in strong, if not poetic, language when he states:

"The I.Q. is a questionable measure of general intelligence and a minor determinant of success. Average differences in I.Q. between blacks and whites can never be conclusively ascribed to heredity until blacks and whites get equal treatment in our society. If a permanent lower class or caste system should develop, inheritance of I.Q. will have a very small role compared to inheritance of social standing and occupation."

We know that children who have low I.Q.'s can improve their grades, stay in school longer, and do better work if they are stimulated, if they receive special help, or are allowed to think of college as an ultimate goal. Since the I.Q. improves under proper stimulation, educators cannot assume that the I.Q. score determines whether the child succeeds or fails in school.

That is what Professor Jencks of Harvard believes, when he comments:

". . . neither a student's academic achievement nor the number of years of school he completes is completely determined by his I.Q. There are all kinds of other things at work, of which family background is the most obvious and personality probably the most important. Taken together, all these have considerably more influence than I.Q. on both academic success and persistence in school. After school, the importance of the I.Q. diminishes even further."

According to Professor Jencks, a precise estimate of the relative importance of heredity and environment in the development of the I.Q. is almost certain to be wrong as well as misleading. He believes that instead of attributing 80 per cent of the I.Q. score to heredity, something in the neighborhood of 45 or 50 per cent would be closer to the facts.

One sixth of white identical twins reared apart shows differences of an average of 15 I.Q. points. This is primarily caused by environment, as identical twins have the same type of genes. Dr. Jencks contends that if white families rearing twins differed that much, it is safe to assume that the typical white home and neighborhood also differ from the typical black environment enough to account for the 15-point spread that some psychologists maintain exists, caused by heredity.

By excluding a person from higher learning on the basis of a mediocre I.Q. score, observes Professor Carl Senna of the University of Massachusetts, educational policy assumes that children inherit not intelligence but opportunity. The injustice of this policy is that prolonged learning experience could raise the I.Q. scores. These tests, the Massachusetts educator contends, should be dropped from the school agenda and relegated to their "proper" status as parlor games.

A further biting indictment of the I.Q. tests is made by Dr. Mercer of California, who observes that if the I.Q. tests were abandoned, it would eliminate their misinterpretation and misuse in educational practice. It would make I.Q. scores irrelevant and unavailable. By abolishing I.Q. testing, educators would be forced to look beyond this convenient label and come to grips with the needs of children in all their individual complexities.

Moreover, Dr. Mercer objects to the reference to I.Q. scores as "intelligence quotients," adding that it is archaic to accept as accurate the relationship between chronological age and mental age. The term "intelligence quotient," or I.Q. as it is known, has acquired a semimystical meaning, rendering it useless as an accurate scientific instrument.

If used at all, I.Q. tests should, in all fairness, be standardized on similar sociocultural and ethnic backgrounds of the children tested. In that way, a child's score could be compared with other children of his own culture and background. A pluralistic, sensitive interpretation of the meaning of how children perform on all standardized tests would prove a sounder basis, than is now possible through I.Q. tests, to determine the youngster's ability.

This point is pursued further by Professor David Layzer of Harvard, who contends that the I.Q. test does not measure an individual's phenotypic (physical) characteristics such as height or weight. Rather, it is a measure of the rank order or relative standing of test scores in a given population. The tests are so constructed that the frequency distribution of the scores conforms as closely as possible to the familiar bell-shaped curve, used to develop "norms" for students. To call the I.Q. a measure of intelligence, Dr. Layzer says, conforms neither to ordinary educated usage nor to elementary logic.

A long-range study of high I.Q. children, undertaken by the late Professor Lewis M. Terman of Stanford, has followed the lives of 1,529 children for the past fifty-three years. The results of the research have been published in numerous articles, monographs, and books. This is an ongoing project and has thrown some light on various aspects of the I.Q. controversy.

Terman and his staff located 1,529 children in California whose I.Q.'s average 150 points. When selected, they were between the ages of eight and twelve. Most came from white, professional, middle-class families.

Later follow-up studies found that the high I.Q. children did better work in school than their classmates, but mainly in subjects such as reading and arithmetic. Courses dealing with vocations, for example, woodworking or sewing, did not appeal to them.

Among the findings of the Terman project are these:

Nearly 70 per cent finished college, compared with 8 per cent of their counterparts in the general population—the 1930–40 generation. Some 40 per cent of the male college graduates earned law, medical, or Ph.D. degrees. They did extremely well in college, a third graduating with honors.

The study showed that the I.Q. is by no means fixed. Some of those tested gained, or lost, as much as 30 points in subsequent retesting. On the whole, though, the 1,529 children (first tested in 1922) with high I.Q. scores outstripped their classmates in almost every measurable category. However, he noted that intellect and achievement are far from perfectly correlated.

Just what the Terman study proves has not as yet been determined. Further studies on the Terman project are now being made by a research staff at Stanford.

Research has shown us that the I.Q. test is amost totally subjective, though it tries to be objective. Another California psychologist, Dr. James O. Massey, found that substantial variations in scoring typical responses on the WISC exist at present. Dr. Massey reviewed numerous tests given by psychologists to children undergoing the WISC and then placed them on one hypothetical exam. This was then sent for scoring to four hundred accredited school psychologists, who would normally administer the WISC to schoolchildren. Since they all followed the WISC Manual, defining ways to score, presumably the variations among the examiners would be minimal. But such was not the case. Quite the contrary. On the verbal scale alone, the psychologists gave the students who were (theoretically) being tested an incredible range of scores, from a low I.Q. of 80 to a high of 117 on the same test for the same student!

In the WISC scoring, a child can get 2 points, 1 point, or zero. In checking the scores returned to him, Dr. Massey was distressed to discover how frequently simple errors of arithmetic or careless reading of the conversion tables in the Manual resulted in significant changes in the total score. He also found errors in addition, computation for chronological age, the child's birth date, and sloppy clerical work.

Writing in *Scoring Criteria—Scoring Supplement for the WISC,* Dr. Massey cites typical items used in the test and the interpretation of the child's answer by the examiners. Among the items are the following examples:

"Where does the sun set?" If the child answers, "In the west," he gets a correct score. If he says, "In the sky," he is marked zero.

"What does C.O.D. mean?" If the answer is "Cash" or "Collect on Delivery," the child again has answered correctly. Or he will be given full I.Q. credit if he answers: "Pay the Postage." But if he answers "A cod fish," the child gets zero credit.

An aside to the WISC examiners: C.O.D. does spell cod. Or, perhaps some children have never had a C.O.D. package delivered to their home.

To the question, "What is a barometer?" the correct answer is "An instrument for indicating atmospheric pressure." Wrong answer with zero credit would be: "Predicts weather, or tells how hot it is and if it's going to rain."

Another item: "What is a lien?" Correct answer would be: "A legal claim on property." A zero answer: "A shack that leans."

Lien? . . . a lean-to? The words sound alike. Many students have read about lean-tos in stories.

"What do you do if you lose one of your friends's balls?" Correct response: "Replace the loss." But a zero answer would be: "Try to find it." That answer sounds logical. Another zero answer: "Tell him you're sorry." Sounds logical, too.

Now we come to the section of similarities.

Question: "You walk with your legs and throw with your. . . . ?" Correct answer: "Arms or hands." Zero answer: "Fingers."

Question: "What is the connection between liberty and justice?" Correct answer: "Social ideas or values." Zero: "Both mean freedom." In a sense they do, in my opinion.

Vocabulary is considered the best measure of the I.Q. The Manual describes the general rule for scoring as being any recognized meaning of the word. For example:

Swords: Two-point answer: "It's like a knife, only it's longer and fancier." One-point answer: "It has a sharp point and is used in the army to fight or kill." Zero answer: "Things to fight with; to have a sword fight." Well, why not?

Gambles: Two-point answer: "Take a chance; try to win by

luck." One point: "Playing cards or checkers." Questionable: "Play for money." Zero answer: "Lose money that way." We sure do!

Chattel: Correct two-point answer: "Belongings." One point response: "A man's money." Zero answer: "Real property or land."

I wonder how knowledgeable most unsophisticated children would be on the definition of chattel. Yet, by getting a zero on this word and the other eight sample items mentioned above, the child's I.Q. might be lowered by 18 points. For an average child it would mean the difference between a score of 100 and one of 82, between being rated normal or listed as retarded!

The best of our I.Q. tests are highly fallible instruments which are extremely difficult to interpret with assurance. Even trained psychologists, as Dr. Massey found, are as uncertain about some answers as are the students themselves.

Various research projects are now under way to determine the value as well as limitation of the I.Q. tests. How do they correlate with cognitive thinking, the typical way a person has of processing the information he receives from the world around him and applying it to life situations accordingly?

An attempt is being made to identify features of teaching and learning behavior that are in turn a function of cognitive learning, and to identify the ways in which teachers adapt their teaching methods to the cognitive style of learning to their students. This can, perhaps, eventually erase the familiar complaint of students about teachers who "rub them the wrong way" or the teachers's observation that "Teddy and I are on two different wavelengths."

What has research found out about the I.Q.? A great deal and, paradoxically, very little. We know only little more today than we did seventy-five years ago when Binet gave us a test to predict whether children should be assigned to special schools for slow learners. But we also know that the I.Q. tests opened a Pandora's box by being labeled as measurements of intelligence.

The University of Michigan's Institute for the Study of Mental Retardation and Related Disabilities conducted a follow-up study of four California communities in which lawsuits had been filed against boards of education on behalf of minority children enrolled, on the basis of I.Q. scores, in classes for the mentally retarded.

Litigation has forced school districts to retest ethnic minority students. Based on the retesting, 20,000 minority children have returned to regular classrooms. Although repeated court action has compelled schools to revise testing and placement procedures, evidence indicates that racial and class discrimination persists.

Many schools, the institute found, have low expectations for ethnic minority students and thus assign them less challenging work. These students then achieve less, work more slowly, and fulfill the schools' Pygmalion expectations.

How much better it would have been had the term Intelligence Quotient not been used to designate this test. Perhaps in time psychologists will find the answer to such questions as the role of environment in developing intelligence, the place that heredity plays in the child's life, the ethnic or racial differences in intellectual attainment, the varied aspects of academic and creative abilities, and the hundreds of other unanswered questions that have clouded the I.Q. picture.

Educators should not plan a child's future on the basis of his I.Q. test. Similar to all school tests, it should be regarded as fallible, transient, and uncertain, subject to change and certainly not an object of academic sacredness.

Now we come to a summary of our discussion of I.Q. testing. I would like to present my reasons for the moratorium that I have urged on all standardized tests, and will follow this with several proposals that might be suitable as a replacement.

16

No more I.Q. testing—and instead...

Not only the I.Q. but all standardized achievement tests should be carefully reviewed and, one by one, eliminated. Why do testmakers assume that all children grow alike mentally and physically? It is impossible to compare, on a nationwide basis, the mental development of children based on age alone.

Therefore, all I.Q. scores should be eliminated from the accumulative record folders of the students so that the teachers who now see the scores will not be able to prejudge their children. Of course, it is sometimes important and useful to know about a child's background, his interests, his physical condition, his behavioral problems, his social and emotional states, and how these traits might affect his schooling. But it is wrong to encourage a teacher to formulate her judgment, in advance, through the I.Q. scores, as to what she can expect from the child when he enters her classroom and joins with his classmates in the learning process.

It is essential, if education is to be improved in this country, and if all children are to receive equality of opportunity, to discontinue I.Q. testing and to weaken the hold it has upon the educational world.

The I.Q. score has become a badge of accomplishment, a medal of honor, a symbol of elitism. Parents boast about the I.Q. scores their children receive as though this was the most important part of the entire educational system. They bask in reflected glory.

But you can't blame the parents. They have been brainwashed and oversold on the value and importance of the I.Q. and have accepted the assessment of teachers, guidance counselors, or psychologists that a high I.Q. score is a magic opening for their children to academic and worldly success.

Testing has become big business in this country. Those who manage and operate the standardized tests—and they are concentrated in a very few hands—are more interested in maintaining the status quo than in developing, evaluating, and preparing better, more equitable tests. Often it is not the true measurement of the student's ability that really holds the greatest concern for test makers and their publishers, but how many tests can be sold that becomes the overriding factor and consideration.

This booming industry should be regulated and reorganized and made accountable to the educational profession, not the market place. With two thousand or more different tests available and now in use, each offering its own brand of testing procedures and claiming for the tests more than they can actually deliver, it is difficult for the average school system, psychologist, teacher, or parent to estimate which test is valid or appropriate for the child who is being tested.

Above all, the I.Q. tests should be re-evaluated, restandardized, and their validity scrutinized. Culture-fair and culture-free tests may not be possible, but an attempt to develop them is certainly in order and long overdue. It is disheartening to find that the most popular tests now used to measure a child's I.Q. have been standardized on student samples of one or two generations back. The first order of business in the testing industry should be a thorough re-examination of the tests now in use, and the elimination of dubious ones, and the strengthening and updating of those that may be salvaged. After that, the tests should be labeled with the warning: CAUTION—THIS I.Q. TEST SHOULD BE USED SPARINGLY AND AT NO RISK TO THE CHILD.

As an alternative to the national I.Q. and other standardized achievement tests, more emphasis should be placed on the teacher-oriented examination. The teacher meets with her students six hours a day, five days a week, forty weeks a year. She becomes acquainted with them, gets to know what they can do, which ones need special help and which are the shirkers. She can prepare her own tests, based on the subject matter that she is teaching and the information she wants from her children. Her tests are usually criterion based, and she can judge the intellectual ability and growth of her pupils on the basis of her daily observation and classroom discussions.

The qualified teacher does not need an I.Q. test to tell her whether Stan and Ellen are reading at the level that they presumably should be reading. Nor does she need an I.Q. score to discover whether Jonathan is bright or Benjamin is dull and needs extra help in math or in Spanish grammar.

A test formulated by the teacher will be more likely to cover the aspects of the subjects stressed in class than will a test prepared in a central office several thousand miles away by test makers who may not have been in a classroom for decades and have lost touch with the needs of children as well as teachers.

Moreover, the teacher-designed test will, as a rule, be more than a multiple-choice instrument in which the student is given a choice of four or five items, one of which is presumed to be the correct one. No thought process of his own is involved. His reasoning power is not challenged when all he is called upon to do is to locate and, if he is not sure, to guess at the correct answer and then put a check mark in front of the item he thinks is correct, or block off a square on the answer sheet that corresponds to the item on the test.

Logical and thought-provoking questions are not asked on the I.Q. tests. It would, in the opinion of the school officials and those responsible for assembling I.Q. tests, be too costly to include essay-type questions. An essay would have to be read and valuated by the teacher or examiner. The answer sheet can be placed in a computer which can score a thousand papers in the time it would take the examiner to read and score one test that required reasoning powers.

An imaginative teacher can, in almost any subject, take the facts involved and, through skillful questioning and provocative prodding, educate her students in a far superior manner, regardless of their I.Q. scores.

One English teacher, trying to get her students to find the essential meanings in high school literature, and confined by a curriculum requirement to teach the rather old-fashioned but beautifully written *Ethan Frome* by Edith Wharton, assigned it to her "dull-average" English class as part of a teaching schedule that also included the very popular *Love Story* by Eric Segal and the rather overwhelming *Farewell to Arms* by Ernest Hemingway.

She showed how the three books had a common theme: Each of the heroes had to make the decision to defy convention or conform to it: whether to leave the army and live with the woman he loved (*Farewell to Arms*), whether to defy his father and marry the girl he loved (*Love Story*), or whether to defy society and leave his wife for the servant girl he loved (*Ethan Frome*).

For the first time, the students saw that there was a direct connection, an underlying theme, among these books that related to a problem which every person must face in his lifetime. The students were challenged to think about issues which could never be brought out in the multiple-choice type questions on the existing I.Q. test. Although science and math are based on exact information and facts, these too can, and should, be given meaning through thoughtful and logical questions which can make the student think, reflect, and surmise.

Moreover, creativity in the child is not discovered by the I.Q. tests. The tests do not, in any way, suggest to the teacher whether the score the child has received stands for ability, experience, or just ordinary lack of information on the questions asked. The tests do not differentiate between the child who has a good memory and can recall readily the information that he has gained, in or out of school, and the one who has cognitive skills, can think through a problem, is ready to be challenged, and is eager to be intellectually stimulated.

Rather than continue with the dubious I.Q. tests, we should place greater emphasis on imaginative and creative school programming, on inspirational teaching, and co-operative, understanding supervisors, guidance counselors, and administrators. All of these steps are far more important than the emphasis now placed on I.Q. scores. Good teaching can bring about greater stress on intrinsic, though often intangible, values not subject to testing.

The classroom can become the forum for enlightenment, for the implanting of integrity and a sense of honesty in our children, an emphasis on decency and moral values, so that another Watergate would be impossible and not tolerated by an educated, alert electorate. Students should gain in the classroom, from their first school day to graduation from high school or college, an education based on analytic thought processes derived from meaningful facts, rather than the goals of "What mark did I get in my test? What is it going to get me, anyhow?"

The teacher can judge the child's capacity in the classroom, his ability to learn. But the I.Q. does not measure this important capacity, as psychologist Bruno Bettelheim, a noted educator, points out, when he reports:

"One boy, who came to us diagnosed as feeble-minded, is today a professor at Stanford."·

We need good schools, not irrelevant I.Q. tests, so that each child can receive the education best suited for him, whether he is gifted, average, slow, or retarded. Not everyone is intellectually bright, but every child has the right to get the educational program best suited to his needs.

These steps, I suggest, should be taken as rapidly as possible and should replace the I.Q. tests as a measuring instrument: Place greater emphasis on better-trained teachers. Give them the available resources they need to do an outstanding job. This would assume smaller classes, not more than fifteen to twenty pupils per class. This will permit the teacher to be in a better position to become personally acquainted with each child, to spend more time with him, and to understand his problems and his needs.

Teacher-training institutions must play their role in educating teachers who can work with all types of children, from every type of environment, and who can cultivate the highest possible achievement in the students.

A good teacher is far more to be desired than a dozen I.Q. tests. But she needs co-operation from her school board, from the parents, and from the community at large. She should have a well-stocked school library available, so that she can work with the children on an individual basis, permitting them to set their own pace, encouraging them to make greater use of the library resources. The teacher should be experienced enough to judge where the child belongs in his class, his capacity for work, and the creative ability, tapped or covered, that he may have and that may come to the fore under her sympathetic handling.

School board co-operation is essential for a good program. The teacher is often circumscribed and frustrated by the type of assistance, or lack of it, that she gets from the school board, from her supervisors and her administrators. The school board allocates the necessary funds, decides on new technological tools, sets the teachers' salaries, and evolves the over-all school policy. A progressive and alert school board does not limit the teacher's imaginative and innovative teaching program with sets of unrealistic and rigid rules.

The board, also, determines whether I.Q., achievement, or other tests are to be used. With the support of board members, the schools can develop new methods, introduce new techniques, build unique school structures, or introduce open classrooms and modern educational design.

In *Crisis in the Classroom,* Dr. Charles E. Silberman reports that for the most part our classrooms are drab and uninviting, the students are uninspired, the teachers resigned to mediocre working conditions. He suggests that the schools be reorganized, that more inspirational and challenging teaching be introduced, and that the students be motivated to a greater desire for effective learning.

I agree. Too few schools have introduced genuinely new teaching programs, such as team teaching, nongraded or open classrooms, individualized instruction, flexible scheduling or an optional program of alternative schooling. Fewer still provide their teachers with an adequate supply of technical tools such as audiovisual equipment, overhead projectors, television sets, computers, or the whole range of helpful teaching aids that are now readily available, at not too high a price. These can be obtained at not much more than the annual cost of providing children with the numerous standardized tests that they are forced to undergo. Certainly the money would be better spent.

Parents are important components of the educational program. Too little utilization is made of the services of many well-qualified parents who could contribute greatly to the school program and the education of the children. They are overlooked, sometimes deliberately, since teachers and, more particularly, the administrators do not want to get involved with the parent who occasionally comes to school to "make a fuss." But the importance of the parents to the schools, even years before the child enters kindergarten, has been underestimated or misunderstood. Yet, as one parent complained unhappily:

"The only time I am asked to come to school is when John gets into trouble or when he fails his math test."

It has always been assumed by those working in the school-parent relations groups that parents are essential factors in the school-home environment and involvement. Now we have specific proof that without parental support and understanding, especially with preschoolers, children often develop a negative, and even hostile, attitude toward their education, their teachers, and their classmates.

This would suggest that parents should be encouraged to come to school long before their own children do. It may be necessary for the teachers to entice, through various means, the parents who are unwilling to come to school for conferences to do so for the benefit of their own children.

The support of the community, as well, is essential in building an effective school program. Teachers should co-operate with the community leaders, with spokesmen of the representative organizations within the community, and attempt to build a strong rapport with all members. In this way, they will be more likely to gain support for the programs that they introduce, assuming that they are sound and worth while.

Too often, differences develop between the school personnel and the community. This may be caused by a teachers' strike, the introduction of a course on sex education, or charges of the use of "obscene" books. Teachers, parents, and community leaders should discuss these differences freely and openly at public meetings and attempt to ameliorate the misunderstandings that usually develop under emotional stress when dealing with controversial issues.

Frequently it is the community, as represented perhaps by a small group of vocal parents, who demand that the I.Q. or achievement tests be given to their children and who, upon learning that their children did not get as high a composite score as those in a neighboring school, demand that the school board take drastic action, even if it means firing or transferring teachers.

But, if the teachers can explain that the scores are not meant to be anything more than one index of achievement, that I.Q. tests are not reliable indicators of what their children are capable of accomplishing, the parents may accept the fact that their fears are groundless, that their children are getting just as good an education as those who made higher scores, and presumably are getting better instruction in the classroom.

We must utilize the best human resources available to improve our teaching programs. In every community we can find men and women, noted authorities in their fields, who stand ready to help work with children, if called upon for their services. There are many retired, energetic, and alert journalists, authors, scientists, mathematicians, engineers, musicians, artists, business executives, and other professional and semiprofessional persons who can contribute constructively to the schools. Many would be more than willing to volunteer to speak, at no, or a minimal fee.

Why not call upon the senior citizens, the retired professionals? They have much to offer. They can be invited to the classroom to meet with and co-operate with the children and the teachers. The journalist, for example, can cite his method of creative writing, or explain how he got that "scoop." The engineer can discuss theories and problems with the chemistry and physics classes, the artist can give an actual example of how he executes a portrait, while the retired musician can relive some of his past "hits" on the piano, encouraging the students to join with him in a "mass sing."

In one school a "Meet the Experts" program was initiated. Twice a month, a parent who was an expert in his field, or perhaps a well-known scientist or a writer, spent a day at the school. He met informally with the students, spoke at their assemblies, lunched with them, and answered numerous questions about everything from water pollution to strip mining.

Sometimes teachers or administrators resent the "intrusion" of retired professionals, or even parents, in their classrooms. They are unhappy because it breaks up the daily school routine. The schedule is rigid, the course of studies fixed, and time is not available for outside activities.

At one school, where the "Meet the Experts" project was successfully introduced, William L. Laurence, former science editor of the New York *Times,* talked about his experiences as the only civilian allowed to watch the explosion of the first atomic bomb in New Mexico.

The class schedule was completely disrupted. The day was spent in a discussion of science. Students listened intently at a presentation, informally given, of the implications to mankind of the newly released atomic power, of the possible cataclysmic violent end of the world. Awed and excited by this actual proof of living history by a man who had been there when it happened, the students learned more about modern science that day than in a month of class work. Moreover, it was knowledge and insight that could never be measured on an I.Q. test.

More of this supplementary teaching can aid and help to motivate even the poorest nonachiever, the student who is merely marking time and will drop out as soon as the law permits him to do so. These students, too, can profit from the vividly recalled experiences of gifted experts and authorities. Not only the poorly motivated students, but all, and especially those who are bright and eager for further information, can find these meetings with experts highly valuable.

Many other ways can be devised to make learning more meaningful, to motivate children, to bring about greater equality of educational opportunity for all. These methods of teaching do not depend upon I.Q. scores, but on the imaginative teacher who can stimulate, challenge, inspire, and motivate her students. Out of the poverty-stricken slums and ghettos have come children who have astounded the educational world with their art and poetry, their mathematical skills and scientific wizardry, encouraged by a far-seeing creative teacher unencumbered by a dependence on I.Q. scores and unwilling to accept these tests as being the determinant of a child's abilities or potentialities.

Parents in the more privileged communities usually want to give their children as fine an education as they can afford and the schools permit. They put it this way:

"I want my child to get a good start in life. Only education can do that."

This attitude does not always exist in poverty areas, where

parents are often more concerned with putting bread on their table than thinking ahead about the education their children will, or should, get. Alert teachers, though, can help these parents understand that the educational progress made by their children will open greater opportunities for them in the years ahead.

Often I.Q. scores are so misleading that they affect the child's future school career. Professor Robert Williams of Washington University, ardent opponent of the current type of intelligence testing, cites this illustration of the basic unfairness of the test when applied to different cultures:

Second-graders in a city school took an I.Q. test in which one portion asked that thirty illustrations be matched with the appropriate words listed. One item showed a *log,* followed by the words: GOAL . . . LOG . . . LEG . . . MAKE. . . .

Never having seen a log or a wood-burning fireplace, the children searched for the word "rug." To them, the picture looked like a rolled-up carpet. But the word "rug" was not among the four words listed. So, most of the second-graders who took the I.Q. test got this word, and many others with which they were not familiar, wrong. Their I.Q. scores suffered accordingly.

As the results went into the child's accumulative record, his inaccurate score, perhaps as low as 75, or borderline, near the mentally retarded range, followed him right through each grade of school. Somewhere along the line, the high school guidance counselor, looking at the score, might call Kevin into his office and say:

"Kevin, I suggest you take a vocational course. You are not, I'm sorry to say, college material. Why waste time knocking your head against a stone wall? There's nothing wrong with being a bus driver or janitor, you know."

And this recommendation was made on the basis of an I.Q. test, taken in the second grade, on questions that did not remotely begin to measure the child's actual intelligence or his learning power!

This incident has been repeated so often in our school system that it has become commonplace. The tragedy is that the child's life is affected, and that instead of getting an opportunity to improve himself and reach higher, he will remain in the lowest economic and cultural levels. Professor Williams recalls that his I.Q. was listed as 82, when he was in elementary school, and he was advised by the guidance counselor to take a vocational trade, as he could never make it in college. Undaunted, Professor Williams continued as a foremost psychologist and a most vigorous opponent of the existing I.Q. tests.

If we eliminate standardized achievement testing, as well as the I.Q. tests, we will curtail the practice now frequently in existence, where teachers, wanting to make as good an impression as possible on their school boards, and fearing the anger of the community and parents, subvert their own teaching principles by making certain that, by whatever means may be necessary, their students will get high achievement scores. The students may not know much about Hamlet, but they will know how to answer a multiple-choice question correctly.

This can be done in many subtle ways, none of which actually help the student: by "teaching to the test," by giving students practice questions that come from immediate or previous tests, and, by special tutoring or coaching, getting the students ready and primed for the test. It is not difficult, through these and other innocent-appearing procedures, to raise the class average substantially. In an achievement reading test, for example, a third-grade class that is found to read on a 3.9-grade level is applauded for its excellence, while a 3.1 average is considered to be below expected standards. There are enough built-in errors in these tests to make an eight months difference statistically meaningless. Yet the public, generally, and parents, in particular, do not recognize this truism.

On one occasion I supervised the reading and arithmetic achievement tests given in a private elementary school. These were state-wide tests, and the results were awaited eagerly. Would our school be on top in the state? Looking over the individual results, I noticed that in a fourth-grade class, Kenneth did not meet the level of his group in arithmetic. In fact, he just about reached the first-grade level.

How could that be? I knew that Ken was an excellent math student. In fact, he startled many of us with his uncanny ability. He could solve difficult mathematical problems, without pencil or paper, doing all the work in his head. Students would stand in awe as they would ask: "Ken, how much is 738 times 212?" A moment's reflection, and then came the answer: "It is . . . it is . . . 156,456." Figuring it out on paper, the children yelled: "Ken's right. He never misses."

Now, to find Ken achieving on the first-grade level was prepos-
terous. It was as though Einstein had failed a high school algebra
test.

But then I looked at his reading achievement scores, and I really
began to wonder. Kenneth's reading also was on the first-grade level.
He appeared to be bright; but no, his I.Q. score stood out ominously
—94. That probably explained everything; his teachers nodded in
agreement.

"Sure," said his reading teacher, "the kid just doesn't have it.
With an I.Q. of 94, what can you expect? And look at last year's
scores, and the year before that. I think he belongs in a special class
for mentally retarded children."

I didn't think so. I called Ken into my office. "Seems as though
you did badly in both reading and math," I began. "Have any trouble
today, Ken?"

"Nope," he answered sullenly.

"But you failed even the easiest answers in the arithmetic test," I
persisted. "They are rather simple, don't you think?"

Ken didn't answer. Just sat staring at the floor.

I opened the arithmetic achievement test and said: "Do this first
problem."

It was a simple one, asking that the student multiply two 2-digit
numbers. A list of five choices were offered. The student was to
check which he thought was the correct one. Ken gazed at the test, at
the ceiling, and then pointing to one of the choices, said: "This one
—the third."

I noticed that he had pointed to an answer at random. I tried
several others, but in each case drew a blank. I saw that the flustered
lad was only guessing.

Then I had a hunch. "Put your pencil down," I said. "Just answer me as I read the questions to you. . . . How much is 175 times
38?"

That was easy. Without a moment's hesitation, he answered:
6,650.

"Good," I said. "Here's another question on the test: If you had
150 apples and gave 25 to Bill, 17 to John, 44 to Robert, and then
Mary added 28 to your pile of apples, and Jill added 34, how many
would you have left?"

A moment's pause. I could hear the wheels ticking. "One hundred and twenty-six," he answered.

I had to add the figures to see if he was right. He was. "But," I said, holding up his test paper, "you checked 23, didn't you?"

"Read the next question to me," I continued, "and give me the correct answer. You're doing great so far."

Ken looked at the question, stared into space, looked down again, and finally said quietly: "You read it for me."

Then I understood. Ken just couldn't read! Somewhere along the line he had come as far as the fourth grade, unable to read at first- or second-grade levels. His teachers, seeing his low I.Q. score, simply accepted the fact that they were dealing with a dull-witted child.

"Very well," I said. "I'll read, and you give me the answer you think is correct."

Then I gave Ken the arithmetic achievement test orally. I asked the questions, read the directions, and got his answer. He gave me the correct answers to every one of the seventy-five questions on the test. Remarkable! Instead of getting a first-grade achievement score in arithmetic, he was on seventh-grade level, as high as the scoring on this test went.

"Guess you're okay in math, but you certainly need help in reading," I told him. "You'll get it, starting today."

And he did. His teachers were still skeptical, insisting again and again: "Look at his I.Q. score. Doesn't that mean anything?"

"Sure, that proves he's dull, doesn't it?" another teacher asked.

"No," I answered emphatically. "It only shows that the boy needs help in reading. Forget the I.Q. score. Teach Ken how to read. I don't know why his other teachers didn't."

After several intensive months of help, Ken, his reading improved, became a more tractable youngster, no longer trying to disrupt activities. His frustrations gradually disappeared. Because he never learned to read properly, he got a low I.Q. score. And, because his score was low, his teachers naturally assumed that Ken was "stupid," so why bother with him?

But as we looked beyond the threatening I.Q., we found that here was a truly bright youngster, eager and happy to co-operate. Perhaps his teachers also learned an even more important lesson: I.Q. scores do not evaluate a student's learning ability.

In the public schools, where individual attention is difficult to get because of large class size, Ken had been labeled a dullard, working below grade level, but, somehow, surprisingly superior when it came to problem-solving that did not require reading.

How many Kens are there in our schools today who are labeled with ominously low I.Q. scores because their more basic problems have been overlooked? The accumulative files showed that Ken was a poor student, his I.Q. test score was low, and his ability, therefore, could not be improved, because the test said so.

It is difficult to convince the educational world, at least that part of it involved in psychometrics and psychological research, that the I.Q. scores should be discarded as part of the permanent records of our schoolchildren.

Too much harm has been done, too many children have been hurt, too many parents have become discouraged, too many teachers have been placed in an untenable position because of these tests. The arguments in favor of retaining an I.Q. testing apparatus have grown weaker with the passing years, as their harmful effects have become increasingly apparent.

The many court cases, the numerous instances of educators who object to children who are being mislabeled, whether bright, average, or slow, indicate that the light at the end of the I.Q. tunnel is in sight. It cannot come too soon to help children everywhere.

Not every child can define a sonata. Music is not a part of every house. But every child has the right to be happy, to be treated with humanity, with compassion, and with respect and honesty.

This will be made possible once we remove the inadequate and inaccurate I.Q. labeling that can strangle him academically and socially.

Bibliography

American Psychological Association, "Standards for Educational and Psychological Tests and Manuals." Washington, D.C., 1966

American Psychologist, 20, 857–992. 1965. Special issue on Testing and Public Policy

Anastasi, Anne, "Heredity, Environment and the Question How?" *Psychological Review,* 65, pp. 197–208. 1958

————— *Psychological Testing.* 2nd ed. New York: Macmillan Company, 1961

Banks, James A., ed., "Heredity, Environment, Race, I.Q.: A Debate Between William Shockley and N. L. Gage." *Phi Delta Kappan,* January 1972

Bayley, Nancy, "Research in Child Development: A Longitudinal Perspective." *Merrill-Palmer Quarterly Behavior Development,* 11. 1965

————— "Comparisons of Mental and Motor Test Scores for Ages 1–15 Months by Sex, Birth, Order, Race, Geographical Location and Education of Parents." *Child Development,* 36, pp. 379–411. 1965

————— "Behavioral Correlates of Mental Growth: Birth to Thirty-Six Years." *American Psychology,* 23. 1968

Bazelan, D. L., and Boggs, E. M., "Report of the Task Force on Law." President's Panel on Mental Retardation, 1963

Bereiter, C., and Engelmann, S., *Teaching Disadvantaged Children in the Pre-School.* Englewood Cliffs, N.J.: Prentice-Hall, 1966

Bettelheim, Bruno, "Teaching the Disadvantaged." *National Education Assn. Journal.* 54, 8–12. 1965

Bloom, Benjamin S., *Stability and Change in Human Characteristics.* New York: John Wiley & Son, 1964

————— *Compensatory Education for Cultural Deprivation.* New York: Holt, Rinehart & Winston, 1965

Braginsky, B. M., and Braginsky, D. D., "Stimulus Response: The Mentally Retarded: Society's Hansels and Gretels." *Psychology Today,* March 1974

Brickman, William W., and Lehrer, Stanley, eds., *Education and the Many Faces of the Disadvantaged: Cultural and Historical Perspectives.* New York: John Wiley & Sons, 1972

Brison, D. W., "Accelerated Learning and Fostering Creativity." Toronto, Canada: Ontario Institute for Studies in Education, 1968

Brophy, J. W., "Mothers as Teachers of Their own Preschool Children: The Influence of SES and Task Structures on Teaching Specificity." *Child Development,* 41, 79–91. 1970

Bryan, Ned J., "Building a Program for Superior and Talented High School Students." North Entral Association.

Burgess, Evangeline, *Values in Early Childhood Education.* 2nd ed. Washington: National Educational Association, 1965

Burks, B. S., "The Relative Influence of Nature and Nurture upon Mental Development: A Comparative Study of Foster Parent-Foster Child Resemblance and True Parent-True Child Resemblance." Yearbook of National Society for the Study of Education, 27, 1. 219–316. 1928

———— Jensen, D. W., and Terman, L. M. *Genetic Studies of Genius, III: The Promise of Youth.* Follow-up Studies of a Thousand Gifted Children. Stanford: Stanford University Press, 1930

Buros, Oscar K., *Tests in Print.* Highland Park, N.J.: The Gryphon Press, 1968

———— *Reading Tests and Reviews.* Highland Park, N.J.: The Gryphon Press, 1968

———— *Personality Tests and Reviews.* Highland Park, N.J.: The Gryphon Press, 1970

———— *The Mental Measurement Yearbooks.* Highland Park, N.J.: The Gryphon Press, 1968, 1972

Burt, Cyril, "The Inheritance of Mental Ability." *American Psychologist,* 13, 1–15. 1958

———— "Intelligence and Social Mobility." *British Journal of Statistical Psychology,* 14. 1961

———— "Is Intelligence Distributed Normally?" *British Journal of Statistical Psychology,* 16, 175–90. 1963

———— "Mental Capacity and Its Critics." Bulletin British Psychology Society, 21. 1968

———— "Inheritance of General Intelligence." *American Psychologist,* 27, 175–90. 1972

California State Department of Education, "Racial and Ethnic Survey of California Public Schools, Part I: Distribution of Pupils." Sacramento, Calif., 1966

Caspari, Ernst, "Genetic Endowment and Environment in the Determination of Human Behavior: Biological Viewpoint. *American Educational Research Journal,* 1968

Cattell, R. B., "The Multiple Abstract Variance Analysis Equations and Solutions: For Nature-Nurture Research on Continuous Variable." *Psychological Review,* 67. 1960

———— "Theory of Fluid and Crystallized Intelligence: A Critical Experiment." *Journal of Educational Psychology,* 54, 1–22. 1963

———— *Abilities: Their Structure, Growth and Action.* Boston: Houghton-Mifflin, 1971

Center for Statewide Educational Assessment, *State Educational Assessment Programs.* 1973 revision. Princeton: Educational Testing Service.

Cohen, David K., "Does I.Q. Matter?" *Commentary,* 53, N. 4. April 1972

Coleman, James S., and others, *Equality of Educational Opportunity.* Washington, D.C.: U. S. Office of Education, 1966

College Entrance Examination Board, *Guide for High Schools and Colleges, 1973–74.* New York: CEEB, 1973

Conant, James Bryant, *Slums and Suburbs: A Commentary on Schools in Metropolitan Areas.* New York: McGraw-Hill, 1961

Conference on Teaching Children and Youth Who are Educationally Disadvantaged. Washington, D.C., 1962

Cordasco, Francesco; Hillson, Maurie; and Bucchioni, Eugene, *The Equality of Educational Opportunity.* Totowa, N.J.: Littlefield, Adams & Co., 1973

Crabtree, Robert K., "Breakthrough in Massachusetts: Getting it Together for the Handicapped. *Compact* magazine, September 1973

Cravioto, J., "Malnutrition and Behavioral Development in the Pre-School Child." Pre-School Child Malnutrition. National Health Science, No. 1272

Cronbach, Lee J., "New Light on Test Strategy from Decision Theory from Testing Problems in Perspective," 53–59. Anne Anastasi, ed. Washington: American Council on Education, 1966

———— "Heredity, Environment and Educational Policy." *Harvard Educational Review,* 39, 339–47. 1969

———— *Essentials of Psychological Testing,* 3rd ed. New York: Harper & Row, 1969

Cutts, Norma E., and Mosely, Nicholas, *Teaching the Bright and Gifted.* Englewood Cliffs, N.J.: Prentice-Hall, 1957

Daniels, V., "Concerning the Validity of Standardized Tests." *Clearing House,* 39: 12–14. September 1964

Darcy, N. T., "Bilingualism and the Measurement of Intelligence: Review of a Decade of Research." *Journal of Genetic Psychology,* 103. 1963

Davis, Junius A., and Temp, George, "Is the SAT Biased Against Black Students?" *College Board Review.* New York: College Entrance Examination Board. Fall 1971

Deutsch, Martin, "Happenings on the Way Back to the Forum: Social Science, I.Q. and Race Difference Revisited. *Harvard Educational Review,* 39, 523–58. 1969

—— and others, *The Disadvantaged: Studies of the Social Environment and Learning.* New York: Basic Books, 1967

—— Katz, I., and Jensen, A. R., eds., *Social Class, Race, and Psychological Development.* New York: Holt, Rinehart & Winston, 1968

Dobzhansky, Theodosius, *Heredity and the Nature of Man.* New York: Harcourt Brace Jovanovich, 1964

—— *Genetic Diversity and Human Equality.* New York: Basic Books, 1973

Dreger, R. M., and Miller, K. S., *Comparative Psychological Studies of Negroes and Whites in the United States.* Psychology Bulletin, 57. 1960

Duncan, O. D., "Ability and Achievement." *Eugenics Quarterly,* 15, 1–11, 1968

Dunn, Lloyd M., Expanded Manual. Peabody Picture Vocabulary Test. Minneapolis: American Guidance Services, 1965

—— Horton, Kathryn, and Smith, J. O., Peabody Language Development Kits. Manual for Level P. Minneapolis: American Guidance Services, 1968

Durrell, D., Murphy, H. A., and Junkins, K. M., "Increasing the Rate of Learning in First-Grade Reading." *Education.* 62. 37–39. 1941

Dyer, Henry S., "Testing Little Children: Old Problems in New Settings." Paper Presented at National Leadership Institute in Early Childhood Education. Washington, D.C. October 1971

—— "Recycling the Problems in Testing." From Proceedings of the 1972 Invitational Conference on Testing Problems—Assessment in a Pluralistic Society. Princeton, N.J.: Educational Testing Service, 1972

Eckland, B. K., "Genetics and Sociology: A Reconsideration." *American Sociological Review*, 32: 173–94. 1967

Educational Policies Commission, "Education and the Disadvantaged American." Washington, D.C.: National Education Assn., 1965

Educational Testing Service, Measurements for Self-Understanding and Personal Development. Proceedings of the 1973 Invitational Conference on Testing Problems. Princeton: ETS, 1973

———— American Education and the Search for Equal Opportunity. Washington, D.C.: National Education Assn., 1965

Eells, Kenneth Walter, *Intelligence and Cultural Differences: A Study of Cultural Learning and Problem-Solving*. Chicago: University of Chicago Press, 1951

Einhorn, H. J., and Bass, A. R., "Methodological Considerations Relevant to Discrimination in Employment Testing." *Psychological Bulletin*, 75, 261–69. 1971

Elashoff, Janet D., and Snow, R. E., *Pygmalion Reconsidered*. Worthington, Ohio: Charles A. Jones Pub. Co., 1971

"Equal Educational Opportunity." *Harvard Educational Review*. Cambridge, Mass.: Harvard University Press, 1969

Erlenmeyer-Kimling, L., and Jarvik, L. F., "Genetics and Intelligence: A Review." *Science*, 142: 1477–79. 1963

Eysenck, H. J., *The I.Q. Argument: Race, Intelligence and Education*. New York: The Library Press, 1971

Fantini, Mario, and Weinstein, Gerald, *The Disadvantaged: Challenge to Education*. New York: Harper & Row, 1968

Feedback, "Newspaper of the New California State Testing Program." Vol. 1, No. 1., January 1973. Sacramento, Calif.

Fehr, F. S., "Critique of Hereditarian Accounts." *Harvard Educational Review*, 39, 1969

Feldman, S, and Weiner, M., "Use of a Standardized Reading Achievement Test with Two Levels of Socio-Economic Status Pupils." *Journal of Experimental Education*, 32: 269–74. Spring 1964

Fincher, Jack, "The Terman Study Is Fifty Years Old." *Human Behavior*, March 1973

Findley, Warren G., and Bryan, Miriam M., *Ability Group: 1970 Status, Impact and Alternatives*. Center for Educational Improvement, Athens: University of Georgia, 1970

Fleming, Elyse, and Anttonen, R. G., "Teacher Expectancy or My Fair Lady." *American Educational Research Journal*, 8. 241–52. 1971

Furfey, P. H., and Harte, T. J., "Reducing the Effects of Cultural Deprivation." Mental Health Program Reports. U. S. Department of Health, Education and Welfare, January 1970

Frazier, Alexander ed., "Educating the Children of the Poor." Washington, D.C.: Association for Supervision and Curriculum Development, National Education Assn., 1968

Fuchs, Estelle, "How Teachers Learn to Help Children Fail." *Transaction*, 5:45–49. September 1968

Gagne, R. M., ed., *Learning and Individual Differences*. Columbus, Ohio: Merrill, 1967

Gallagher, James J., "Research Summary of Gifted Child Education." Illinois: Dept. for Exceptional Children: Gifted Program, 1966

——— Aschner, Mary Jane, and Jenne, William, "Productive Thinking of Gifted Children in Classroom Interaction." Research monograph. The Council for Exceptional Children. Washington, D.C., 1967

Gesell, Arnold, *Wolf-Children and Human-Children*. New York: Harper & Bros., 1940

Getzels, J. W., and Jackson, P. W., *Creativity and Intelligence*. New York: John Wiley & Sons, 1962

Gilliland, A. R., "Socioeconomic Status and Race as Factors in Infant Intelligence Test Scores." *Child Development*, 22, 271–3. 1951

Ginandes, Shephard, *Inequality in Education*. Cambridge, Mass.: Harvard Center for Law and Order, July 1973

Glaser, R., and Nitko, J., *Measurements in Learning and Instruction in Educational Measurement*. R. L. Thorndike, ed., 2nd ed. Washington: American Council on Education, 1971

Glass, D. C., ed., *Genetics*. New York: Rockefeller University Press and Russell Sage Foundation, 1928

Goodenough, F. L., "New Evidence on Environmental Influences on Intelligence." National Society of the Study of Education, 39, Part I. 1940

Gordon, Edmund W., "Programs of Compensatory Education," in *Social Class, Race, and Psychological Development*, 381–406, Deutsch, Martin, Katz, Irwin, and Jensen, A. R., eds. New York: Holt, Rinehart & Winston, 1968

——— and Wilkerson, Doxey A., "Compensatory Education for the Disadvantaged: Programs and Practices—Preschool Through College." New York: College Entrance Examination Board.

Gordon, I. J. ed., *Reaching the Child Through Parent Education:*

258 Bibliography

The Florida Approach. Gainesville: Institute for Development of Human Resources, University of Florida, 1969

Gough, H. G., "A Nonintellectual Intelligence Test." *Journal of Consulting Psychology,* 17, 242–6. 1953

Gowan, John C., and Demos, George D., eds., *The Disadvantaged and Potential Dropout: Compensatory Educational Programs: A Book of Readings.* Springfield, Ill.: C. C. Thomas, 1966

Gray, Susan Walton, *Before the First Grade: The Early Training Project for Culturally Disadvantaged Children.* New York: Teachers College Press, 1966

Guertin, W. H., "Differential Characteristics of the Pseudo-Feeble Minded." *American Journal of Mental Deficiency,* 54, 394–98

Guilford, J. P., "Creativity." *American Psychologist,* 5, 444–54. 1950

———— *Fundamental Statistics in Psychology and Education.* New York: McGraw-Hill, 1965

———— *The Nature of Human Intelligence.* New York: McGraw-Hill, 1965

———— "Minority Subcultures and the Law of Effect." *American Psychologist,* 25, 313–22. 1970

———— Hoepfner, R., *The Analysis of Intelligence.* New York: McGraw-Hill, 1971

Halpern, Ray, and Halpern, Betty, "The City That Went to School: Integration in Berkeley." *The Nation,* 206: 632–36. May 13, 1968

Harrell, R. F., Woodyard, E., and Gates, A. I., *The Effects of Mothers' Diets on the Intelligence of Offspring.* New York: Bureau of Publications, Teachers College, 1955

Harter, S., "Mental Age, I.Q. and Motivational Factors in the Discrimination Learning Set Performance of Normal and Retarded Children." *Journal of Experimental Child Psychology,* 5. 1967

Harvard Educational Review, "Environment, Heredity and Intelligence." Harvard Reprint Series No. 2, Cambridge, Mass., 1969

Haseman, J. K. and Elston, R. C., "The Estimation of Genetic Variance from Twin Data." *Behavior Genetics.* L: 11–19. 1970

Havighurst, Robert J., *Unrealized Potential of Adolescents.* Bulletin of National Association of Secondary School Principals, 50: 75–114. May 1966

—— and Levine, Daniel U., *Education in Metropolitan Areas,* 2nd ed. Boston: Allyn & Bacon, 1971

Heber, R. F., "A Manual on Terminology and Classification in Mental Retardation." 64. Monograph supplement. 2nd ed.

—— "Rehabilitation of Families at Risk for Mental Retardation." Madison, Wis., 1969

Hellmuth, Jerome, ed., *Disadvantaged Child.* 3 vols. New York: Brunner/Mazel, 1969–70

Herber, Rick, and others, "Rehabilitation of Families at Risk for Mental Retardation." Rehabilitation Research and Training Center in Mental Retardation. Madison: University of Wisconsin, 1972

Herrnstein, R. J., "I.Q." *The Atlantic,* September 1971

—— *I.Q. in the Meritocracy.* Boston: Little, Brown & Co., 1973

Hess, R. D., and Shipman, V. C., "Maternal Influences Upon Early Learning: The Cognitive Environment of Urban Preschool Children." In R. D. Hess and R. B. Ball, eds., *Early Education.* Chicago: Aldine, 1968

Hillson, Maurie, "The Nongraded School: An Organization for Meeting the Needs of Disadvantaged and Culturally Different Learners." Hillson Letter ⌗17: The nongraded elementary school. Chicago: Science Research Associates, 1967

Holmen, Milton G., *Educational and Psychological Testing: A Study of the Industry and Its Practices.* New York: Russell Sage Foundation, 1972

—— and Doctor, Richard F., "Criticisms of Standardized Testing." *Today's Education,* Washington, D.C.: National Education Assn., January/February/1974

Houston, Susan H., "A Re-examination of Some Assumptions About the Language of the Disadvantaged Child." *Child Development,* 41:947–63. 1970

Hunt, J. McVicker, *Intelligence and Experience.* New York: Ronald Press, 1961

—— "How Children Develop Intellectually." *Children,* 11: 83–91. May 1964

—— *Human Intelligence.* New Brunswick, N.J.: Transaction Books, 1972

Hunt, Kellog W., "Synthetic Maturity in School Children and Adults." Monographs of the Society for Research in Child Development, 35:1. 1970

Inequality in Education, "Testing and Tracking Bias in the Classroom." Harvard Center for Law and Education. Harvard University. No. 14. July 1973

Inhelder, B., and Piaget, Jean, *The Growth of Logical Thinking from Childhood to Adolescence.* New York: Basic Books, 1958

Jencks, Christopher, and others, *Inequality.* New York: Bobbs-Merrill, 1972

Jensen, Arthur R., "How Can We Boost I.Q. and Scholastic Achievement?" *Harvard Educational Review.* Vol. 39, No. 1. Winter/Spring 1969

———— *Race and the Genetics of Intelligence: A Reply to Lewontin.* Bulletin of the Atomic Scientists, 26. 1970

———— "Do Schools Cheat Minority Children?" Educational Research Bulletin. November 1971

———— "I.Q.'s of Identical Twins Reared Apart." *Behavior Genetics,* 1, 133–48

———— "Reducing the Heredity Environment Uncertainty." *Harvard Educational Review,* 39, 449–83

———— *Educability and Group Differences.* New York: Harper & Row, 1973

———— Rohwer, W. D., Jr., *Experimental Analysis of Learning Abilities in Culturally Disadvantaged Children.* Final report on OEO Project No. 2404. U. S. Office of Economic Opportunity. Washington, D.C., 1970

Kagan, J. S., "Inadequate Evidence and Illogical Conclusions" *Harvard Educational Review,* 39, 274–77, 1969

———— "I.Q., Fair Science for Dark Deeds. *Radcliffe Quarterly,* March 1972

Kamin, Leon, "The Misuse of I.Q. Testing." *Change* magazine, Vol. 5. New York, 1973

Karnes, M. B., *A New Role for Teachers: Involving the Entire Family in the Education of Preschool Disadvantaged Children.* Urbana: University of Illinois, 1969

Kidd, Aline H., and Rivoire, Jeanne L., *Perceptional Development in Children.* New York: International Universities Press, 1966

Klaus, R. A., and Gray, Susan, "The Early Training Project for Disadvantaged Children: A Report of Five Years." Monographs of the Society for Research in Child Development, 33, No. 4. 1968

———— "Early Training Project: Seventh Year Report." Monograph, 1970

Klineberg, Otto, *Negro Intelligence and Selective Migration*. New York: Columbia University Press, 1935

———— "Negro-White Differences in Intelligence Test Performance: A New Look at an Old Problem." *American Psychologist*, 18, 198–203. 1963

Koenig, Peter, *Psychology Today*, June 1974

Kohlberg, L. "Teaching the Disadvantaged." Report by Gertrude Noar, Washington, D.C.: National Education Assn., 1967

———— "Early Education: A Cognitive Developmental View." *Child Development*, 14. 161–63. 1968

Leahy, A. M. "Nature-Nurture and Intelligence." Genetics Psychology Monographs, 17. 1935

Lesser, G. S., Fifer, G., and Clark, D. H., "Mental Abilities of Children from Different Social Class and Cultural Groups." Monograph from the Society for Research in Child Development, 30, 4. 1965

Lewontin, R. C., "Race and Intelligence." Bulletin of the Atomic Scientists, 26, No. 3. 1970

Light, R. J., and Smith, P. V., "Statistical Issues in Social Allocation Models of Intelligence: A Review and a Response." *Review of Educational Research*, 41, 351–67. 1971

Loban, W. D., *The Language of Elementary School Children*. Champaign, Ill.: National Council of Teachers of English, 1963

Loretan, Joseph O., and Umans, Shelley, *Teaching the Disadvantaged: New Curriculum Approaches*. New York: Teachers College Press. Columbia University, 1966

McCall, Robert B., "Intelligence Quotient Pattern Over Age: Comparisons Among Siblings and Parent Child Pairs." *Science*, 170. 1970

———— "Similarity in I.Q. Profile Among Related Pairs: Infancy and Childhood." Proceedings, 80th Annual Convention, American Psychological Association, 1972

———— Applebaum, Mark I., and Hogarty, Pamela S., *Developmental Changes in Mental Performance*. Monographs of the Society for Research in Child Development. Chicago: University of Chicago Press, 1973

MacLeon, Gordon A., "Does Creativity Lead to Happiness and More Enjoyment of Life? *The Journal of Creative Behavior*. Vol. 7, No. 4, 1973. Buffalo, N. Y.: The Creative Education Foundation

McNemar, Quinn, "Lost: Our Intelligence? Why?" *American Psychologist*, 19, 871–82. 1964

Manachek, Don E., *Today's Education,* Spring 1974. Washington: National Education Assn.

Mehrabian, Albert, "Measure of Vocabulary and Grammatical Skills for Children Up to Age Six." Washington: U. S. Public Health Services Grant, MH 13509

Menyuk, P., "A Preliminary Evaluation of Grammatical Capacity in Children." *Journal of Verbal Learning and Verbal Behavior,* 2, 429–39. 1963

Miami *Herald,* April 3, 1974

Miller, C. H., "Counselors and the Culturally Different." *Teachers College Journal,* 37: 212–17. March 1966

Mercer, Jane R, "Sociocultural Factors in Labeling Mental Retardates." *The Peabody Journal of Education,* 48. April 1971

——— "Who Is Normal? Two Perspectives on Mild Mental Retardation." E. G. Jaco, ed. Glencoe, Ill.: Free Press

——— "Anticipated Achievement: Computerizing the Self-Fulfilling Prophecy," Paper Presented at the Meetings of the American Psychological Association, Honolulu, September 1972

——— *Labeling the Mentally Retarded.* Berkeley, Calif.: University of California Press, 1973

National Council of Teachers of English, "Uses, Abuses, Misuses of Standardized Tests in English." Urbana, Ill.: National Council on English, 1974

National Education Association, "How Schools Test Your Child's Potential." Publications Division, Washington, D.C.: National Education Assn.

——— "Interim Report of the Task Force on Testing." Washington, D.C.: July 1973

——— "Research Summary . . . Ability Grouping." Washington, D.C.: National Education Assn. Research Division, December 1968

——— "What Parents Should Know About Ability Grouping." Washington, D.C.: National Education Assn.

——— "Tests and the Use of Tests: Violations of Human and Civil Rights." Tenth National Conference, Center for Human Relations. Washington, D.C.: National Education Assn. 1972

National Leadership Institute/Teacher Education. "Infant and Toddler Programs." Storrs, Conn.: University of Connecticut, 1974

——— "High I.Q. Minority Children." Report by William F. Brazziel, University of Connecticut, January 1974

National Society for the Study of Education, "Committee on the Educationally Retarded and Disadvantaged." Paul A. Witty, ed. Part 1, Yearbook 1966. University of Chicago Press, 1967

Naueye, R. L., and others, "Urban Poverty: Effects of Prenatal Nutrition." *Science*, 166, 1026. 1969

Oden, M. H., "The Fulfillment of Promise: Forty-Year Follow-up of The Terman Gifted Group." Genetic Psychology Monographs, 77, 3–93. 1968

Offenbacher, Deborah I., "Cultures in Conflict: Home and School as Seen Through the Eyes of Lower-Class Students." *The Urban Review*, 2:208. May 1968

Ornstein, Allan C., "Teacher Training for the Difficult School." *Peabody Journal of Education*, 41:235–37. 1964

——— "Effective Schools for Disadvantaged Children." *Journal of Secondary Education*, 46:105–09. March 1965

——— "Learning to Teach the Disadvantaged." *Journal of Secondary Education*, 41:206–13. May 1966

——— and Vairo, Phillip D., *How to Teach Disadvantaged Youth*. New York: David McKay, 1969

Osborne, R. T., "Racial Differences in Mental Growth and School Achievement: A Longitudinal Study." *Psychological Reports*. 7. 1960

Osser, H., Wang, M. D., and Zaid, F., "The Young Child's Ability to Imitate and Comprehend Speech: A Comparison of Two Subcultural Groups." *Child Development*, 40, 1063–75. 1969

Passow, A. Harry, ed. *Developing Programs for the Educationally Disadvantaged*. New York: Teachers College Press, Columbia University, 1968

Piaget, Jean, "The General Problem of the Psychobiological Development of the Child." In *Discussions of Child Development*. Vol. 4. New York: International Universities Press, 1960

——— *Six Psychological Studies*. New York: Random House, 1967

President's Committee on Mental Retardation. "Report to the President: A Proposed Program for National Action to Combat Mental Retardation." Washington, D.C., 1962

——— "The Six-Hour Retarded Child: Report on Conference on Problems of Education in the Inner School." Washington, D.C., 1969

Radin, Norma, "Some Impediments to the Education of Disadvantaged Children." *Children*, 15:170–76. September/October 1968

Rees, Helen E., *Deprivation and Compensatory Education: A Consideration.* Boston: Houghton-Mifflin, 1968

Report by the Task Force on Children Out of School, *The Way We Go to School-The Exclusion of Children in Boston.* Boston: Beacon Press, 1970

Report of the Commission on Tests. "Righting the Balance." New York: College Entrance Examination Board, 1970

Reymart, M. L., and Hinton, R. T., Jr., "The Effect of a Change to a Relatively Superior Environment upon the I.Q.'s of One Hundred Children." Year Book of National Society for the Study of Education, 39. 1940

——— "Briefs." New York: College Entrance Examination Board, 1970

Rist, Ray C., "Student Social Class and Teacher Expectations: The Self-Fulfilling Prophecy in Ghetto Education." *Harvard Educational Review*, Vol. 40, No. 3, August 1970

Roberts, Joan L., *School Children in the Urban Slum.* New York: Macmillan, 1967

Rosenthal, Robert, and Jacobson, Lenore, *Pygmalion in the Classroom.* New York: Holt, Rinehart & Winston, 1968

Rude, H. Neil, and King, Donald C., "Aptitude Levels in a Depressed Area." *Personnel and Guidance Journal.* 43. 769–785

Samuels, S. Jay, and Dahl, Patricia R., "Relationships Among IQ, Learning and Reading Achievement." Technical Report No. 5. Minnesota Reading Project. Minneapolis: University of Minnesota, 1973

Scales, Eldridge, "Measured: What Is the Standard? *Clearing House*, 39. December 1964

Scarr-Salapatek, Sandra, "Unknowns in the I.Q. Equation." *Science*, 17. 1971

Senna, Carl, *The Fallacy of I.Q.* New York: The Third Press, 1973

Shuey, A. M., *The Testing of Negro Intelligence.* 2nd ed. New York: Social Science Press, 1966

Shockley, William, "Negro I.Q. Deficit: Failure of a 'Malicious Coincidence' Model Warrants New Research Proposals." *Review of Educational Research*, 41, 227–48. 1971

——— "Offset Analysis Description of Racial Differences." Proceedings of the National Academy of Sciences, 64, 1432. 1971

———— "Models, Mathematics, and the Moral Obligation to Diagnose the Origins of Negro IQ Deficits." *Review of Educational Research,* 41, 369–77. 1971

Sigel, Irving E., and Perry, Cereta, "Psycholinguistic Diversity Among 'Culturally Deprived' Children." *American Journal of Orthopsychiatry,* 38, 1122–26. 1968

Silberman, Charles E., *Crisis in the Classroom.* New York: Random House, 1970

Smilanksy, Sara, *The Effects of Sociodramatic Play on Disadvantaged Preschool Children.* New York: John Wiley & Sons, 1968

Smith, James A., *Setting Conditions for Creative Teaching in the Elementary Schools.* Boston: Allyn & Bacon, 1972

Sontag, L. W., Baker, C. T., and Nelson, V. L., "Mental Growth and Personality Development: A Longitudinal Study." Monographs of the Society for Research in Child Development, 23, 1–85. 1958

Sorgen, Michael S., "Testing and Tracking in Public Schools." *The Hastings Law Journal,* Vol. 24, May, 1973. Hastings, Calif.

Stalnaker, John M., "Scholarship Selection and Cultural Disadvantage. Bulletin of the National Association of Secondary School Principals, 49:142–50. Washington, D.C. March 1961

Stanford Research Institute, "Compensatory Education and Early Adolescence." Educational Policy Research Center. Stanford, Calif., 1973

State Testing Programs, "Educational Resources Information Center," 1973 Revision. Princeton, N.J.

Steinberg, E. R., "Middle-Class Education for Lower-Class Students." *Education,* 86, 67–74. October 1965

Stone, James C., and DeNevi, Donald P. eds., *Teaching Multi-Cultural Populations.* New York: Von Nostrand Reinhold, 1971

Stott, D. H. "Interaction of Heredity and Environment in Regard to Measured Intelligence." *British Journal of Educational Psychology,* 30. 1960

Strom, Robert D., *Teaching in the Slum School.* Columbus, Ohio: C. E. Merrill, 1965

Taba, Hilda, *Teaching Strategies for the Culturally Disadvantaged.* Chicago: Rand McNally, 1966

Taylor, Calvin W., *Creativity: Progress and Potential.* New York: McGraw-Hill, 1964

———— ed., *The Third Research Conference on the Identification of Creative Scientific Talent.* Salt Lake City: University of Utah Press, 1959

———— and Barron, Frank, *Scientific Creativity: Its Recognition and Development.* New York: John Wiley & Sons, 1963

Temp, George, "Test Bias: Validity of the S.A.T. for Blacks and Whites in Thirteen Integrated Institutions." Princeton: Educational Testing Service. January 1971

Terman, L. M., *Genetic Studies of Genius,* Vol. 1. "Mental and Physical Traits of a Thousand Gifted Children." Stanford Calif.: Stanford University Press, 1926

———— and Ogden, M., *The Gifted Group at Mid-Life.* Stanford, Calif.: Stanford University Press, 1959

———— and Merrill, M. A., *Stanford-Binet Intelligence Scale.* Boston: Houghton-Mifflin, 1960

Tests and Educational Materials, American Guidance Services. Minnesota, 1974

Thorndike, Robert L., "Intellectual Status and Intellectual Growth." *Journal of Educational Psychology,* 57. 1966

Thurstone, L. L., and Thurstone, T. G., *Factorial Studies of Intelligence.* Chicago: University of Chicago Press, 1941

Tiedt, Sidney W., ed., *Teaching the Disadvantaged Child.* New York: Oxford University Press, 1968

Torrance, E. Paul, *Education and the Creative Potential.* Minneapolis: University of Minneapolis Press, 1963

———— *Guiding Creative Talent.* Englewood Cliffs, N.J.: Prentice-Hall, 1963

———— *Rewarding Creative Behavior.* Englewood Cliffs, N.J.: Prentice-Hall, 1965

———— "Career Patterns and Peak Creative Achievements of Creative High School Students Twelve Years Later." *Gifted Child Quarterly,* Summer 1972. Cincinnati, Ohio

———— An Alternative to Compensatory Education. *Educational Horizons,* Vol. 50, No. 4. Washington, 1972

———— "Is Creativity Research in Education Dead?" Paper Delivered at Invitational Conference of Creativity: A Quarter-Century Later. Greensboro, N.C. May 24, 1973

———— "Creativity: An Overview." Presented in Critical Appraisal of Research in the Personality-Emotions-Motivation Domain. Washington, D.C.: U. S. Office of Education, September 1973

Tuckman, Bruce W., and O'Brien, John L., eds., *Preparing to Teach the Disadvantaged: Approaches to Teacher Education.* New York: Macmillan, The Free Press, 1969

Tyler, Leona E., *Intelligence: Some Recurring Issues.* New York: Von Nostrand Reinhold, 1969

U. S. Commission on Civil Rights, *Racial Isolation in the Public Schools.*" Vol. 1, Washington, D.C., 1971

U. S. Department of Health, Education and Welfare, Office of Child Development: "Case Studies of Children in Head Start Planned Variation, 1970–71." Bureau of Child Development Services, Washington, D.C., 1972

U. S. Office of Economic Opportunity Project Head Start. "An Invitation to Help Head Start Child-Development Programs: A Community Program for Young Children." Washington Office of Economic Opportunity, 1965

U. S. Office of Education, "A Chance for a Change: New School Programs for the Disadvantaged." Washington, D.C.: U. S. Government Printing Office, 1966

Vandenberg, S. G., ed., *The Nature and Nurture of Intelligence in Genetics.* New York: Rockefeller University Press and the Russell Sage Foundation, 1968

——— "What Do We Know Today About the Inheritance of Intelligence and How Do We Know It?" In *Intelligence, Genetic and Environmental Influences.* R. Cacro, ed. New York: Grune & Stratton, 1971

Venezky, Richard L., *Testing in Reading.* National Council of Teachers of English. Urbana, Ill., 1974

Vernon, P. E., "Ability Factors and Environmental Influences." *American Psychologist,* 20. 1965

Wallach, Michael A., "The Psychology of Talent and Graduate Education," Paper Presented at Invitational Conference on Cognitive Styles and Creativity in Higher Education. Sponsored by Graduate Record Examinations Board. Montreal, November 1972

Waller, J. H., "Achievement and Social Mobility: Relationships Among IQ Education and Occupation in Two Generations." *Social Biology,* 18. 1971

Warden, Sandra A., *The Leftouts: Disadvantaged Children in Heterogeneous Schools.* New York: Holt, Rinehart & Winston, 1968

Watt, Lois B., and others, "The Education of Disadvantaged Children: A Bibliography." Educational Materials Center, U. S. Office of Education. Washington, 1966

Weber, George, *Inner-City Children Can Be Taught to Read: Four Successful Schools.* Sponsored by Council for Basic Education, Washington, D.C., 1971

——— *Should Group I.Q. Tests Be Abolished?* Council for Basic Education. Washington, D.C., October 1973

Wechsler, David, *The Measurement and Appraisal of Adult Intelligence,* 4th ed. Baltimore: Williams & Wilkins, 1966

———— "WISC Manual. Wechsler Intelligence Scale for Children." New York: The Psychological Corporation, 1949

Weir, M. W., "Developmental Changes in Problem-Solving Strategies." *Psychological Review,* 71. 1964

———— "Age and Memory as Factors in Problem Solving." *Journal of Experimental Psychology,* 73. 1967

White, Burton, L., "Preschool: Has It Worked?" *Compact: Education Commission of the States.* Denver, Colorado. July/August, 1973

Williams, Robert L., "Abuses and Misuses in Testing Black Children." *Counseling Psychologist,* Vol. 2, No. 3. 1971

———— "Bitch—100: A Culture-Specific Test." Paper Presented at American Psychological Association, Honolulu, September, 1972

———— and Rivers, L. Wendell, "The Use of Standard Versus Non-Standard English in the Administration of Group Tests to Black Children." Paper Presented at Annual Meeting of the American Psychological Association. Honolulu, September 1972

Wise, Arthur E., *Rich Schools, Poor Schools. The Promise of Equal Educational Opportunity.* Chicago: Chicago University Press, 1968

Wisniewski, Richard, *New Teachers in Urban Schools.* New York: Random House, 1968

Witkin, Herman A., "The Role of Cognitive Style in Academic Performance and in Teacher-Student Relations." Princeton, N.J.: Educational Testing Service, 1972

Young, Michael, *The Rise of the Meritocracy.* Baltimore: Penguin Books, 1958

Zach, Lillian, "The IQ Debate." *Today's Education,* National Education Assn. Journal. Washington, September 1972

INDEX